THE 12 WEEK MIND WORKOUT

FOCUSED TRAINING FOR MENTAL STRENGTH AND BALANCE

WOUTER DE JONG AND
MAUD BEUCKER ANDREAE

JOHN
MURRAY
LEARNING

First published in the Netherlands in 2018 by Maven Publishing B.V.

First published in Great Britain by John Murray Learning in 2022
An imprint of John Murray Press
A division of Hodder & Stoughton Ltd,
An Hachette UK company

1

A CIP catalogue record for this title is available from the British Library

Trade Paperback ISBN 978 1 529 33873 7
eBook ISBN 978 1 529 33875 1

Typeset by KnowledgeWorks Global Ltd.

Printed and bound in Great Britain by Clays Ltd, Elcograf S.p.A.

John Murray Press policy is to use papers that are natural, renewable and recyclable products and made from wood grown in sustainable forests. The logging and manufacturing processes are expected to conform to the environmental regulations of the country of origin.

John Murray Press
Carmelite House
50 Victoria Embankment
London EC4Y 0DZ

www.johnmurraypress.co.uk

For Ava

CONTENTS

INTRODUCTION

Isn't it odd that adverts for watches often feature those 'timeless' moments when you wouldn't dream of checking the time? A man and a woman engaged in a deep and meaningful kiss, each wearing a sparkling watch; a muscular rock climber hanging from a cliff edge by one arm, with an attractive timepiece around his wrist.

Such timeless moments, unfortunately, tend to be an exception to the rule. Our lives are ruled by the clock: we dash from one appointment to the next. And if we're not eagerly looking forward to the future, we may be melancholically longing for the past. My uncle in The Hague used to say: 'If you have one foot in the future and the other in the past, you are urinating on the present.' I am sure we all know that irritating feeling of always wanting to be somewhere else – or be somebody else. Most of us are used to this sense of dissatisfaction lurking at the back of our minds. Maybe you, too, have convinced yourself that this is what life is about. Just imagine how it would be if we could feel a sense of *peace* instead in our minds. If that were possible, what would it be worth to you?

HEALTHY CONSCIOUSNESS

In today's world, we are continually looking forward to something, waiting for that magic key, experience, achievement or somebody that will free us from our chronic dissatisfaction. The British writer and Zen practitioner Alan Watts compared this to impatiently listening to music longing to hear the final note, or heading towards a particular spot on the dancefloor. Of course we dance because we like dancing, but don't we sometimes live in hope to find 'that special "something"'.

But what is 'that special "something"'? Is it material things, wealth, sex? I am convinced that it means feeling at home in your own consciousness. After all, your mind is the only home you will occupy permanently.

Are you not convinced? Just imagine you were promised access to a superpower which would allow you to acquire anything you wanted – money, cars, lovers, status, skills and power – but on one condition: you have to give up your consciousness. Would you agree? No, of course you wouldn't: without consciousness, all these things would be worthless. Ask yourself this, too. Whose life would you prefer – that of Professor Stephen Hawking, the paralysed genius who said he wasn't afraid of death, but wasn't in a hurry to die either, because there are so many beautiful things to live for; or that of the extremely healthy Markus Persson, the Swedish multibillionaire and inventor of Minecraft who suffers from bouts of deep depression because he thinks life is pointless?

THE IMPORTANCE OF A HEALTHY MIND

You might easily fill a book with all the goals and ambitions you'd like to achieve in your life, but the main objective – whether you go camping, start a political party, read this sentence, attend a meeting or take some pain relief – is that you feel at ease in your own mind. Even people who commit suicide want only to be free from pain and suffering, to be happy. Of course, material circumstances are important, especially the basic needs that must be met if we are to survive, but in the end true happiness does not depend on possessions or ephemeral emotions, but on your outlook on life, on your mindset.

A healthy, happy mind, then, is invaluable – we wouldn't want to swap it for anything – and yet we don't treat it accordingly or give it its dues. Isn't it amazing that everything we do passes through the filter we call consciousness but we pay so little attention to the actual filter?! In the West, we have never been as affluent as we are today, but if you consider that in the UK, for example, one in four people experience mental health conditions every year[1] and that mental ill health is responsible for 72 million working days lost and costs £34.9 billion each year,[2] then it looks as if the progress inside our heads is not keeping up.

TRAINING THE MIND

It surprises us that in the Middle Ages food was not yet linked to health. In the 1950s, physical exercise was not yet linked to health: if someone saw a jogger in the park, they'd think: 'Why is she in such a hurry? She must be late for her train.'

Today it's quite acceptable for us to pay attention to what we eat and to exercise our bodies. But still we don't link mental training to health; often, we don't even think about our brain until something goes wrong (and go to a clinical psychologist for help). Isn't this rather strange? If you want to join the gym, you don't need to prove you have physical ailments first.

Fortunately, a third revolution is gaining momentum: mental training. A whole raft of scientific evidence is telling us that mental training can help us lead more meaningful and enjoyable lives (and create a better world). In ten years' time (we hope), a mind workout will feel just as natural as brushing your teeth. In other words, if you're not doing any mental training, others may complain of the foul air swirling around your head.

MIND WORKOUT

'Life is like a camera,' wrote the financier and activist Ziad K. Abdelnour. 'Focus on what's important. Capture the good times. And if things don't work out, just take another shot'. Perhaps you always take good photos, and if so, you might as well close this book now. But it's more likely that, just like anybody else, your camera sometimes fails. In theory, most of us will say that we want a meaningful and happy life, but we don't live accordingly. This book offers you the handles to get to grips with the nature of a 'meaningful and happy life' and put it into practice.

The 12 Week Mind Workout offers you the resources to maintain a constant healthy mental condition in all life's moments – the happy, the sad and the downright dull. If your mind is clear and sharp you know where you can make an impact and what you should accept. You will not learn to be free *from* certain (inner) experiences, but you will discover freedom *within* your experience. It will help you maintain inner peace, even when you are sad or angry, or when things aren't going quite as you like. You will learn to maintain or change your behaviour, which will help your life to be aligned with what really matters to you.

This book isn't based on blind faith, quackery or waffle. It's based on a rich, pragmatic bedrock of science on how we can influence our minds. Of course, research is always provisional and debatable, but it's all, for the moment, that we have. This is why I have tried to cite evidence from multiple scientific studies as well as, of course, my own experiences and those of participants on my training courses.

HOW TO HAVE A HAPPY BRAIN

We have been talking about a healthy mind, but in order to train a healthy mind we first need to understand what this might mean without becoming mired in esoterica. Science can help us. Richard Davidson, a professor in psychology and psychiatry at the University of Wisconsin–Madison, has investigated what makes our brains clear, effective and happy. Four independent brain circuits are responsible for what he calls 'the happy brain':

1. *Attention.* Our ability to maintain our focus; a distracted mind is an unhappy mind.
2. *Resilience.* Our ability to recover quickly from negative states of mind.

3. *Positivity.* Our ability to create positive emotions and thoughts and to nurture them.
4. *Altruism.* Our ability to give unconditionally; generosity.

Interestingly, these circuits can operate independently. It means that you have the ability to have really good conversations with a friend, but at the same time be quite poor in patching up the relationship after a disagreement with that same friend. It also means that the quantity of positive and negative emotions are fairly unrelated: you may experience many positive emotions and still find that you are frequently overwhelmed by unpleasant feelings. Research also shows that all these circuits are malleable. In other words, they can be exercised like you train muscles.

HOW TO APPROACH THE MIND WORKOUT

These brain circuits are the foundation of the Mind Workout. The book is divided into three parts: covering attention, power of compassion and happiness skills. Part 1, about attention, provides the foundation for the other two parts: attention training will give you more self-awareness and self-control. You learn to focus your attention where and how you want it. This is how you build up a basic level of readiness to perform the exercises in Parts 2 and 3. In Part 2, about compassion (your resilience circuit), you will learn to deal constructively with the difficult things in life. You will build up the resilience to stand strong in the midst of pain and suffering.

This will give you support for the following part, because you will have learned how to relinquish the behavioural patterns that stop you from living a happier life. Part 3, which is about happiness (the positivity and altruism circuits), will introduce you to the techniques you need to flourish and thrive in life.

Each part consists of four weeks, each with its own training suggestions. Of course, those 'weeks' are just guideline time periods. If you want to spend more time practising exercises in a particular week, please do. It's important you don't rush through the exercises. They are not quick fixes or miracle remedies; their value will become noticeable only after frequent practice and consolidation.

Each week begins with a warm-up (the theory), followed by training (the practice) and a cooling-down exercise (reflection). It's good to know why something is beneficial, and if you put it into practice and then reflect on it, you will optimize your efforts. You can choose from three practice levels: light, medium and (for the diehards) intensive. Light training exercises will take up no extra time; you will do these exercises during your daily activities (such as taking a shower, making a phone call, or waiting at traffic lights). If you would like to do some more training, you could choose the medium level where there are plenty of audio tracks and additional exercises. These exercises require you to put in 20–30 minutes per day. If the intensive training is your thing, then expect to put in 30–45 minutes.

YOUR APPROACH
In *The 12 Week Mind Workout* it's important that you trust only your own experiences and intuition. Don't fall into the trap of thinking everything can be looked up in books. Knowledge does not equate with experience. You should absorb your experiences to recognize and get to know the deeper value of the exercises. Just reading a doctor's prescription is not likely to make you better. If you think you're short of time, remember that the average British person spends three hours and 23 minutes watching television or using the laptop per day. That's more than a whole year of staring at screens for every eight years of your life. And what is more important to you: a better quality of life or keeping up to date with your Facebook friends?

It takes courage and discipline to look inside yourself. Taking a step inside and letting go of old habits and ideas that have become ingrained is more exciting than skydiving, climbing Everest or travelling to the moon – especially if you're prepared to let go of that most dangerous of perspectives on personal growth, 'It's just the way I am and I can't change it.'

IN CONCLUSION

In my opinion, striving for material prosperity isn't the real problem; in fact, having a bit of money and enough things can actually give us an advantage! The real challenge is how we use our material prosperity to support mental progress and create a more sustainable world.

I fully realize that we can't always make the world serve our purposes. Mind Workout is based on my belief that we do have the option to adopt an alternative view of our world. And if we introduce more clarity and definition into our consciousness, we should – paradoxically – be more able to shape the world the way we like. A clear and content mind will make you want more from life than just lazing in a hammock. It will make it more likely that we will be more involved in others than in ourselves. We will be more helpful and loving if we feel comfortable in ourselves and in our mind. We will spend more money on others, do more voluntary work, be more prepared to share and help, compared to unhappy people.[3] In summary, a better world begins in your mind.

If we were to invest all the often unnecessary effort we put into our appearances, social media presence or binge-watching on training a healthy mind, it would not only make us happier but also create the right conditions for a society in which we pay attention to what matters most – each other.

Wouter de Jong

PART 1
ATTENTION

> *'If you try to chase two rabbits,*
> *both will escape.'*
> CHINESE PROVERB

Eight seconds. That's the length of time you can focus on something or somebody. After that, you lose concentration and your mind turns to something else: a bag of chips, an app, your thoughts, whatever. In 2000, the average individual's attention span was 12 seconds; since then our smartphone era has shaved another third off this (are you still with me?). Now even goldfish have a longer attention span: this little creature can keep focus for no fewer than nine seconds.

Attention is the foundation of all our activities, from hitting the alarm clock in the morning to setting it in the evening and anything else in between: driving a car, attending work meetings, kissing, cooking... As a child you could spend hours playing with LEGO bricks, but now you're grown up, it's much harder to give your undivided attention to one single activity. This is first because, as adults, there are more demands on your attention. Today, attention is like gold dust: brands and adverts vie for our attention, colleagues expect us to keep focus, our children want us to play with them, a friend in distress would like us to listen. Second, it's because every day our digital age exposes us to a deluge of information that craves your attention. The number of images we need to process (from newspapers, our computer, our smartphone or simply out in the street) has increased a hundredfold compared to a century ago. We are subjected to 300 items of advertising, of various forms, every day.[4]

ATTENTION INJURY

All these 'attention seekers' play havoc with your attention. And your own brain is complicit, because it is addicted to information: the more input it gets, the greedier it becomes and the more it devours.[5] Just as you can injure your body through excessive exercise, you can also overload your 'attention muscle'. As a consequence, you can switch off during even the simplest of activities. Your mind drifts off into the future (while eating the appetizer, you are already anticipating dessert; during a massage session, you're already feeling sorry it will soon be over), or alternatively back in time (why was your friend so unkind to you yesterday?). These meanderings of your brain into the past or into the immediate future don't help you; they merely distract you from your current activity, which means that you can't fully enjoy it and you are more prone to making mistakes.

How many times have you heard the expression 'Be more in the now'? It's so overused, it just sounds hollow, doesn't it? It stands to reason that everybody is in the now – it's impossible not to be. What really matters is *how* you are present in the now. Making plans for the future can only be useful if you can enjoy them when that future presents itself. And it too will require all your attention.

If you ignore a wrist or knee injury, it will lead to other problems, and the same applies to an overloaded attention muscle. To avoid this, we need to find out how we can bring that undivided, LEGO-attention we enjoyed in our childhood back into our lives. It's this that we'll be working on in the coming four weeks.

A LIFESAVING LUNCH

If ever you were to end up in prison and decided to ask for early release, cross your fingers that you will be heard at eight o'clock in the morning or just after lunch. A revealing study into early release showed that judges granted 65 per cent of all requests in the morning, but only 10 per cent at the end of the day. After lunch there was another peak of 65 per cent. Why was this? The researchers concluded that the decision to grant early release demanded a high level of attention. Just before lunch the judges had little battery power left, and the same applied in the late afternoon. This explains why there were significantly fewer early releases at those times.

SIT-UP

Did you notice a typo in the second paragraph? If so, you're pretty smart! If you didn't, the mistake was in the sentence 'This is first because, as adults, there are more demands on your attention', which should of course have been 'an adult'. You most likely missed it because mistakes like that just aren't important to you. It would require more energy if you had to dot the *is* and cross the *ts* in addition to paying attention to content. Your attention muscle is trying to save energy. Unless, of course, you are a book editor (and spotting errors is your job).

ATTENTION TRAINING

It is interesting that, when we learn new skills (painting, driving a car, management efficiency), 'Module 1: Attention Training' is not on the curriculum.

Yet attention is at the core of everything we do – as well as when we learn (something new) at school. Unfortunately, the only words we were used to hearing about paying attention at school were something like 'Pay attention, otherwise I'll have to ask you to leave the classroom!' or 'If you don't stop talking now, I'll put you in detention!' Paying attention was just something we had to do if we didn't want to get punished. Isn't that weird, because how do you pay attention? And yet attention should be part of the curriculum, as it's at the very core of constructive learning.

So how can you strengthen your attention muscle? Answer: by practising mindfulness. If the idea of mindfulness doesn't appeal to you and just hearing the word makes you want to chuck this book into the recycling bin, please hold on! Yes, I know, the whole concept of mindfulness has become tarnished. It might remind you of a bunch of dishevelled hippies in an ashram, or you might be thinking of a bunch of spoiled hipsters on a retreat or trendy midlifers trying to impress with Eckhart Tolle quotes.

It's great that mindfulness has gained popularity over recent years – we no longer bat an eyelid if our CEO takes time off to go to a 'retre- at' – but its popularity has led to an indiscriminate and often incorrect usage of the term. A common misconception is that being 'mindful' is equal to feeling relaxed or Zen, or that nothing or nobody will ever be able to upset you again. However, the literal meaning of mindfulness is 'having full awareness [i.e. attention]' – being attentive and registering what is happening moment by moment without prejudice – everything from pain and joy to anger and that itch on your big toe.

If your lifestyle is mindful, it means that you have consciously decided where and how you want to centre your attention. Your attention muscle will become stronger, you will gradually notice that you are finding it easier to focus and consequently you will not only feel more content, but have a resilient and constructive approach to dealing with unpleasant situations.

Isn't each of your seconds the most important moment of your life?
There is no later... Later is now.'

DE DIJK

THE BENEFITS OF ATTENTION TRAINING

One of the earliest studies looking at active attention training (the 'traditional' eight-week mindfulness programme) and its impact on the workplace even surprised the researchers. The participants, they found, were less stressed and restless, had a more positive mood and worked more efficiently than the control group.

The (unexpected) bonus was the physical impact: at the end of attention training the participants were given a flu injection to test the response of their immune system. Those who had practised their attention control developed significantly more antibodies than the untrained group.[6]

The benefits of attention training are huge. Many studies show that it helps against fear, physical pain, anxiety and depressive feelings, and that it leads to increased happiness, health, concentration, decision-making and self-control, among other things.[7] And if we consider that attention is the foundation of everything we do, a (more) attentive life must be the first step towards growth in everything we do.

In a ground-breaking study carried out by the neuroscientist Christopher deCharms, patients suffering chronic pain were shown a real-time fMRI (a type of X-ray) of their brain activity. In the image, their pain was visualized as fire: the heavier the pain, the more the activity in their brain, the greater the flames. The patients then practised the type of attention they wanted to pay to the flames (their pain) and they concentrated on making the flames smaller. As a result, their experience of pain decreased, and the flames grew smaller. The patients had consciously and actively changed the structure of their brains; the flames grew smaller or even died out.[8]

INTENT

Daily exercises will burn belly fat and the fat rolls may become a six-pack, but stop exercising and all the fat rolls back. This is how attention works, too: if you regularly exercise your attention muscle, it will help you be more attentively in daily life, but if you live without being attentive – by multitasking, allowing your mind to wander, or constantly picking up that smartphone – the muscle will become as weak as the proverbial kitten. This will lead to a less mindful life (you will forget appointments, increasingly mislay objects, take less notice in traffic, etc.), which in turn will have an even greater negative effect on the muscle. Attention training breaks this vicious circle: paying more attention strengthens your attention muscle, which in turn makes you more attentive. Actually, it is quite straightforward: pay attention to your attention, and your attention will grow.

You will be working on exactly this over the next four weeks. Each week begins with a warmup (theory), followed by training (practice) and a cooling down (reflection).

It's good to know why something is beneficial: if you put something into practice and then reflect on it, you will optimize your efforts.

'A poor attempt is better than no attempt at all.'

ANONYMOUS

Do consider beforehand which level of training is feasible for you – and be realistic. If you take up running, you won't be ready to join a marathon immediately; it probably won't be possible straightaway. A slow build-up is crucial to attention training: short exercises can really boost your attention muscle. If you discover after a while that the additional exercises are too much for you, don't worry. Don't give up – just go back a step. The main thing is to practise. The 'training lite' version is also adequate. And if you happen to think you have let the side down, then stop and consider what you have achieved – don't think about what you should have achieved. This in itself is a good attention exercise.

WEEK

01

THE BASICS

> *'Life is what happens to you while you're busy making other plans.'*
>
> JOHN LENNON

How does attention work and what makes it so difficult to lead a mindful life? Drifting and acting on autopilot in particular tend to reduce your attention, but why does that matter and what are the consequences? And why can a little bit of drifting and certain automatic behaviours even be quite helpful? This week you'll find the answers to these questions, so that you understand why you need to strengthen your attention muscle. The starting point of this week is focusing on the foundation of attention training: your breathing.

WARM-UP

A strong attention muscle is indispensable if you want to lead a happier life. We all have enough time – everybody gets the same 24 hours in a day – but we don't have enough attention. Unfortunately, multitasking is pretty much par for the course in the contemporary world, even though scientific evidence has shown it just doesn't work: the quality of our output during multitasking appears to be the same as when we perform tasks while drunk.[9] Research, and possibly our own personal experience too, shows us that, if a task is to be successful and/or productive, we need to keep focus. This also applies to sex.[10] Thinking about the washing-up or putting out the bins out during foreplay is fatal. Or at least it won't result in a new life.

Take a look at this cube. Is the little ball at the front or at the back?

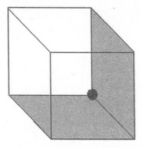

SIT-UP

It's a trick question of course: there's no correct or incorrect answer. There happen to be visual interpretations of the so-called Necker cube. The human brain cannot see both at the same time. Likewise, it is impossible to have two conversations at the same time.

THE ATTENTION MODEL

You cannot split your attention. It is like a spotlight: if it lights up an object (say a chair), then something else (a table) will be in the shade. Similarly, giving your full attention to your foot means that you will temporarily be unaware of your hand; if you are listening to an exciting podcast, your attention will not be on your sick mother. Just like a spotlight, you can change the direction or span of your attention: are you focusing your attention internally or externally? And, in doing so, are you focusing on something specific or are you open to more stimuli? The suitability of each type of attention depends on the circumstances and the moment. I will try to make all this clearer by providing examples and benefits for each attention type.

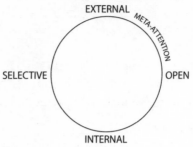

Figure 1.1 Meta-attention makes you aware of your attention direction and span.
Source: © Wouter de Jong

SELECTIVE ATTENTION
In selective attention, the beam of light is as fine as a laser beam. You focus your attention on one aspect: an episode of your favourite TV show, an itchy foot, Vivaldi's *Four Seasons* (without simultaneously reading or sending text messages!). You focus all your attention on that one single activity.

Advantage: selective attention is effective. You have a good likelihood of completing the project (preparing a meal) and the risk of making mistakes (burning the pine nuts) is greatly reduced.

OPEN ATTENTION
Open attention is the opposite to selective attention. Here the beam is like a construction lamp that lights up the entire room in a broad sweep. You open yourself up to all the stimuli in and around you. If you are sitting enjoying a coffee at one of the outdoor tables at a café, there will be all kinds of internal and external stimuli: a busker, the comings and goings of the waiter, the sun on your skin, a conversation at another table, an itchy ear and your mulling over an argument you've had with your brother.

Advantage: you are open to (new) information that will boost the creative part of your brain.[11] After racking your brains for days, this one hour of open attention has presented you with five ideas for the birthday present you would like to give to your friend.

EXTERNAL ATTENTION

You turn your spotlight outward: to the tennis match, freshly baked apple pie, train departure times, the waiter's or waitress's pleasant smile.

Advantage: external attention increases your adaptability, your ability to notice changes in your surroundings. It helps you avoid an approaching tram or notice your partner's smile.

INTERNAL ATTENTION

Internal attention means focusing on your thoughts, feelings or physical sensations. Do you feel any tingling sensations? Are you feeling hot or cold? Is it a stab of jealousy? Are you happy or are you feeling stressed?

Advantage: internal attention informs you about your state of mind and helps you control your impulses. Thoughts and feelings give rise to appropriate action: the knot in your stomach tells you that the new job might not be a good idea, and by reflecting on your goosepimples you realize that it is due not to cold but emotion.

Start a timer on your phone and pay full attention to your sense of touch for two full minutes (external selective attention): what does the texture of the cover of this book feel like, what do the pages feel like? Each time you find yourself distracted, refocus your attention.

How did that go? Did you feel anything new, any surprising textures? Did your mind often drift? If so, what were your thoughts? Did you manage to refocus on the book?

SIT-UP

THE COLOUR OF YOUR ATTENTION

An important addition to the attention model is the colour of your focused beam. This is because attention isn't just about the subject of your attention, it's also about your relationship to the subject. Are you offering an accepting type of attention (green coloured); are you showing resistance (red), or are your feelings neutral (white)?

For example: one person might give a porn film a red light and a monastery a green light, but somebody else might do the opposite. Likewise, you could also be feeling frustration (red) at your own emotions, such as jealousy, sorrow or anger, or you could approach them more constructively and see them in a neutral (white) or accepting (green) light.

META-ATTENTION

We have a special type of attention that often occurs in attention training: meta-attention. We use this phrase when you are paying attention to your attention. You are reflecting on your attention: first, you notice the *type* of attention you have used and subsequently the colour of your beam. Your subconscious often tends to adopt a favourite attention type, one that is not always suitable for a particular moment. For instance, you might be adopting open attention when you should be focusing on your work (selective attention), or selective attention when you might benefit from a creativity boost (open attention).

Employing meta-attention helps you realize that you are focusing on your colleague's heavy breathing (external and selective) and that the colour of your spotlight is red (irritation); or that you are paying attention to all the stimuli in and around you (open attention), such as a crying baby, your hunger pangs and bright sunlight in your eyes. Meta-attention is a first step towards modifying the direction, breadth and colour of your attention.

SIT-UP

Focus for 30 seconds on the sensation in your right hand (internal selective attention). Also be aware of the type of attention you use (meta-attention). Did you manage to focus your attention on your hand? If not, what drew your focus away? Were there external distractions, such as a barking dog? Or were there distracting thoughts (I'm hungry; how much longer?) and feelings (satisfaction, irritation, impatience)? Were you conscious of straying (meta-attention)?

LEAVING THE NOW (ON AUTOPILOT)

In an ideal world, you would be consciously switching between selective and open attention, from red to green, from internal to external, and back again. But as you have read in the Introduction and maybe have experienced in the sit-ups, there are quite a few attention seekers that can disturb this consciousness.

Distraction, such as incoming emails, a cool track on Spotify, work, a colleague blowing his nose or a street fundraiser tapping your shoulder, takes your mind off the activity you want to or should be doing at that particular moment, requiring all your attention. All these external factors weaken your attention muscle and draw you away from the now.

Although you may occasionally be distracted by external factors, you yourself are the greatest distractor. How many times have your thoughts drifted while reading this chapter? People's thoughts tend to drift 20–40 per cent of the time while they are reading.[12] You may think this is high, but on average we daydream half the time and on top of that we sleep approximately eight hours each day. This means that by the time you are 30 you have lived about 20 years of your life unconsciously!

OUR CHATTERING MONKEY

In Eastern philosophy, there is a term for this – monkey mind. Your monkey mind is this infinite chattering in your head when you subconsciously jump from thought to thought, from emotion to emotion – like a monkey swinging from tree to tree. *What are my other appointments this afternoon? Oh dear, I forgot to ring my mother yesterday. I should renew my phone subscription and I mustn't forget to book our summer holiday.* Before you know it, your monkey mind is in China – and it's three hours later.

Recently, brain scientists have discovered what your monkey mind in your brain looks like: it is a network of interconnected parts of the brain that is inactive when focusing but overactive when straying. At such times the *default network* works non-stop,

looking for solutions to tasks and problems: what you are going
to have for dinner that evening, contacting the babysitter or more
serious concerns such as job loss or a sick relative.

DISADVANTAGES

One disadvantage of an overactive monkey mind is that you miss a
significant part of your pleasant experiences. You kiss your loved one
while your mind is on some piece of admin that needs doing, or you
miss feeling the warm spring sunshine on your back because you are
worrying about a deadline.

Another disadvantage is that your chattering monkey also causes
you to miss many unpleasant experiences. You're probably thinking,
what's so bad about that? Well, if you want to deal constructively with an
unpleasant event (like arguments and criticism) and painful emotions
(anger and sorrow), you need to experience them consciously. Otherwise they will eventually come back and hit you like a boomerang.

A third disadvantage is that when you drift you miss an opportunity to make repetitive activities more interesting. If you cycle
to work and your mind is already at your office desk (or still in
bed), you are living from peak moment to peak moment without
appreciating the time in between.

> **EYE-OPENER**
>
> In an attention test, a random selection of passers-by were asked the way.
> While each passer-by was giving directions, two removal men carrying a
> huge door passed between the passer-by giving directions and the person
> receiving them. As they did so, the person asking the way was replaced by
> a different person. Interestingly, half the passers-by did not notice they
> were talking to someone else and ended the conversation as if nothing
> had happened.[13]

A further disadvantage of monkey mind is that the chattering often
has a dark focus. Even if the day is full of positive events, you are
probably not continually thinking thoughts like 'Aren't I lucky that
my train is on time?' or 'Don't I have a fun life?' People are troubled

by a *negativity bias*: a natural tendency to focus on (the prevention of) risk, which the mind often translates into focusing on the negative: 'What a lot of things I've got to do'; 'Oh no, not again, my phone's died'. Alternatively, you draw negative conclusions. Without realizing, you are pulling yourself down, you are passing judgements on others, you are interpreting somebody else's remark as an attack, and so on.

Try to be curious about everyday things like a bike ride, for example the pedal movement (internal selective attention) or whatever comes into your mind: the trees, the wind, people waiting at traffic lights, the technical ingenuity of the bicycle (external open attention). Does this change your cycling experience? Did you consciously manage to select a type of attention (internal selective, external selective, internal open, external open)? And did you manage to hold your attention, or did it often stray? If so, where did it go? And, don't forget the attention colour is important, too. What was the colour of your attention: green or red? In other words, did you accept what you experienced or did it irritate you?

SIT-UP

UNHAPPY

The disadvantages of drifting have a major consequence: an unhappy mind. This was confirmed in a study by Harvard University during which participants using a Track Your Happiness app scored their actual feelings and thoughts. The results confirmed that people tend to daydream almost half of their daily life (46.9 per cent), but also that an improved sense of wellbeing did not depend on the quality of the activity, but on the participants' level of attention to the activity.[14] This means that washing-up can make you much happier than a theme park or a performance by the Berlin Philharmonic (or an outing that makes your heart beat a little faster) as long as you are focused on the washing-up brush, the cups and saucers, and your movements. One of the explanations might be that when you are giving something your full attention, you cannot possibly drift away in the infinite stream of (critical and negative) self-chatter. In other words: you're focusing your spotlight on a chair (the washing-up) and moving the table (the chattering of your monkey mind) into the shade.

ADVANTAGES

Now, I'm not trying to argue that the drifting mind is all bad. Evolutionary experts think our drifting mind was a great leap forward in human evolution; just like conscious planning and reflection, subconscious drifting is one of the skills that probably distinguishes us from other animals. Here is a list of some of the positive aspects of the drifting mind:

- Drifting can be an innate version of the Facebook alert or a reminder on your smartphone. Because your thoughts are briefly elsewhere, you suddenly remember to wish your little niece a happy birthday.
- Drifting makes space for creativity. Imagine you're having a shower and – ping! – you suddenly have this bright idea on how to deliver your presentation. It seems to appear from nowhere, but in fact that 'nowhere' is your default network. Your subconsciousness has just been sitting on it.
- Drifting is like taking a break from focusing. From time to time, the selective attention muscle needs a bit of rest so it can recharge.
- Finally, it can be fun to allow yourself to drift, such as daydreaming about your new love, about a sabbatical, or that vintage car you want to buy.

Even after you undertake attention training, don't think you will never stray again. However, it will happen less frequently and more consciously. Why is that so hard? Einstein's answer: 'We can't solve problems by using the same kind of thinking we used when we created them.' In other words: the part of the brain that is responsible for straying is also responsible for noticing that you've just strayed.

Attention training will help you improve your awareness of drifting. You will make friends with your monkey mind. Instead of having to process its endless round of 'to dos' and nagging problems, you'll learn to ask it to do real tasks (points of focus) that you have thought of yourself.

LEAVING THE NOW (ON AUTOPILOT)

After a fair amount of repetition, you will find things happen automatically: almost 90 per cent of everything you do is on autopilot. It's like the grooves worn by a waterfall that finds its way down a rockface.

> Fold your arms. Now fold them the other way round. Did you notice how difficult this is? Whether you cross your right arm across the left arm or the left arm across the right arm, you do this on autopilot, without thinking, because that is how you trained yourself. It is only when you change a habit that you stop to think about what you are doing.
>
> **SIT-UP**

Automatic actions and behaviours are useful. It's possible to perform different tasks simultaneously if you're doing one automatically (e.g. walking), so that you are able to fully focus on the other (e.g. having a conversation). Unfortunately, your autopilot has its downsides, too: it will lead you back to all those destructive patterns, unwholesome and unproductive activities that poke their heads up from time to time: thoughtlessly lighting a cigarette, eating chocolates after dinner, and of course reaching for that smartphone.

'We are what we habitually do.'

ARISTOTLE

We do not consciously decide to display 'poor' behaviours; we do so without noticing. The autopilot is tuned in to what it is used to doing; it takes no account of bad weather or an unexpected change of direction. I'm sure you know a Mr or Ms Grumpy in the office who goes into meltdown every time work procedures change; his or her argument 'But we've always done it this way!' stems from a fear of the unknown and a resistance to change.

That autopilot of yours is a pretty comfy flight, so you can even take a nap every once in a while.

SIT-UP

Find out if you can manage four hours without your smartphone today and make a mental note of each time you feel the urge to grab it. Here's a trick to help you notice: write the word 'attention' on the thumb you use to work your phone.

How did that go? Did you find you were frequently holding the phone in your hand without noticing? How often did it happen? Are you pleasantly surprised or are you disappointed?

ARRIVING MORE OFTEN IN THE NOW

Your autopilot is tuned in to what you are used to doing. If you want to live with more awareness, you may want to turn off that autopilot more often and consciously plan your route – without a navigation system, on an old-fashioned map. This starts with attention training. By taking note of your attention (meta-attention) you become aware of your automatic behaviours (initially, you'll do this without implementing changes). This is the first step towards deciding definitively to phase out destructive habitual behaviours.

> Research shows that on average we make 227 decisions a day on food alone (usually unconsciously).[15] Try to be aware of this today – as you make a choice between a muesli bar or an apple, whether you put that extra item not on your shopping list in your shopping basket, whether to sprinkle dressing or olive oil over the salad and so on. At the end of the day, check to what extent you have managed to do this. How often did you put something in your mouth before you realized what you were doing? Did you find yourself at the checkout with a basket full of food items instead of only the salmon steak and salad you had intended to buy? Did you really taste that cherry tomato or chocolate biscuit?
>
> **SIT-UP**

Just as with the drifting mind, my intention here is not to encourage you to renounce automatic behaviours. After all, you can make them work to your advantage, such as training yourself to have a salad for lunch every day. Not only is it healthy to automatically choose a salad instead of a toasted sandwich, this automatic choice (but also your automatic chewing and swallowing of food) helps you make time and energy for trickier things that do require thought, like playing a new piece on the piano or trying to understand a computer program.

Research into the brain activity of top athletes confirms that they show less brain activity during difficult tasks compared to amateurs and semi-professionals, which gives them more mental energy to excel.[16]

BREATHING

Your first step to saying goodbye to those (destructive) automatic behaviours and to frequently silencing that monkey mind is attention training, which means paying attention to what happens at a certain time without intending to change it immediately. We'll start to train the attention muscle by paying selective attention to our breathing: you'll focus on the rise and fall of your stomach or the inhalation or exhalation of your breath through your nose or mouth.

You must be wondering why you concentrate on your breathing, and not on your little finger or the tip of your shoe? The main reason is that your breath is always there, in the here and now, and causes bodily movement that's easy to detect. Moreover, your breathing is at the interface of control and non-control: you are in control, but you can also let go and leave it to manage itself. And finally, your breathing changes, depending on your mood. For instance, if you're stressed, your breathing will be high up in the body and fast; if you're relaxed, your breathing will be calm and more likely to come from your stomach.

Sit up straight and relax. Focus on your breathing for one minute.

What did you feel? Is your breathing in the chest or the abdomen? Did you manage to continue your focus or did your mind wander? If so, what did it turn to? To worries or pleasant thoughts? Did you feel irritations or physical sensations like itching?

SIT-UP

During the training sessions in the coming weeks we'll find that the monkey mind often takes you off course. The trick is to notice as soon and as often as possible, and then to realize what you are focusing on and bringing your focus back to your breathing (or your activity at that moment).

LOST FAITH IN YOURSELF?

If you find yourself drifting in this exercise, you may become annoyed with yourself and tell yourself off. You may find yourself being overly critical as you bring your attention back to the breath.

Don't! This kind of self-condemnation doesn't help with behavioural change (here, living in a more attentive way). The effect, in fact, is the opposite: being angry with yourself will ultimately lead to more drifting of the mind. So, don't beat yourself up, but congratulate yourself on having noticed your monkey mind. You are giving yourself an opportunity to bring back your focus. Be polite and say goodbye to the monkey and return your focus to what you were doing: breathing. Attention training is not about completely stopping your mind from drifting, but taking a positive approach to your meanderings and bringing them back into the now.

HOW TO PREVENT INJURIES TO YOUR ATTENTION MUSCLE

Just like athletes need water and protein to improve physical fitness, your attention muscle also needs support to develop more quickly and be injury-free. Try the following recipe for the perfect 'attention-protein shake':

1. A *splash of light determination*. If you are too frantic in the way you focus your attention, it will cost you a lot of energy. And if your focus is too slack, you will often find yourself daydreaming. Try to keep your attention light and loose. Think about the strings of a guitar: they sound best when they are not too loose and not too tight.

2. A *pinch of judgement*. One of the biggest misconceptions about attention training is that you should never judge (I'll return to this in Week 3). This isn't true: it's extremely useful to make judgements and important to be able to make distinctions and choices. Attention training isn't about practising living without making judgements; it's about delaying judgement, so that you can make a more sensible judgement later on. The caveat here is that the further you progress in attention training, the more you'll notice the infinite stream of prejudices you indulge in – about that new colleague at work, your sister's new partner, that new footballer who's signed up to your football team. You may begin to condemn yourself for making such off-the-cuff judgements, but beware, and avoid the snowball effect. Just be aware of your judgements and pat yourself on the back if you notice yourself making one.

3. *A handful of generosity.* Accept that you make mistakes and allow yourself to be a slow learner. In the coming weeks, you should focus on all the things you've done instead of being worked up about all the things you didn't do.

TRAINING

This is the first week of your attention training. As with all types of
training, you'll start slowly. Living attentively is still relatively unknown territory; it needs to be explored gradually. This week's focus is
on our awareness of the moment, of our breathing and our attention.
Think in advance about what you would like to achieve by training
your attention muscle. Do you mainly want to reduce stress, worry
less, feel fitter, communicate more effectively or be more resilient?
Once you know your intention, you can track your progress more
easily and increase your chances of achieving it. The following actions
and thoughts may help:

↔ Write down your intention, preferably using pen and paper.
   Phrase it positively, and do not write 'I'm aiming for a
   reduction in negative self-criticism', but rather, 'I want to be
   kinder to myself'.
↔ State your intention several times, out loud or in your head.
↔ Don't push yourself too much. You don't try to create a fun
   atmosphere for a party by forcing things – 'At eight o'clock
   tonight we'll have a good time' – as it often has the opposite
   effect. Instead, you create the right conditions: by putting
   on music, inviting nice people, providing tasty snacks. The
   condition for attention training is above all that you have no
   expectations, just an open mindset.
↔ And don't forget: an intention is just a direction, not
   something set in stone or measurable. Try to let go of a desired
   result.

▮▮▮ LIGHT
EXERCISE 1: BREATHER

Do three 'breathers' during the day: each time pay attention to three
full inhalations and exhalations. Choose a set time, for example
when you're starting up your computer or doing the washing-up.
Focus on your physical sensations during the breather, such as the

rising and falling of your stomach, your chest going up and down, or the airflow through your nose. The aim here is not to slow down your breathing, nor to deepen and lower it – in other words, to change it. Neither is it to aspire to a special feeling. All that matters is that you are aware of your breathing process, regardless of whether it is superficial or fast; it doesn't need to make you feel more relaxed. If you notice passing thoughts or feelings, just observe them. Try to delay making any judgement; instead, refocus your attention on your breathing.

TRAINER'S TIP

If you prefer not to focus on your breathing – because it disturbs you or you have experienced (panic) attacks from breathing – you could choose another point of focus. Choose something that is very noticeable – for example the soles of your feet, the backs of your hands, your chest or maybe your facial muscles. In Weeks 2 or 3, when your attention muscle has had some training, try to focus on your breathing as well.

EXERCISE 2: ACTIVITY

Choose an activity you would normally do on autopilot, such as shaving, climbing the stairs or opening the curtains. From now on, you should perform this activity every day while giving it your full attention. Focus on the senses involved during these actions. For example, notice your first bite at mealtimes. Study that piece of salmon, feel the muscle power required to lift your fork to your mouth, be aware of the flavour, chew consciously, investigate the texture in your mouth, and notice any automatic behaviours and thoughts without any judgement. Give the activity your full attention for a maximum of five minutes.

TRAINER'S TIP

There may be some problems here such as lack of time and/or motivation or unpleasant feelings. This is how to deal with them:

1. Lack of time? Just one breath or micro-action will do for a practice. Check which time of day would suit you best to practise and put it in your diary.

2. Lack of motivation? Have another look at your intentions and define why you want to do this.
3. Unpleasant? Attention training does not need to be pleasant. It is rewarding if you don't give up even during difficult moments; unpleasant experiences happen in real life, too. If an activity like this starts to feel unpleasant, just remind yourself that it's all good training material.

ıllᴵ MEDIUM

EXTENSION TO LIGHT If you managed the preceding exercises without any problems and you would like to do a bit more, you can intensify your training by trying some sitting meditation focusing your attention on breathing. In the coming weeks, we will add new points of focus to this style of meditation every week. You will use an audio track for this meditation.

🎧 Audio track 1. Focus on breathing

ıllᴵ INTENSE

EXTENSION TO LIGHT If you want to do some intensive training, then do the meditation for breathing and body this week and use the audio track. Your first point of focus will be your breathing and then your body. In the coming weeks, we will continue to extend these attention exercises with new points of focus.

🎧 Audio track 2. Attention to breathing and body

🎧 You can download the audio tracks from www.12weekmindwork-out.com

COOL DOWN

This was the first week in which you focused on your attention. How did it go? Maybe there were times that you didn't feel like it or forgot to do an exercise? Or did you practise and notice that it sometimes made you more relaxed or gave you a clearer mind? You may have noticed yourself becoming restless during the exercises, either because you weren't sitting comfortably or you found the voice on the audio track annoying. In short, your monkey mind was chattering away again. All this doesn't matter. In fact, it's all part of the process and offers fantastic training material.

Ask yourself whether you have achieved any of the following in Week 1:

- Are you more aware of your breathing during the day?
- Have you found a few daily activities, such as eating, washing up or brushing your teeth, which offer suitable training material for attention training?
- Are you more aware of your autopilot and your monkey mind?
- Are you more aware of your subconscious judgements?

Any first week of training, at a sports centre, a boot camp or on a tennis court, will give you lots of conflicting feelings, ranging from pride to 'I don't feel like it', and from aching muscles to a sense of satisfaction. Attention training is the same. You have completed Week 1 and you are now heading for a totally healthy focus.

IN CONCLUSION

After two years of study, a student of Buddhist metaphysics was ready for his exam. He entered his teacher's room with confidence. His mind was full of thoughts and ideas about the complicated subject he was about to be examined in. 'I am ready,' said the student. 'I have only one question,' said the teacher. 'The flowerpot in the entrance, was it to the left or to the right of the coat rack?'

WEEK

02

YOUR BODY, YOUR
LOGBOOK

> '*Those who see any difference between soul and body have neither.*'
>
> OSCAR WILDE

Your body is your logbook, it tells you how you are doing. That is, it tells you how you are doing if you read it. Often you may not read the information your body provides at all, because your unconscious behaviour and habits draw your attention (far) away from your bodily sensations. In this, the second week of your Mind Workout, you will find out why this happens and how it can lead to national disease number one: stress. And of course I will explain, and you will practise, how you can return your focus to your body. You will then start to open your body logbook more frequently.

WARM-UP

Imagine driving down the motorway. You look at your dashboard and see that you are almost out of fuel. After a mile, you stop at a service station to fill up. After an hour, another indicator begins to flash. It shows a spanner: maintenance needed. What should you do? Do you grab the emergency hammer to smash the flashing light, or do you take the car to the garage to investigate the problem? I imagine the latter. But isn't it strange that we often turn off our body's warning lights or ignore them? Often we don't even notice (unpleasant) sensations in our bodies, like tingling or raised shoulders. We just keep on going, sometimes even when the engine is overheating.

STUBBORN HABITS

We keep on going because most of the day we rely subconsciously on a range of automatic behaviours which we deploy (you may remember) 90 per cent of the time! During the deployment of these behaviours your attention is not focused internally but externally. This

30

unconscious state might make you unaware of important internal information, like a shiver, tension, or a knot in your stomach. For you to understand how to stop those instinctive automatic behaviours now and then – to give your body back the attention it deserves – you first need to know what causes them.

THE THREAT SYSTEM AND DRIVE SYSTEM

It may not surprise you to learn just why those automatic behaviours are so stubborn and ingrained when you realize that they originate from a part of your brain which is millions of years old. It consists of two systems that are crucial for survival in the short term. The oldest part is the instinctive threat system. It is aimed at self-preservation. The threat system came about at the time of the sabre-toothed tiger, and it automatically concentrates external attention on whatever causes your fear – ranging from an angry boss to the honk of a carhorn – and prepares you to fight, to flee or to freeze.

The second system, the more recent drive system, also focuses on an external factor, but this time as a reward. In prehistoric times that reward might have been a good meal. In modern times your search for a reward may be focused on food and drink, but also on a myriad of other possibilities – a hedonistic tendency towards drink and drugs, the desire for love, the pursuit of a six-pack or a better job. In both systems your attention is focused entirely on your surroundings and the exterior world, rather than turning inwards towards internal physical sensations.

Today, try to be aware of the instinctive regulation systems to which you automatically return. Was it your drive system telling you to chew and swallow a handful of sweets, or keep checking in for 'likes' on your social media accounts? Does your threat system take over sometimes, ensuring you jump in fright as a car-horn sounds from the street, or are you quick to anger?

SIT-UP

THE SOOTHING SYSTEM

But if those systems have been around for such a long time, is there anything that can remove us from their grip? Certainly! The answer is the soothing system. This system is aimed at ensuring our long-term survival. Unlike your instinctive systems, with the soothing system your responses will no longer be entirely determined by autopilot – they will be conscious and balanced. The soothing system provides recovery, it helps you seek connection with (and care for) others, encourages you to take breaks when necessary and go to sleep when you are tired. In the soothing system your attention is wide open to receive whatever presents itself to your senses – also your physical sensations.

SIT-UP

Ask yourself which regulatory system you are using while reading this book. Is it the threat system (you're afraid of being told off – by someone else or by yourself)? Is it the drive system (you want to improve yourself through your reading), or is it the soothing system (you feel you deserve to take this time out and don't feel the need to perform)? Or are all three systems alternating? Each reader will have a different answer. Just like every person reacts differently to a rollercoaster: one might be petrified with fear (threat system), the other thrives on the adrenaline (drive system) and a third takes care of a frightened passenger next to him or her (soothing system).

BALANCE AND ERROR

The sun is shining, and Harry is stretched out in the garden. He hears the leaves on the trees rustling gently, a few butterflies are fluttering around him: life is good. Harry's soothing system is clearly in control at this moment. He jumps up when he hears the neighbour's dog, Mia, bark. His fur bristles, and he is now completely focused on the chocolate Labrador, ready either to attack or run away. The threat system is now in the ascendant. Fortunately, Mia's owner drags her away. Harry has a good stretch and starts to purr (soothing system). He is feeling a little hungry. An unsuspecting sparrow draws his attention (drive system). He keeps his body low and his paws mark time, as he fixes his focus on the bird, observing his prey. After a run and a pounce, he misses his target – for the second time this week! – and lazily walks inside to his bowl of cat food. He nibbles contentedly, and after he rubs his head against the chair leg, it's time for a nap (soothing system). While he dreams of catching a dozen blackbirds, Harry the tomcat is giving himself plenty of time to recover from the afternoon's excitements.

Harry is a good example of how the regulatory systems work: he experiences brief moments of stress – which are necessary for short-term survival – and repeatedly deploys his soothing system to calm himself down. However, as we've seen, other than Mia and the sparrow, there have been few triggers to provoke Harry's systems this afternoon. For us busy, fully occupied humans, it's a bit different – our drive and threat systems are frequently on high alert. The threat system is the most powerful: in a split second it can take full control of your brain when it suspects danger. This is a good thing: if you're happily eating a handful of blackberries and a burly-looking bear comes along, it would be unwise to decide to pick a few more berries (drive system) or put on a jumper (soothing system) before running away.

That said, we often respond with the threat system even when it's not necessary, and this can be harmful. The modern environment is chockful of stimuli. Your computer or smartphone screen, that work appraisal you're about to go into, even the sound of a car revving up are all innocent enough stimuli but are interpreted by your trusty old threat system as potentially life-endangering threats, and so you are kept constantly on red alert. Another trigger is the expectations imposed on us by our western society and culture and our uncertainty about whether we can live up to them. Your primal brain interprets this lack of control as a life-threatening 'jungle' and instinctively reverts to the familiar pallet of responses. This explains why you become tense just before a deadline or angry when you are criticized.

SIT-UP	Think about whether you are troubled by a hypersensitive drive or threat system. If so, which of the two is dominant?

If you find yourself consistently in 'survival mode' or 'drive mode', your attention is constantly focused on external stimuli. The soothing system, which causes your attention to be more open and thus makes you susceptible to physical sensations, is always the loser here and reports an 'error' – in other words, you suffer (chronic) stress. This affects large numbers of people: more than 7.5 million work days are lost owing to stress each year, at the cost of 1.6 billion pounds (2.1 billion US dollars).

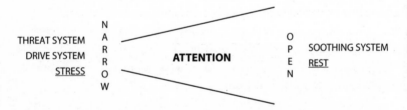

Figure 2.1 Attention and your emotion regulatory systems: an overview of your attention span at times of stress and rest, including the prevailing systems.
Source: © Wouter de Jong

STRESS

However, it's not the triggers themselves – the angry customer, the argument with your partner, the expectations imposed on you by your environment – that are the primary cause of chronic stress, but rather your *interpretation* of them. It's your perception that causes you to panic when your inbox is overflowing and your diary is packed to the rafters, or makes you, by contrast, able to deal with these things calmly and happily; it's your perception that makes you feel stressed in a traffic jam or alternatively makes you feel relaxed ('Great, a moment for myself at last!').

Research has shown that the amount of stress you experience is less important than how you perceive that stress.[17] We find that people who consider stress useful have physical responses to stress that correspond to what happens in the body when we feel joy: the heart is beating faster, but the blood vessels stay relaxed. There's an interesting aside here: stress doesn't trigger health problems in such people; on the contrary, people who find stress useful have a high(er) life expectancy.

Your perception – your internal experience – is the thing over which you have the most influence. Even if you do experience stress, how you perceive it is crucial. Does stress make you (more) upset? Or can you take a step back and perceive it as something that could even help you at times? As something that enabled you to perform better as well as act as a wonderful alarm system?

> Do you usually divide up your time? Do you set aside eight hours for work, an hour for your children, an hour for your partner, half an hour for preparing a meal and some time for yourself? If you think about it, sharing out your time in this way is a bit strange, because all time is your time, isn't it? Why don't you look at your to-do list for today from a different perspective? Could you unite the must-dos and want-to-dos?

SIT-UP

READ YOUR BODY

It may sound contradictory, but you can distance yourself from your own stress by focusing on your body, especially on the area in which your stress first becomes apparent. This is something you haven't done sufficiently because of the stress... But why not reverse the flow? If you pay green (accepting) attention to your physical sensations, you will trigger the soothing system (calmness), which means that you open your attention and are susceptible to physical sensations, which in turn activates your soothing system...

If we go back to how we were tearing around in the beginning: treat yourself in the same way as you treat your car. Pay attention to your 'empty tank' and your 'warning lights', and to the message your body is giving you. And, just as you do with a car, maintain your body by giving it a check-up every now and again, especially also at times of (relative) peace and quiet. Ask yourself: What am I actually feeling? Read your logbook – it will help you activate your soothing system.

SIT-UP	Focus your attention on the physical sensations in your right hand (temperature, dryness, tingling). Now consciously transfer this accepting attention to your whole body. Which sensation comes to the fore? You might notice that you are thirsty, or your feet are cold, or there's some tension in your neck. Notice what's going on, but don't pass any judgement – *why is my neck so bloody stiff again* – just accept that it is! And if (such) thoughts pop up, make a note of them without passing any judgement and quietly return your attention to your body.

THE MONDAY MORNING MODEL

The 'Monday morning model' (Figure 2.2) explains why, and how, focusing conscious and accepting attention on the body has a calming effect.

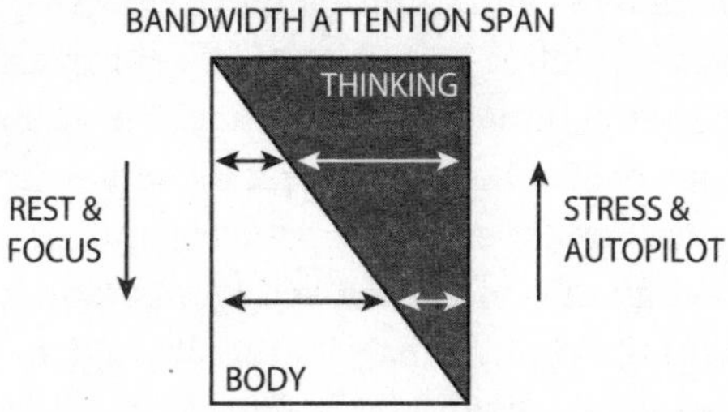

Figure 2.2 The Monday morning model: at the top of the 'funnel', attention consists mainly of thoughts, while at the bottom it consists of sensory stimuli.
Source: © Wouter de Jong

It's 8.30am, you haven't slept well, you've left home after an argument and have arrived at work with a headache; what's more today's diary is chock-a-block. There's a whirlwind of thoughts in your head: you're worrying about the argument, all the to-dos are playing ping-pong, concerns are piling up. In short, your attention is subconscious, it is red (resisting), narrow and completely taken over by thinking. You are in the top right corner of the diagram. In addition, you've received an irritating email from a pushy client. Your fingers are ready to type an angry response.

But then you remind yourself about the warning lights in the car and you allow yourself to focus your attention on your body. You focus on the warmth of the cup of tea against your hand and on the light tension of the muscle needed to lift it to your mouth. You also notice your headache and the adrenaline rush through your body. Although not all of these sensations are nice and some are decidedly unpleasant, you try to approach all your sensations with green (accepting) attention.

Because you can only focus on one thing at a time – think back to the Necker cube – your attention gradually shifts from stressful thoughts to sensations in your body. In terms of the diagram, you are now progressing to bottom left. Your whirlwind of thoughts weakens and becomes a light breeze, and slowly but surely your soothing system takes over.

By quietly focusing your attention on your physical sensations you have been able to distance yourself from stressful thoughts instead of responding immediately to them. This allows you to make a conscious decision about your next action. You might still decide to write that angry email, but at least you are making a conscious decision and you are not acting on autopilot.

Your body can give you a lot of sensible advice, but you need to be capable of recognising such advice. By training your attention you will learn how to be aware of those invaluable physical signals. Listen to and act on the wisdom of your body! The body's wisdom was made clear in an experiment conducted by the University of Iowa in which subjects were linked to a detector that recorded the activity of sweat glands in their hands: the more stress they felt, the more sweat their hands produced. They were playing a card game in which the cards had been stacked: subjects always won with the pack of blue cards and lost with the pack of red ones. After drawing approximately 50 cards, most participants began to realize what was going on. What was most interesting, though, was that, on average, they started to get sweaty hands after they took the tenth red card – that's 40 cards before they knew consciously that something was fishy. Their body was smarter – quicker – than their conscious thoughts.[18]

BONUS

Your posture gives your body an attention bonus. Your mind simply follows physical actions; like a docile sheep, it virtually replicates what happens in your body. For example, it appears that open inviting movements make you more receptive to someone's story. The way you sit, walk or stand also affects your mind: a closed posture (crossed legs, bent shoulders) increases stress, while an open posture reduces stress. In addition, an open posture will help you develop more positive feelings and creates clarity in your mind. And, finally, if you are very busy, don't forget to lift the corners of your mouth.

Regardless of whether you are feeing genuinely happy, smiling has been found to have a strong reductive impact on stress.[19]

In an experiment at the University of Michigan, participants had to read a story while simultaneously stretching and bending specific fingers. They were told that this was to test the hypothesis that the use of muscles affected reading comprehension. What the researchers were trying to measure was whether raising your middle finger led to a negative perception of the story and whether raising your thumb would have the opposite effect. Both hypotheses were confirmed. The thumb and middle finger, respectively, also had a positive and negative effect on the participants' feelings of happiness.

EYE-OPENER

TRAINING

This week you will train your attention muscle by focusing on physical sensations, which will make you less dependent on the automatic preferences of your attention that arise from the threat and drive systems. A stronger body awareness gives you the opportunity to recognize stress signals sooner and to deal with them more constructively.

▮▮▮ LIGHT

This week, I'm going to give you four exercises that you can do at different times of the day.

EXERCISE 1: BREATHER 2.0

Last week you consciously practised inhaling and exhaling three times; this week you will focus on taking the breather. You can practise the breather anywhere and at any time of day (in the shower, in the lift, waiting at traffic lights). Do breather 2.0 at least three times a day, from 30 seconds to a few minutes.

Check with yourself:

↔ What is the focus of my attention? Then ask yourself: What am I experiencing at this moment? Are there any thoughts, feelings, emotions, a particular mood? What am I experiencing in my body? All you need to do is notice; don't make any judgement.

↔ What is my breathing like? Then focus on your breathing. Pay full attention to your inhaling and exhaling from beginning to end. You don't need to change your breathing; you only need to notice it.

↔ What does my body feel like? Then widen your attention to the physical sensations in your whole body. Whatever you find, let it be.

EXERCISE 2: CONSCIOUS WALKING

Once a day, walk for a few minutes and be conscious of the physical sensations this gives you. Try to feel every step instead of just moving towards your destination. It's helpful to focus on a specific anchor, for example what you feel in your knees or on the soles of your feet as you take each step. If you find yourself losing your attention, becoming distracted and/or having thoughts popping up, refocus your attention on the sensations on the soles of your feet or another point of focus in the body.

EXERCISE 3: YOUR BODY

Next week, take notice of pleasant events (from a compliment to an unexpected bonus) and unpleasant events (from a delayed train to an argument) and pay attention to how they feel in your body. Focus your attention on concrete sensations as much as you can. A useful tool is to name those sensations, for example, tingling, shuddering, numbness, shooting pain or warmth. If thoughts pop up, recognize them and return to your physical sensations.

EXERCISE 4: STRESS

Try to recognize stress at an earlier stage:

- ↤ Be aware of physical sensations such as a knot in your stomach, a headache, tingling or raised shoulders.
- ↤ Also try to identify stressors – work, your mother/father, the dog – and then find out the impact they are having on your body. Do you experience stress because your drive system is dominant (I *want to, I must, I shall*) or is your threat system taking over (*I don't want this, I find it scary, I want to hide/ disappear*)?
- ↤ In addition, try to be aware of what feelings and thoughts arise and cause stress, and the impact of stress on your actions.
- ↤ If you notice stress patterns in yourself, don't blame yourself. Instead, realize that it's great that you have noticed them. After all, it gives you the chance to put the attention and breathing

exercises into practice. Remind yourself that stress (within reason) can be useful in some situations.

⟩ TRAINER'S TIP

1. Use reminders to help you keep practising. For example, use your screensaver, put yellow stickies on the mirror, or invent passwords such as 'Iwillnowconsciouslyinhalethreetimes'.

2. Reflect on the exercises at the end of the day. Before you hit the pillow, ask yourself: Did I manage to focus my attention for at least five minutes today? If you didn't, do another (couple of) exercise(s).

3. Do not perceive attention training as a punishment, but as a gift to yourself.

▮▮ MEDIUM

EXTENSION TO LIGHT If you would like to do some extra training, you could alternate every other day with the sitting meditation, the Attention to Breathing and Body in week 1 and the Body Scan. When you are doing the body scan, you literally scan different parts of your body. This is to check what you are feeling, from the tip of your toes to the top of your head. Remembering not to pass judgement, notice when your monkey mind comes on stage and return your attention to your bodily sensations. Use the audio tracks for both sets of training.

🎧 Audio track 2. Attention to breathing and body

🎧 Audio track 3. Body scan

⟩ TRAINER'S TIP
Did you find it difficult to do any additional exercises in Week 1? Here are some tips and tricks to help you keep going:

. Plan the attention exercises like any other appointment in
  your diary.
₂. Apply healthy habits: plan to do the exercises at set times.
₃. Do the exercise in a place where you feel comfortable. This
  will make doing your exercises more appealing. Create a corner or area in your home for you alone. Display some objects
  that make you feel relaxed, such as a photograph, candle or
  ornament.

Are you still finding it a lot or too much to cope with? In that case,
remember that the light training alone will give you enough exercise!

ıİІ INTENSE

EXTENSION TO LIGHT + MEDIUM If you are aiming to do
some intensive training this week, then alternate daily between
the Body scan and the Attention to breathing and body meditation,
and immediately follow up with the Attention to sound exercise.
It is highly likely that performing two meditations consecutively
will seem more difficult, perhaps because you become impatient or
because you get fed up of hearing that voice. An increase in thoughts
and automatic behaviours that distract your attention is a good thing:
it means there is more for you to pay attention to. Especially when
you experience resistance, you can learn many things about the way
in which your attention works and how you can regain control.

🎧 Audio track 2. Attention to breathing and body.

🎧 Audio track 3. Body scan

🎧 Audio track 4. Attention to sound

🎧 You can download the audio tracks from 12weekmindworkout.com

COOL DOWN

No matter how many times you move house in your life, your body is the only place in which you will permanently reside. Just as you have to maintain your home from the roof to the foundations, your body also deserves your full attention – not only by exercising and eating healthily, but also through body awareness. This week you've laid the foundations for strengthening this awareness. It helps you learn – even when it feels unpleasant – to be at ease with your physical sensations, without being captivated by the autopilot in your threat or drive systems.

So how did it go this week? Maybe you found it difficult to keep your attention on body signals during the training exercises. Maybe you enjoyed your mind wandering off into a stream of consciousness during your sitting meditation, without stepping out of your thoughts. Or did you fall asleep during a Body scan? Perhaps it was even more difficult to notice what you were feeling without being judgemental, and maybe you thought impatiently, 'Yes, I know all about that toe!', and then became annoyed about your impatience. Or maybe you didn't feel anything at all and this made you doubt yourself or the exercise. In this phase, you've taken the first step from unconsciously unskilled – when you haven't a clue about attention, drifting or automatic behaviours – to consciously unskilled, when you are aware how attention works and of the pitfalls. This learning phase can be frustrating, and it's certainly not always pleasant or easy. But believe me, it will all improve through practice and you'll reap the benefits.

> *'Whatever you sow in your unconscious mind,*
> *you will reap in your body or life.'*
>
> JOSEPH MURRAY

Ask yourself if you have achieved any of the following in Week 2:

↔ Can you distinguish between the threat, drive and soothing
systems?
↔ Do you know which system you often resort to automatically?
↔ Has your overall awareness of bodily sensations improved?
↔ Are you able to identify your stressors and the effect they have
on your body?

IN CONCLUSION

Treating body and mind as separate entities is likely to cause trouble. Our body and mind are caught up in an intimate, never-ending
tango. If we let them get out of step with each other, we ruin the
harmony.

A busy man was asked how he could be so relaxed, despite all his
activities. He answered: 'When I stand, I stand; when I go, I go; when I
sit, I sit; when I eat, I eat; when I speak, I speak.' 'But we do that too,'
exclaimed the inquirer. 'What else do you do?' He repeated his answer.
And again, the author of the question said: 'But surely we all do that?' The
man said: 'No, you don't. When you sit, you're already standing; when you
stand, you're already walking; when you walk, you've already arrived; and
when you eat, you've already finished.'

EYE-OPENER

03

DEALING WITH THOUGHTS AND EMOTIONS

> *'The thoughts have us instead of*
> *us having the thoughts.'*
> DAVID BOHM

After the basics (breathing) in Week 1, we discussed last week how you can check your own condition (both physically and mentally) by paying attention to your body. The focus on your body grounds the focus on your thoughts and emotions, which you will be working on this week. I will show you how thoughts and feelings can be an obstacle to your attention and can cause you to involuntarily revert to autopilot. Of course, I will also show you what you can do about it.

WARM-UP THOUGHTS

Thoughts are wonderful. Because we can think, we have medicines and technological developments, and we can communicate and make music. We have an extraordinary number of thoughts – researchers estimate about 50,000 per day.[20] For the sake of comparison, we generally utter about 16,000 words per day.[21]

Read the following:

Charles goes to school. He's worried about the maths lesson. Yesterday he didn't manage to control the class. After all, that's not the janitor's job.

Most likely, in your mind Charles progressed from student to teacher to janitor. Without noticing, you put labels on Charles that turned out to be incorrect. You usually do this unconsciously, mentally, in your thoughts. Half of your thoughts are unconscious, and they do not always match reality – look at the example of Charles. Often your stream of thoughts is like a Monday-morning meeting, long-winded, not leading anywhere, seeming to last weeks, in which your most boring colleague always shows you the same presentation or – even worse – PowerPoint slides. About 90 per cent of our thoughts consist of repetitions.

OBSTACLES

When it comes to living with more attention, thoughts can be obstacles. For example, it's not easy to distinguish between your stream of thoughts and observations. You regard your thoughts as 'the truth' and follow them blindly. You think you have thoughts, but instead the thoughts have you. Three mechanisms play a part here: interpretation, judgement and rethinking.

Ceci n'est pas une pipe.

SIT-UP

Look at this painting by René Magritte. What do you see? A pipe with the text: 'This is not a pipe.' Now you may be thinking, but surely this is a pipe! And yet Magritte is right: it isn't a pipe, it's a collection of brush strokes representing a pipe. In fact, because this is a reproduction of Magritte's painting, it's actually thousands of pixels on a piece of paper.

INTERPRETING

Your thoughts are an interpretation of what is happening around you, all your experiences, ranging across taste, touch, smell, sight and hearing. These experiences connect with previous experiences. The word 'pipe' or the painting of a pipe is not a pipe, but our mental concept of a pipe. Likewise, the word 'apple' is not the apple itself, but a reference to that apple. Have you ever taken a bite out of the thought of an apple? The interpretation mechanism saves precious mental energy because it allows you to assess situations quickly.

> **SIT-UP**
>
> Listen to a sound and make a note each time you notice you are thinking *about* the sound. Note how difficult it is to listen without interpretation or judgement.

Interpretation generally happens unconsciously. When you hear a loud roaring sound outside (*vroom vroom*!) it is also linked to duration, volume and pitch, among others. The vroom sound is usually not the only part of the whole story.

When you hear the sound, it immediately invites associations (with, for example, a car, truck, moped, hedge trimmer, drill) or maybe you immediately have a picture of a Saab or your grandfather's vintage car, or thoughts about mopeds in general (*oh, how annoying they are*).

At first, we only hear something, but very soon we have a succession of thoughts about (the interpretation of) what we hear. It is difficult to separate hearing – or any other sensory perception – from thinking. If you want a more mindful life, you need to be clear about the thoughts that shape your reality. What helps is your ability to separate your sensory stimuli from your thoughts – especially if they are mixed with negative emotions. For example, after a conversation with your mother, your thoughts may run like this: 'She's always critical, I can't do anything right in her eyes!'

JUDGEMENTS

And this brings me to the second mechanism that makes thoughts an obstacle to your paying attention: judgement. This goes a step further than interpretation; after all, you are also going to have an opinion about your observations.

I'm not going to tell you to stop making judgements; life would become very boring if we did. What's more, your personal judgements can be very useful. For example, they play a part in your decision to take another path through the park at dusk when you see someone with a long raincoat is coming straight towards you. Better safe than sorry.

It becomes troublesome, however, when your personal judgements become an obstruction. *Why hasn't my boyfriend/girlfriend replied to my text messages, he/she's probably not interested in me. I'm more entitled to that bonus than my colleague is. He/she is hopeless, I'll do it myself. I am not likely to have another stable relationship.* These kind of implicit conclusions are usually incorrect, and such thoughts affect your behaviour or create stress: I can't do this, I am superior to others, I am no good, I have no time, I will never manage, he/she must hate me.

Try to view the following things objectively: your partner or boyfriend/girlfriend, your work, your appearance. How quickly do you get caught up in judgements? Note how difficult it is to be objective. We even stick labels on 'concrete' objects, such as a phone (cool, old, slow, useful).

SIT-UP

Judging thoughts can lead to fantasies. An objective observation ('These are my legs') ends up being given a subjective label and thus stray far from the truth ('They are fat/thin/short'). Within nanoseconds, reality is coloured by a subjective judgement, and consequently you lose your ability to perceive objectively.

The following experiment shows that even the smallest of animals can be trapped inside their minds: an ant is placed on a piece of paper inside a circle coloured in black ink. For hours the little creature walks around inside the circle, without crossing the black 'border'. The ant is trapped in its self-created delusion – the idea that it cannot cross the black line.

EYE-OPENER

RETHINKING

You might say that chocolate, Instagram or running is your greatest addiction, but in fact everything is superseded by thinking. We have thought after thought, judgements encourage fantasies, and before we realize it our mental activity consists only of an unconscious, infinite stream of thoughts. For most people, 95 per cent of their attention is filled with thoughts. This 'addiction' leaves us with little room to pay attention to other things, such as our senses – what we hear, feel, taste and see – which are more objective than thoughts.

Like most addictions we would prefer to get rid of this persistent thinking process, so we often push annoying thoughts aside. However, this isn't a desirable way to pull yourself out of a (frequently negative) spiral of thoughts – and very often not a successful one either. Although thoughts can lift us up to incredible heights, they can also make us so mad, even kill us.

A recent study at the University of Virginia showed that many preferred getting an electric shock to being alone with their thoughts. Participants remained on their own in an empty, bare room for six to fifteen minutes without any form of distraction. It was found that 67 per cent of the male and 25 per cent of the female participants preferred to have an electric shock than having to sit out their time.[22]

You probably didn't need a study to tell you this. You just have to consider how angry airline passengers can be if their in-flight entertainment system doesn't work and they have to spend five minutes with their own thoughts.

Our method of dealing with annoying thoughts (if we are aware of them!) is to follow them blindly (that bag of crisps is empty before you know it) or to suppress them. But are you in complete control of your thoughts? Just try to avoid thinking about a white bear or a pink elephant. Pushing thoughts aside just doesn't work. What about avoiding thoughts by distracting yourself? It may help and can certainly be highly effective temporarily: watching a film or doing some sport may be necessary, and can feel good, too! And yet in the long term your unconscious stream of thoughts will take over your awareness. It's not until you manage to refocus your attention on your senses – your body focus – and subsequently on your thoughts, that you might be able to keep them in control.

> '*Eventually, we become our thoughts. The thought manifests itself as a word. The word manifests itself as an action. The action develops into habit and habit perseveres and becomes character.*'
>
> BUDDHA

TAKE THAT OBSTACLE

The best way to find more focus in your stream of thoughts is to get some distance from your thoughts. Ask yourself: in which thoughts would I like to invest? You need to have a clear idea of what your thoughts are before you can answer this question and to recognize them as *thoughts* and not as facts. You want to register your thoughts without judgement, and be above your thoughts so that you can make a conscious decision about which thoughts will help you take action and which ones you should ignore: your own fantasies.

You can focus on your breathing, your body, a ticking clock, a howling wind or the construction of the kitchen table without judgement. You can do this with your own thoughts, too. Your challenge is to be aware that they are your thoughts, without becoming lost in them, without analysing them (reflection on thinking), without wishing to understand, or daydream, or push them aside – without, even, wanting anything of them. It's actually simple: put a sticker on 'thinking' which says THINKING.

Thoughts pop up each and every moment. The realization that you are thinking precedes the actual thought. Just compare it to a wide screen in the cinema. You lean back in your comfy seat and watch the thoughts appear on the screen. You're not part of the set (your thoughts), you remain a spectator (you have open attention). And whether you see a fire, a sunrise or a waterfall on the screen, it's not actually on fire, warming up or wet. In other words, your thoughts are not facts.

BEING AWARE OF YOUR THOUGHTS

The thought 'What a strange guy!' and then thinking about this thinking ('It's rather unkind of me to think that' or 'He must be stone drunk, I think') is different from 'Hey, a thought has just popped up about that man', or 'I am making assumptions about him'. The latter two prove you are aware of your thoughts, which is necessary to determine (from a distance) which thoughts are helpful and which are not. Unlike the first two, they make sure you are not unconsciously drawn into a story or an analysis. If you look at a piece of clothing from half a centimetre away, you will only see a piece of fabric; if you take a large step back, you will clearly see that it's a T-shirt. The same applies to thinking: when you think about thinking, you are right on top of it; your awareness of thinking will give you more insight.

SIT-UP

Observe your thoughts arising without wanting to change, understand or analyse them, or allowing yourself to be drawn in by them. If you have a surge of thoughts, name them with a sense of curiosity – 'Interesting, I have thoughts!' – so that it's as if you are labelling them with a 'thinking' sticker. Don't let the content of your thoughts absorb you and try not to think about thinking. Also take notice if no thoughts arise. During the exercise, try to have (some) awareness of your breathing. And remember that the thought 'I am not thinking now' is a thought, too.

If you found the sit-up difficult, don't get discouraged: practice makes perfect. Losing focus, getting caught up in your stories and thoughts and (eventually) noticing is good practice. In fact, it's what the exercise is about! Or did you find the exercise a piece of cake? Well, maybe you've got a natural talent, but it's more likely that you've confused thinking about thinking with being aware of your thoughts.

For example, many people who meditate don't actually meditate; they just think with their eyes closed. Even if you feel that you suddenly have no thoughts at all, chances are that you are simply not aware of them. This isn't a problem – the advice is the same: keep practising. You will only experience the difference between thinking about thinking and being aware of your thoughts by doing a lot of practice. That is how you learn to distinguish and create a distance between these two things.

Sometimes a situation is too intense to deal with it through attention training only. It might be that your colleague has done you wrong and stopped you from getting a promotion, or a teacher has told you that your daughter is being bullied. Even if you remind yourself in such situations to view your thoughts from a distance, you can't get away from them; you become your thoughts. In that case, you can use a different technique based on cognitive behavioural therapy: question your thoughts at that moment with other thoughts to determine whether they're helpful. This is not your being aware of thinking, so it does not fall under attention training; this is about thinking about thinking. There are three key questions you could ask yourself in such a situation:

1. Is what I think true?
2. Is my thought helpful?
3. Is my thought kind and/or wise (and does it match your values)?

Obstructive thoughts are the stories you keep telling yourself and you strongly believe in. Here are five common types of obstructive thoughts to help you spot them more easily.

1. The love junkie: 'Everybody must like me.'
2. The disaster thinker: 'It can't go right; I don't want to risk it.'
3. The perfectionist: 'I shouldn't make any mistakes.'
4. The moralist: 'Everybody must follow my standards; you should never cancel an appointment.'
5. The victim: 'I am in that traffic jam again; I will probably fail again, like always.'

> **SIT-UP**
>
> Which of these five obstructive thoughts do you have? Or are there others? What would be a helpful alternative thought for you?

WARM-UP EMOTIONS

Any emotion can blind you, not just love. It might be that terrible fear that tells you to leave the stage during a presentation, or the resentment that prevents you from forgiving a close friend for some idiocy or other, or the excessive anxiety that causes a mother to constantly say to her child: 'Be careful!'

The more intense your emotions, the harder it is to be objective. If you are hopelessly in love, you may see your partner as a visionary, whereas other people may think he or she is just a know-it-all. And if you are distraught because you have a broken heart, you may be convinced that you'll never love somebody again. If you are still fuming with anger, it makes it difficult for you to assess to what degree you were responsible in an argument. Many people consider 'Because I feel this emotion it's the truth.' Apart from thoughts, feelings are the second factor that can get in the way of your paying attention.

BASIC EMOTIONS

There are six basic emotions, each with a clear function:

Fear: survival. In dangerous situations, we try to stay safe.

Anger: movement. This motivates us to protect what we believe to be valuable.

Sadness: acceptance and strengthening of relationships. If we show we are sad, we appeal to someone else for help or comfort.

Joy: encouragement. This provides us with the motivation to hold on to what we enjoy and to do it more often.

Disgust: abstinence. This keeps us away from things that aren't good for us.

Surprise: open to new information. This you can literally see in someone's face: their eyes grow big, the eyebrows rise and the mouth opens.

Any feeling we experience can be traced back to one of these six basic emotions or a combination thereof. Consider melancholy, which is a mixture of sadness and joy, or shame, which combines anger and fear. For example, disappointment is a part of sadness, calmness belongs to joy, and irritation belongs to anger. Every human being – wherever he or she is from, the UK, USA, France, Japan – feels these basic emotions and uses the same facial muscles.

The animated film *Inside Out* (2015), created with the assistance of leading emotion scientists, takes you inside an eleven-year-old girl named Riley's mind as she deals with an emotional event in her young life – moving to a different city. In the film, Riley's head is presented as a control room, in which five basic emotions dominate: joy, fear, anger, disgust and sadness (to keep it simple they omitted the sixth fundamental emotion, surprise). The emotion control room advises Riley on her decisions.

It can be helpful to think of an emotion and what arises from that emotion as like four nesting dolls. The smallest doll in the centre represents the physical part, the physical sensations: the shudder you feel when you look down from a mountain peak or a high bridge, or that knot in your stomach when you say goodbye to your loved one. Then follows the doll that gives value to those feelings. Is the feeling strong or weak, pleasant or unpleasant? The third little doll represents your thinking and/or talking about those feelings. You might think, I am so sad, or you shout because you are furious. The fourth little doll is the action linked to your feelings: hiding away, lashing out, crying.

STIMULATING ACTION

Just like your thoughts, your emotions therefore also have a leading function. You listen (often unconsciously) to their orders and organize your whole life in such a way that you experience as many pleasant emotions and as few unpleasant ones as possible. Emotions stimulate action; they help us act (quickly). If they feel pleasant, they teach you to do this more often, or to continue doing so; if they feel unpleasant, the message is to keep away or to change the situation. Emotions mean well, even the unpleasant ones.

When Riley moves house in the film, everything in her head is turned upside down. We see how her emotions cope with this enormous change. For Riley, joy is the dominant emotion in the control room: 'Everything should be fun.' The others aren't allowed to join. This leaves less space for other emotions, such as sadness. So, because the move isn't fun, chaos breaks out in the control room.

HAPPY?!

Whatever may be happening in Riley's head, her frantic holding on to positive emotions is something we all do. This is especially the case in the West, where being happy has almost attained religious status, with the smiley emoji its cult symbol. Although we tend to ban negative (unpleasant) emotions, feelings generally surface without our having any say in the matter. Just try not to feel fear when you are threatened in the dark by two big, broad-shouldered men.

Humans are deeply programmed to avoid pain, but pain is inevitable. After all, we can't help but fall ill, get fined, suffer relationship breakups, fall off our bikes or unexpectedly lose our jobs. Whatever those self-help books tell you, *life sucks* (now and then). Imagine you trip over a jutting-out pavement slab and badly scrape your knee. Ouch! Instead of tending to the wound, though, you start to worry. Why was that pavement slab sticking up? Why was it me who tripped? In many instances of suffering (physical and psychological), this is exactly how we behave; instead of looking after ourselves, we resist. It is how we fight our darker moods, drown our sorrows, or push past setbacks. This kind of *fight–flight–freeze* response can be effective: sometimes you have to fight back if there's a (serious) physical risk, you have to run away or freeze. However, if we want to fight or flee from our pain, it is counterproductive. This applies especially to emotions. Consider a mosquito bite. The more you scratch, the more it starts to itch. The bite means *trouble*; the scratching – resistance – *double trouble*; and our annoyance because we find ourselves scratching and blaming ourselves for resisting means *triple trouble.*

We need negative (unpleasant) emotions as well as positive (pleasant) emotions. But it can be difficult to estimate the value of how negative emotions can help us. Of course, you can distract yourself when you have difficult emotions or wrap yourself up in them.

In the short term, this is fine. Difficulties arise if you suppress or bury your unpleasant feelings on autopilot – say if you start to grumble about your employees every time you feel stress, or grab your smartphone to start texting someone. These actions are like adding fuel to the flames: they will lead to increased emotion (in this case stress and anger). If you want to benefit from your emotions, it is important to realize that they are not here to annoy us. You need to keep an appropriate distance to separate your objective observations from your emotions. That is the ideal situation, but let's have a look now at the reality.

TO SUPPRESS OR TO SUBMIT, THAT'S THE QUESTION

Like thoughts, emotions can be uninvited guests; there's not much you can do about them. You can, however, influence them depending on whether and how you welcome them. Do you slam the door in their face and push a heavy chest so there's no way they can get in? Or maybe you open the door wide and give your guest complete freedom, allowing them to put their feet up on the table. Often, we do one or the other: either we suppress our emotions or we wallow in them.

Suppression allows our fear of feeling to play a part. It means you will miss out on a lot of valuable information. Your emotions tell you what you find important in life. If you have feelings of guilt towards your family, suppression probably means you won't go and watch your little boy take his swimming certificate but spend yet another Saturday in the office.

When you wallow, you are overwhelmed by a wave of emotions that sweeps you along because you've lost control. You are not in control of the action. Giving the finger on the motorway, slamming your fist down on the table, obsessively checking your phone... this is also not the way to recognize the underlying messages that your emotions are trying to convey.

SIT-UP

How do you deal with your emotions? Do you double-lock your door or do you keep it open? Would you rather suppress your emotions or drown in them? Most people prefer one or the other, but of course it can vary between situations and emotions. Maybe you lock the door after a break-up but open it when you are angry with your boss. Perhaps you're often suppressing your financial fears.

The whistling kettle theory was popular for quite a while: the idea was that by completely absorbing yourself in your emotions you could apparently process and get rid of them. Think of training sessions where participants vent their anger by thrashing boxing balls. Studies show that bashing a boxing ball may give you temporary relief, but in the long term it will only accelerate and intensify your anger.[23]

WHAT'S THE SOLUTION? - DANC(E)

You, the feeler, want to be the boss, not your feelings. As with thoughts, you need to get some distance here, too. You need to detach your feelings from the way in which you deal with them. But how? The most straightforward way – but also the most difficult – is by doing nothing, feeling your emotions and letting them be. In this way, you stay in control by fully feeling your emotions and keeping in touch with them. The four-step DANC(E) plan can help you too DANC(E) in harmony with your emotions:

↔ Determine: determine and recognize emotions.
↔ Accept: investigate with an accepting mind.
↔ No/t: do not identify, no need to act.
↔ Calm down: calm yourself and make conscious decisions.
resulting in
Emotion becomes Encouraging: to take wise action.

DANC(E) isn't a tool to make your emotions disappear (although that could feasibly happen), but it helps you stay in control of your emotions. You are no longer afraid of your fear. In Riley's terms, in *your* control room *you* determine what happens, not your emotions.

DETERMINE

The core of your emotions lies in your body. In this step, you localize your feeling (e.g. anger) in your body, accept it and then stick a label on it (internally or out loud): for example 'Anger', 'Shame'. This is also called *affect labelling*. It's worth adding here that you can also apply this step to positive emotions.

In an experiment, subjects were shown photographs of emotional faces. Group A was asked to think of a first name for each face, such as Marcel or Lola, while Group B was asked to label the emotion (angry, frightened, etc.). The researchers discovered that the amygdala, which is a part of the brain that is active in emotions, did not light up as much in Group B (who applied a label to the emotion) as in Group A (who suggested a first name). By contrast, the parts of the brain responsible for actively *investigating* our emotions showed more activity in Group B than in Group A. It seemed that the subjects who labelled their emotions were not held hostage by their feelings to the same extent as those in Group A. The study also showed that the more experienced a subject was in meditation and attention training, the greater their ability to label their emotions, and the less control those emotions exerted over them.[24]

So, localizing feelings (once again, we can see the importance of body focus!) and giving them a name will increase your grip on your emotions. There are various ways to do the labelling – you can...

↔ Focus your attention internally (on your body).
↔ Write about your emotions – and then try not to concentrate too much on facts or what you should be doing or feeling but, instead, maximize your focus on your emotions and how they *feel*.
↔ Talk – the challenge is not to analyse and look for solutions, but to feel and verbalize what your feelings are doing to you and your level of acceptance.

SIT-UP

Think of the latest compliment you received. See if you can locate your current feelings about that compliment in your body and label them. Now do the same regarding the time you were severely criticized or did a stupid thing that really annoyed you. Labelling helps you be aware of your feelings at a specific moment.

If you feel your feelings moving, it is a sign that you are labelling them accurately and appropriately. The emotion feels fluid instead of fixed, changeable instead of static. Think of an unlabelled emotion as a block of ice. Precise affect labelling makes the emotion melt; it becomes flexible, feels lighter and can be washed away more easily. You will then experience an 'aha' moment, or relief. It is not because you've suddenly stopped being jealous/angry/appalled, but because you understand what's going on.

You will find that the time you are absorbed by an emotion has shortened (science calls this the 'refractory period').[25] If you are having a serious disagreement with your sister that has been on your mind for several days, there will be less room for other things. Your work suffers, your children or friends suffer; you are generally less attentive.

Affect labelling and focus without resistance will shorten the refractory period of emotions. You will still feel the emotion, but the intensity decreases more quickly.

Be careful: if you *think too much* about labelling your emotion, you risk losing the focus on your body that enables you to *feel* the emotion. You are then more likely to think of a label that doesn't match your body signals. The refractory period might even increase.

> *'What you can feel, you can heal.'*
>
> ANONYMOUS

ACCEPTING AND INVESTIGATING

Once you have recognized your feelings, the second step is to accept and investigate them. Accepting emotions isn't the same as resigning or surrendering like a helpless beetle on its back. Should I accept someone verbally abusing me? Should I accept someone preventing me from being promoted? Should I hold my emotions at bay when my partner is late for the umpteenth time? Of course not! It is about learning to understand and accept your internal experience, so that your response to the outside world becomes less of an automatic response. If someone jumps the queue, you will now be more aware of the irritation in your body and you can make a conscious decision as to what would be more constructive: telling the person politely that they've pushed ahead or simply to ignore what they've done. Your feelings are there to accept; problems are there to be solved. This will give you space to see what you can and what you cannot solve.

Imagine you've had a quarrel with your best friend. You did something that was wrong in her eyes, and you can see her point. Although you talked it over and said sorry, she's still angry. You have done everything possible to solve the problem, but you haven't been successful. You turn what's happened over and over in your mind, and you can't get to sleep, even though you know there's nothing more you can do about it. Here's the way out of the impasse: allow the feeling of guilt to enter your body, and experience the knot in your stomach with green investigatory attention. This will mean that you do not unconsciously resort to suppressing the emotion or drowning it out. You're in control, not the emotion.

EYE-OPENER

In a research experiment, two groups were asked to keep their hands in a bowl of ice as long as possible. One group was asked to focus with curiosity on the physical sensation of pain; the other group was asked to distract themselves from the pain by thinking of, for example, their loved ones, a favourite dish or a dream vacation. The study showed that during the first few minutes the latter technique seemed to be most effective, but it soon became apparent that the group who were focusing on the pain could keep their hands in the bowl of ice much longer.[26]

Feeling an unpleasant emotion can sting or burn, in other words hurt. Think of pain as being like a beach ball bobbing in the swimming pool: the harder you try to push it down, the harder it hits your nose when it forces itself to the surface again. The exercise and challenge are to be open to the pain and to feel it fully in your body without immediately wanting to get rid of it and even being prepared to investigate it. No, it's not pleasant, but it's necessary – in the second instance, in the longer term, you'll find it easier to deal appropriately with what feels unpleasant, with nasty events and annoying emotions experienced in your body at that moment. Attention training does not teach you to feel *good*, but to *feel* good.

NO IDENTIFYING

The penultimate step of DANC(E) is about making sure you do not identify with your emotion. An easy trick is to repeat to yourself: 'I have feelings, but my feelings aren't me.' This is about letting go. Admittedly, this can sometimes sound like a bit of a hollow phrase. 'Let it go,' says your friend when you are upset about a missed opportunity, or feel sad because a love affair hasn't worked out. Thanks for nothing. So how on earth do you let go? It's all about your focus. Don't focus on the verb itself, the *letting go* part, but what you are desperately *clinging on* to.

Native peoples hunting small monkeys do not use nets or bullets but peanuts. The hunters dangle an empty coconut filled with peanuts from a rope, with holes just big enough for an eager monkey's hand to slip through. Once an unsuspecting hungry monkey has got hold of the peanuts, the monkeys are stuck, as its fist, now clutching the peanuts, is too big to be pulled out if the coconut again. Although the monkey could easily release itself by dropping the peanuts, it continues to hold on stubbornly. This makes them easy prey for the hunters.

You, too, can often be like an eager monkey, clinging frantically to an emotion and your judgement. It may sound contradictory, but by clearly registering what exactly you are holding on to, it is easier to let go. Until then, accept your own frantic response; it will also help you let go all the sooner.

What are your peanuts? What are the stories you tell yourself, which ideas do you cling on to? For example: 'I am never going to find a new job. That's why I continue to do this work (even though it takes all my energy).' Or: 'My mother is so critical; she doesn't approve of anything I do.' Or: 'I have every right to be heartbroken – it was only a year ago, after all, that I was ditched!'

CALMING DOWN AND MAKING CONSCIOUS DECISIONS

The first three steps, DAN, are about your current emotions; the C (calming down) is about you. Whereas DAN is about 'what I am currently experiencing', the C of calming focuses on 'what I need'. In this fourth step, you will activate the soothing system to calm down and reassure yourself. In Part 2, we'll take a closer look at the calming techniques in DANC(E), and you will learn how to consciously appeal to your soothing system.

If you apply DANC(E) in its entirety, it will help you determine the wise course of action (the Encouragement in DANC(E)): constructive intervention or doing nothing (the power of the latter is often underestimated). The questions you should ask yourself at this stage are 'What do I need?' and 'What does the situation require?'

Let's look at a case study so we can see DANC(E) in practice. Karen is 42 years old. She has had a difficult relationship with her father. She finds him eccentric and preoccupied with his own wellbeing. The emotions she is fighting against are shame and anger. Karen thinks that she shouldn't be feeling this way; after all, he is her father. She is ashamed of her anger, but at the same time she remains angry with him. Her contact with her father has been difficult for years. In a coaching programme, Karen learns about affect labelling. She locates the anger in her body, then puts a label on it (internally or aloud), such as the labels 'Shame' or 'Anger', and practises accepting and investigating the emotion in her body. Karen continues to do so in the following weeks whenever she feels anger towards her father. Karen notices that she is clinging on to her anger. She repeats her mantra in her head again and again: 'I feel angry, but I am not the anger itself.' Gradually, she no longer feels overwhelmed by her emotion, and it begins to trouble her less. Karen's C, 'what I need', is that she wants to be recognized – by her father but also by others. She wants to feel an arm around her shoulders. Now she finds it easier to console herself. Although the relationship with her father continues to be difficult, she is more accepting of the situation.

You don't have to follow the DANC(E) steps in strict order, but it is the natural one. Sometimes a step passes very quickly, sometimes slowly. You cannot force your progress through the steps, and sometimes you may even have to go back a step. Accept where you currently are. Investigate how the current step feels with an open mind and curiosity, and sooner or later the next step will follow on naturally.

TRAINING

This week you will be training how to get a distance between you and your thoughts and feelings in an unassuming manner. This is to prevent you suppressing or drowning them out. How you go about achieving that is exactly what you were practising last week: focusing on physical stimuli.

▮▯▯ LIGHT

EXERCISE 1: BREATHER FOCUSED ON THINKING

Practice time: 30 seconds to two minutes. Take occasional breaks from what you are doing each day, breathe consciously and note your thoughts. When you become aware of a thought, label it internally as thinking. Don't allow yourself to be dragged along in the stream of your thoughts. You might notice a tendency to analyse, to delve into the origin of a particular thought. This isn't necessary; this exercise is only about registering your thoughts. I'm not asking you to fight the urge to analysis; just to take note: 'Hey, I'm analysing.' If you begin to feel trapped inside your thoughts, then focus on your breathing. When you feel more space, return your focus to registering thinking as thinking.

EXERCISE 2: BREATHER FOCUSED ON FEELINGS

Practice time: one to three minutes. This exercise follows on from the previous one.

Focus your attention on potential feelings and follow the first three steps in DANC(E): determine ('I feel jealousy/surprise, etc.), investigate with an accepting mind (don't push your anger/sadness/disgust aside, but allow it to happen and don't judge) and don't identify with your feelings ('I have feelings, but the feelings aren't me').

Practice related to emotions can raise many questions. You might not be used to this and it may even seem that you don't have any feelings. The feeling may be deep down and needs time to surface. If this is the case, try noticing whether you find something pleasant or unpleasant. Gradually, a strong focus on your body will help you learn how to feel and specify that feeling.

EXERCISE 3: AUTOPILOT

Take note of your autopilot under difficult circumstances. The more stress you experience, the harder it is to be present and alert. Register your thoughts, feelings and physical stimuli without judgement.

ıll MEDIUM

EXTENSION TO LIGHT

EXERCISE 1

🎧 Audio track 5. Attention to thoughts and feelings

If you find you are overwhelmed by your feelings and it feels unsafe to continue, it is recommended you ask an experienced coach to help you.

EXERCISE 2:

Focus your attention on your breathing for ten minutes every day without using an audio track. Use a timer.

ıll INTENSE

EXTENSION TO LIGHT + MEDIUM Every day:

🎧 Audio track 5. Attention to thoughts and feelings

If you are ready, you could choose four days of this week on which you follow up Attention to thoughts and feelings with a sitting meditation without audio track, as described below. It is advised to set a timer for 20 to 25 minutes.

The silent sitting mediation can be performed as follows. Go through all the focus points that are necessary to train attention, taking a few minutes to focus on each of them. Start with your breath, then proceed with your body, sounds, thoughts and emotions. This exercise takes a little longer, so you will be training the flexibility of your attention muscle. The advantage of the light and medium variations is that they are easier to access and practise. The great advantage of the intensive exercise, however, is that more resistance and obstructive patterns will arise. Attention exercises are not meant to make you feel relaxed or give you a pleasant feeling of wellbeing; they are intended to help you keep hold of an inner peace as soon as an obstructive pattern emerges, so that you can also apply this technique in your daily life. Remember: if the exercise becomes harder to do, it means you are actually learning!

🎧 You can download the audio tracks from 12weekmindworkout. com.

COOL DOWN

So how did this week go? Was it difficult? Bear in mind that you haven't trained your attention for umpteen years. Patience is paramount; you wouldn't pull on a seedling to make it grow faster. Do watch out for one thought in particular: 'I can't do it.' This will undermine all your efforts to continue practising. 'I can't do it' soon changes to 'I don't want to do this' or 'This fuss isn't my cup of tea.' 'I can't do it' is an obstructive thought we often encounter in our daily life.

If you notice this happening, then respond with a smile: 'Gotcha, this is a thought!' Don't judge, don't try to analyse or understand it. Keep things as simple as possible.

Something else that needs dealing with is a feeling of resistance. If you experience this, you could try investigating it by using the four DANC(E) steps. Welcome each phase; real acceptance is respecting to what degree you are open to, or closed to, feelings.

Ask yourself if you have achieved any of the following in Week 3:

↔ Have you managed to separate interpretation from sensory perception?
↔ Can you create a distance from your thinking by labelling thoughts with the 'thought' sticker?
↔ Have you succeeded in registering feelings with the DANC(E) technique, without getting lost in them or suppressing them?

IN CONCLUSION

If we *have* our thoughts and feelings instead of *being* our thoughts and feeling, we no longer need to be slaves to our automatic behaviours.

04

OPEN ATTENTION

> *'You don't have to give the river an extra push to make it stream.'*
>
> CHINESE PROVERB

You have now reached the concluding week of attention training. This final week has an 'open end', as the focus is on open attention. For the past three weeks you have been exercising the attention muscle, honing your selective attention, with the focus on specific things, ranging from your breathing to your little toe and your thoughts and emotions.

This week you will consciously let go of this strong spotlight by opening up your attention, without drifting off unconsciously. In this instance, you don't concentrate on anything or anybody in particular, but you are nonetheless aware of what's happening in and around you. Having a more open attention will improve your awareness of impulses and how to control them.

This week, then, we will train our open attention and we will learn how we can use impulse control effectively in what we do most of in a day: communicating.

WARM-UP: OPEN ATTENTION

During the past three weeks you have mainly exercised your selective attention by paying attention to different focus points: your breathing, your body, the sounds and images around you, and your thoughts and emotions. Your six-pack of selective attention is beginning to show. But in the gym you don't just train your torso. You also want to improve the glutes and muscles in those spindly legs of yours! Therefore, a mind workout will not be complete until you practise open attention in addition to selective attention. It will help you develop your full attention muscle and you can then respond consciously instead of unconsciously. Numerous studies have shown hat open attention is a catalyst for creativity and self-control. It also helps you determine your values. We will return to that later.

In an experiment, 'Mind the Trap', participants were asked to solve rather complicated puzzles. After completing several of the puzzles they found the best strategy to deal with the questions. Next, the subjects were given puzzles that could be solved in the same (complicated) way but also through much simpler methods. Those who were trained in open attention were not as rigid in their thinking and were much quicker in discovering the easier solution than those who had not had any experience in open attention training.[27]

EYE-OPENER

So, let's have a recap of what open attention is. Open attention means having an awareness of everything that's happening, moment by moment. Selective focus is like a spotlight: it focuses on a single item (a chair, a sofa, a table). Open attention is the floodlight that illuminates the entire room. Just as with selective attention, open attention doesn't mean you have to try to change or judge your experience, nor should you allow yourself to be carried away (remember, the light of the construction lamp is green). Imagine, you open your attention and feel stress in your body: a stiff neck, raised shoulders. You also hear your neighbour playing the trumpet. To become aware of the passing by stimuli is sufficient; you don't need to change anything.

The threat and the drive systems make your attention narrow and selective (you feel you have to take action). Open attention is driven by the soothing system. In contrast to other two systems, this system is not performance based (you are neither escaping nor chasing after something); you are open to what is arising. You will let thoughts, sounds, feelings, images and smells pass without paying them any specific attention. The trick is not to drift and to stay alert (though without putting in much effort).

So how do you do this? Through training. A pianist doesn't improvise until he or she knows a piece thoroughly. This also applies to attention: if you are well trained in both focused and open attention, you can let go of the focus and register where your attention goes of its own accord. Your attention will then improvise and wander at will. Your focus may first be on hearing, then slowly move to thinking, suddenly jump to looking and then transfer to feeling, or step back to thinking again, and so on. In short, you welcome whatever arrives. It is not a matter of doing something; it is just a matter of being – *just* being, no matter what turns up.

SIT-UP | Set a timer for five minutes, sit still, and without any judgement be aware of what happens from moment to moment, in terms of thoughts, feelings, sounds, sights and smells.

OPEN ATTENTION AND CREATIVITY

Brainstorming sessions are often used to generate creative ideas, which is odd because they appear to be extremely ineffective. We don't dare suggest any out-of-the-ordinary ideas or plans because we worry about what other participants might say or think. We have similar inhibitions inside our own head. We find it difficult to let go of conventional frameworks and constructs; we don't easily leave the beaten track. If we opened our attention more often, it would be easier to take a different path or even build a new bridge or dig a tunnel.

Scientists may not yet agree on how it works, but in a state of open attention ideas tend to pop up much faster. One explanation claims that in this state it becomes easier to notice what is going on in your subconscious. You allow uncertainty and doubt to enter, without being afraid or feeling the need to push them back with facts and arguments. This is sometimes known as 'negative capability'.[28] Walt Disney was one of the first to deploy (open) attention training in the workplace because of its positive effect on creativity.

'Ideas come from space.'

THOMAS EDISON

A seasoned expert sees a few possibilities; an impetuous beginner sees thousands. By training your open attention, you will always be an enthusiastic novice, even if you are an expert in the making. You will see different ways, more solutions, new possibilities.

> To train your inquisitive open attention, today you will pretend that you are an alien who has come to snoop around on Earth. Look at everything you see in amazement, as if you have never tasted, felt, smelled or heard it before. Be surprised and see what this form of attention does for you. As you practise this, you will notice how difficult it is to approach objects, people or events without judgement.

SIT-UP

Fortunately, we sometimes experience open attention without any training – those soaring of moments of inspiration, ranging from 'Bollywood will be the theme of our wedding party!' and 'I'm going to buy a cat for my lonely grandmother' to an idea about how to market your work. One person will have their best ideas in the shower, another while cycling, and a third while walking the dog. If you train your open attention, these moments of inspiration will increasingly enter your mind.

> Think of a solvable problem that has been bothering you. Let it go and practise open attention for ten minutes. Don't expect this open attention exercise to immediately bring the perfect solution. But just as you often find your keys after you stop looking for them, the same happens in the brain: forget about the problem for several days, practise open attention, and chances are you will come up with a solution or new idea.

SIT-UP

OPEN ATTENTION AND SELF-CONTROL

In a well-known study, children were asked to wait before eating the tempting-looking marshmallows set out in front of them. If they did, they were told, they would be rewarded with a second marshmallow. Of course, a (large) number of those children didn't manage to wait; they ate the marshmallow almost immediately. All the children who took part in the experiment were followed by researchers in the following years – guess what – those who had waited before eating were significantly happier and more successful than the children who had been unable to control themselves.

Can you see yourself in those greedy children? Well, the good news is impulse control can be trained. Between your craving for something sweet (your impulse) and actually putting the marshmallow in your mouth (your response), there is a short moment, also known as the 'magic quarter-second', because this is the only time when you can decide whether to follow your impulse. The Austrian psychiatrist and Holocaust survivor Viktor Frankl witnessed how, out of compassion, his starving fellow prisoners were able to control their impulses and share their last piece of bread with another person. During his internment, he gained one of his most important insights: 'There is space between stimulus and response. In that space lies our freedom and power to choose our response. Our growth and freedom lie in our responses.'[29]

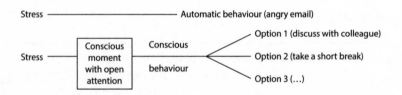

Figure 4.1
Source: Rob Brandsma

TAKING ACTION

The decision to act (or not to act) can be split into three steps. First, we observe the situation: the marshmallow. Then we make a rational estimate regarding the short- and long-term rewards: one goody or two goodies? Finally, there is an act of willpower: do you or don't you conform with the intended behaviour.

In recent decades psychologists have mainly focused on the second and third steps and (their impact on) decision making. For example, governments often talk about the potentially deadly consequences of smoking in its campaigns, appealing mainly to people's rationality and willpower, but often fails to get the message across. The same applies to the importance of exercise and the damaging effect of consuming too much fat and sugar, and yet the number of people with obesity continues to increase (along with the number of fad diets and lifestyle coaches). Apparently, we find it difficult to control our impulses: the impact of willpower – the third step in decision making – is clearly limited.

Meanwhile, the importance of observing the situation, the first step in decision making, is often overlooked. While observation may seem to be the easiest of the three stages, its apparent simplicity conceals complexity. During the past few weeks you have seen the muddying effects of thoughts and feelings on observation and the incredible power of your autopilot. Months, even years, of those 'magic quarter-seconds' pass without us taking conscious decisions. Our awareness often comes only in retrospect – and we say 'if only'.

It is a challenge to be alert to that quarter-second, to keep a clear awareness at that critical moment. You've probably already guessed how we meet this challenge. If we approach the world with open attention, if we separate judgement and observation, we will be better placed to catch our impulses (the being modus) and we can then decide if we will (or won't) listen (the action modus). Remember the C in DANC(E) which focuses on 'What do I need?' and 'What does the situation require?'

SIT-UP

Sit still and take note of those initial impulses you have to move, but without acting on them. You might catch yourself wanting to reach out to scratch your foot, for your phone to send a message, or for a mug of tea to take a sip. Only when you are aware of them, do you notice your impulses and realize how unconsciously you usually carry such actions out.

SELECTIVE AND OPEN ATTENTION

Open attention is by far the best technique to notice the start of the impulse at the actual moment it occurs. This impulse can express itself mentally, physically and/or emotionally. Your aim is to be present as quickly as possible, to make full use of the limited time provided by your quarter-second.

Here we see how selective and open attention work closely together. Selective attention training has made you capable of noticing thoughts, feelings and physical signals more immediately. Open attention will give you an overview so that you notice all three. Selective attention focuses on one point like a TV camera operator, whereas open attention is like the director who can see all the camera images and automatically notices which screen draws his or her attention.

Open attention therefore gives you more control over your actions. You are alert to the magic quarter-second, you keep all your lenses in focus and then choose your behaviour more consciously. There is more space between your impulse and your action, allowing you to make more conscious choices that match your values.

Does one of your values happen to be 'peace and quiet' (regardless whether this is a correct value)? Isn't it great to have that quarter-second to get rid of your irritation after your mother makes that comment and not snap back? Or does your value happen to be 'the truth always comes out'? In which case, use that quarter-second to make a conscious decision to express your annoyance.

OPEN ATTENTION AND VALUES

If a lake is muddy you can't see what's on the bottom. If you try to push the mud aside with your hands, the water will likely become even cloudier. It will not be clear until the sediment has settled.

Our mind is just like that lake. For example, if you try to force clarity – for example, by ignoring the knot in your stomach – or you judge your thoughts and push back your emotions, your mind, heart and body will continue to be agitated and you won't see what's on the bottom of the lake, in other words your deeper values. Open your attention, and the disquiet will settle and a clear mind will arise. You'll see what's lying on the bottom and link with what is profoundly important to you.

Numerous studies show that attention training and open attention give you more clarity about your values. At the same time, you increase your ability to act on those values, thanks to your stronger impulse control.[30]

WARM-UP: ATTENTION AND COMMUNICATION

On average, we spend 70–80 per cent of our waking hours on some form of communication. Apparently, 9 per cent is spent writing, 16 per cent reading, 30 per cent speaking and the greatest part, 45 per cent, listening.[31] In other words, in terms of communication, there's a lot to be gained through attention training.

'Think twice before you speak, because your words and influence will plant the seed of either success or failure in the mind of another.'

NAPOLEON HILL

SPOTTING FILLERS

Okay, you probably don't need telling that, er, most automatic behaviours totally occur – yes, you've guessed – when we actually talk, you know. Fillers such as 'er', 'you know', and 'well' or phrases such as 'so I was like...' show how automatic our speaking is. We use fillers like these to make clear to the listener that it is still our 'turn'. But often they minimize and make it less important. Have you ever heard former US president Barack Obama, a gifted speaker, ever use fillers, in addition to his mantra 'Yes we can!'? The advantage of leaving out this kind of automatic behaviour is that it increases the impact of the message; it makes your story stronger and more credible.

SIT-UP

Make a note of all your speech fillers today (though don't judge yourself!). If you are serious about ending your use of fillers, then ask your child, a friend or colleague to raise their hand every time you use one, even to the point of irritation. Usually, you are not aware you are using them.

Spotting fillers is extremely helpful if we want to hone our attention. It does need discipline, self-kindness and daily practice. Do you remember how there's a degree of automatism in the sort of words we use? Some may prefer doubt words such as 'maybe', 'actually' and 'rather'; others use words with a negative connotation, such as 'no', 'but' and' however'; while others still use more positive words such as 'and', 'cool' and 'that's great'. Your use of words has a powerful effect. You often start to *think* the words you frequently use, use them even more, and then behave accordingly: you become your words. It is easy, for instance, to adopt a 'yes, but' attitude.

EYE-OPENER

It appears from studies that the expression of negative words not only causes a stress response in the speaker but also in the listener. Increased fear and annoyance were also noticed in the latter, which undermines trust and potential cooperation.[32] In Part 2 about compassion, we will return to the power of words.

THINK!

How can you become more conscious of your speech? How do you choose your words instead of them choosing you? Use the following mnemonic aid: THINK. Pause. Stop the urge to speak, pay attention to your breathing and physical sensations. And question yourself about what you want to say. Is it:

TRUE

HELPFUL

INSPIRING

NECESSARY

KIND?

Have you had an argument with a loved one? THINK! Are you fed up with a company's customer service? THINK! Are you disappointed with your adolescent daughter? THINK! Are you afraid of your boss' response? THINK. THINK only works with a strong attention muscle, because it allows you to increase the space between your impulse and your action, which in this case is speaking.

You use the magic quarter-second to communicate more effectively. It does not mean that emotions such as fear or anger will be absent, but that you communicate from a broader perspective than just your emotion. It helps you understand the other person and makes you easier to understand. Open attention allows you to create a clear mind and helps you clearly express your needs, verbalize your point of view and lay down the line – all while showing respect for the other person.

LISTENING

Communication consists of speaking and listening, both verbally and non-verbally. However, in discussions of communication the voice receives much more attention than the ear. There are countless presentation training courses available, but how often do you hear about people attending a listening course? Although a lot of us spend much of our days listening, it's an activity that receives little attention. There isn't a subject called 'listening' at school, universities do not issue listening instructions, and even the average communication training course devotes only 7 per cent of its time to listening.[33] So it's not surprising, then, that we are also fairly poor at remembering, which is the next step after listening.

During an experiment that tested auditory memory, it appeared that subjects could recall only 17.2 per cent of the contents soon after watching the news. Even hints from the researchers did not help the majority achieve more than 25 per cent.[34] Similarly, on average, the listener heard, understood and remembered only up to 50 per cent immediately after a ten-minute presentation. Within 48 hours it appeared that only half was retained. Just imagine how little would be left after a week.[35]

There is an explanation why we are such poor listeners: a speaker speaks 125 to 175 words per minute on average, while the listener can listen to 450 words per minute. The difference between speaking and thinking speeds gives the listener's monkey mind every opportunity to become distracted.[36]

In short, there's a lot of room for improvement in our listening skills, because listening to each other is the best way to connect with as well as to influence others. Here's a mantra we should all keep saying out loud: "Want to be heard? Then listen."

STYLES OF LISTENING

You need to know your listening style to improve your listening attention. When communicating, are you usually only thinking of yourself, or, more likely, the other person? Or maybe you are someone who concentrates on both parties. Roughly speaking, there are four different styles of listening, which we could consider in a hierarchic order:[37]

1. *Automatic listening*. You listen on autopilot and are mainly looking for confirmation of what you already know or think you know. Any communication that goes with it is superficial chatter.

2. *Listening distinctively*. You check whether the information matches your own world view and you mainly listen out for anything that deviates from that world view. The focus is usually on what's wrong or missing. Lawyers use this form of listening to their advantage. The corresponding form of communication is the debate or discussion.

3. *Empathic listening*. You imagine yourself taking on the perspective and feelings of the other person, without making any judgements. This dialogue is the corresponding form of communication.

4. *Generative listening*. In the other styles of listening you are thinking of either yourself or the other person. In generative listening, there's room for both your perspective and somebody else's, and even for the broader perspective. With generative listening, you combine and optimize the other levels of listening. You are sensitive to the atmosphere, you listen and read between the lines, and understand the true message behind the words. You are open to whatever arises, without judging. This form of listening – a kind of open attention – often leads to a shared perspective and cooperation.

'Perception ends where judgement begins.'

DAVID DEWULF

So, be aware of the style of listening you generally use. Is it automatic listening? Try switching up to the second level of listening. And then take another step: empathize with the other person, while (at least initially) keeping your own point of view to yourself. If you take another step, to generative listening, it means that you are switching between the first three levels of listening. Switching back one level is usually quite easy, but taking a step forward requires conscious attention. For example, if you find yourself listening distinctively, practise switching up to empathic or generative listening.

SIT-UP

Today, listen to other people like a sponge; soak up everything that's said without giving an immediate response or opinion. Don't start forming a reply in your mind until you're asked, or it's required. Try switching between the different levels. Note which style of listening you tend to use most of the time. Also note how difficult it is to listen without judgement.

PRACTISING EFFECTIVE LISTENING

The key to effective listening is letting go of your opinions, point of view, and even self-righteousness. Ideas and judgements are useful, but the problem arises when we stick to them doggedly, regardless whether they're positive or negative. Have you noticed how quickly our little voice tells us to label something or someone: as beautiful or ugly, interesting or uninteresting, good or bad, agreeable or disagreeable?

In such cases, we are not listening beyond the limits of our own point of view. We need to keep in mind, too, that any point of view is fluid, however fixed it may seem. We all tend to renege on a point of view from time to time: the former cat hater who now dotes on Fluffy the tabby cat, the hardcore Conservative who used to vote Labour in his younger years, your sister who used to ridicule tattoos and now has them all over her body, and so on. In short, standpoints – however static that notion sounds – are never fixed. So, let go more often and try to listen with a completely open mind to someone else's story.

TRAINING

This week we started working on open attention. You probably remember the end of last week's warm-up: I still owe you the C in DANC(E). But maybe you've already understood the link between open attention training and conscious action?

▮▯▯ LIGHT

EXERCISE 1: BREATHER WITH AN ACTION STEP

If a door gets slammed in your face, you may continue to stare at the closed door, or you try to force the door open again. All the while you've not noticed that, to the left and right, other doors are open. A breather with an action step helps you see those opportunities. This week you will do the same exercise as in Week 3, but with the 'action step' as a bonus. This is the C in DANC(E), the C of calming down and taking conscious action.

Take occasional breaks from what you are doing each day, breathe consciously and note your thoughts. If you become aware of several thoughts, label them internally as part of 'thinking'. Don't allow yourself to be dragged along in the stream of your thoughts. Focus your attention on potential feelings and follow the first three steps in DANC(E): determine ('I feel jealousy/surprise/etc.'), investigate with an accepting mind (don't push your emotion of anger/sadness/disgust aside, but allow it to happen and don't judge) and don't identify with your feeling ('I have feelings, but the feelings aren't me'). Calm yourself by asking yourself: what do I need or what does the situation require? What is wise?

Without attention training you immediately move to the last step, which is action. But by practising the first three steps you can act more effectively and wisely in the last step: you ask yourself what the situation requires and what your needs are. When you get to the second question, what is wise, you should try to let your 'smart subconscious' do the job. Try not to answer the question only from an analytical perspective, but be open to the response that emerges, without judgement. In other words: do not frantically look for a right answer. Remember how you won't find your lost keys until you stop searching – it's the same thing here. If circumstances mean you don't have enough time for this, then practise during your activities. You need to be aware of your breathing, body, thoughts and feelings every now and again.

EXERCISE 2: OPEN ATTENTION DURING THE DAY

Take a break of a couple of minutes three times a day. First pay attention to your breathing, then release the concentration on your attention to register where your attention is going (breathing, body, sound, thinking, feeling).

EXERCISE 3: SPEAKING EXERCISE

Practise 'THINK' before you speak several times a day. Try to smother your kneejerk responses and take advantage of that magic quarter-second. Do not get annoyed with yourself if you don't succeed.

EXERCISE 4: LISTENING EXERCISE

Try listening a few times each day and delay your judgement on the other person and what they're saying. It's just as important to notice that you are judging – without judgement of course. Catch your judgements in the act with a subtle inner voice: 'Yes! I see you!'

▮▮ MEDIUM

EXERCISE 1: OPEN ATTENTION EXERCISE

Would you like to give your attention muscle some extra training in addition to the light version? Then practise the daily Open attention exercise (Audio track 6). Alternate this with doing the same exercise without the audio track. Set your timer for 15 minutes, focus your attention on your breathing and your body during the first few minutes, and then practise open attention.

🎧 Audio track 6. Open attention exercise

EXERCISE 2: ATTENTION IN COMMUNICATION

In addition, be aware of your level of listening (automatic, distinctive, empathic or generative) every day. Are you looking for confirmation (automatic listening) or are you predominantly analysing (distinctive listening)? Are you focusing on the other person (empathic listening) or are you also considering the atmosphere and interests and listening between the lines (generative listening)? Consciously switch between these four listening levels.

▮▮ INTENSE

Maybe you're really getting into it, in which case you may want to opt for intensive training this week. If so, combine your daily Open attention exercise with a complete attention exercise without audio track. In this silent exercise, for which you can use a timer, your focus should be successively on breathing, body, sound, thinking and feelings and open attention. Experiment to figure out how long you'd prefer to focus on each of these points before proceeding to the next. If you've experienced trauma in the past (and need to work through it), you should do the exercise as carefully as possible and at your own pace, especially the part of the meditation that concentrates on emotions. If you find yourself overwhelmed by your feelings and you feel unsure about continuing, it's recommended you ask an experienced trainer to help you.

🎧 Audio track 6. Open attention exercise

In addition, do Exercise 2: Attention in communication, as described in the Medium training section.

🎧 You can download the audio tracks from 12weekmindworkout. com.

COOL DOWN

Attention training can be immensely helpful, but you may be wondering how on earth you cram it into your already brimming diary? Chances are that such a thought has passed through your mind several times while reading and practising the exercises during the past four weeks. Alternatively, you might be thinking 'I have the self-discipline of a shrimp. I just cannot manage the practice.' It's important to remember that being more aware is a way of life, something you can practise at any time of day. Do you remember those drawings when you were a child, when you had to connect dots with your pencil and only at the end did you see that it was a bear or a house? This is how attention training works, too. You start with a conscious first bite when having lunch or brushing your hair, and then you expand your conscious moments and eventually you'll notice that it becomes a way of life.

If you want to continue exercising your attention muscle, keep your goal realistic and keep the threshold sufficiently low. Three hours of exercise on a Sunday is less effective or healthy than half an hour every day. This also applies to a mind workout: five minutes a day is a better workout than one hour once a week. If it's part of your daily life, you're taking advantage of the power of your automatic pilot.

Is there a limit to the training? This depends on the individual. It will not help if you overload your attention muscle until you are absolutely fed up, because you will not feel like starting afresh the following day. If you fall into the trap of imposing an excessive self-discipline when undertaking the exercises, you may start to hate practising. Don't overdo it and give yourself some time off. Keep in mind that some resistance is normal, and longer exercises such as a sitting meditation of 15 minutes plus are valuable to help you see clearly what's happening inside you. You might be able to practise these techniques at an 'attention boot camp' (a kind of attention training retreat) for a day, a week or even longer, and for maybe several hours at a stretch. These often give participants many insights and answers to issues that they had not been able to resolve. They can be life-changing.

The attention techniques you've practised in the past four weeks correspond largely to the eight-week mindfulness training workout known as mindfulness-based stress reduction (MBSR). If you are looking for more depth, this kind of training is recommended. The big advantage is that you can exchange experiences in a group, and the social cohesion of a group is an extra motivation to do training. The coach can also help you with obstacles and blind spots during the practice.

There are many good mindfulness trainers. To find a qualified/ accredited mindfulness trainer/teacher, consult the British Association for Mindfulness-based Approaches (bamba.org.uk), the Mindfulness Teachers Register (mindfulnessteachers.org.uk), or the International Mindfulness Teachers Association (imta.org).

Ask yourself if you have achieved any of the following in Week 4:

↔ Do you recognize open attention and can you apply it in daily situations?
↔ Are you able to be less impulsive in your speaking or responses?

↔ Can you postpone your judgement when listening to someone else?
↔ Are you able to consciously switch between the different levels of listening?

IN CONCLUSION

Continue your attention training, bearing in mind that you are the one who decides whether you will do so and to what degree. Meditation teacher Cheri Huber puts it like this:

'If you want to call yourself a tennis player, you can borrow a racket and a few balls and hit a ball anywhere. If you really want to play tennis, you will buy a racket, take a few lessons, and play when you have time. If you want to play tennis well, you will find a teacher, take lessons, exercise and play regularly. You take time. If you want to be a top tennis player, you will find a teacher, absorb every piece of advice like a sponge, exercise every moment and devote your life to training. Our life is the way it is because we choose it that way. We can say: "I don't have time to stop. I'm too busy to be conscious of what I'm doing." That's fine. You just need to know who is making the decisions. Life is not beyond your control.'[38]

PART 2

THE POWER OF COMPASSION

'If you want others to be happy, practise compassion; if you want to be happy yourself, practise compassion.'

DALAI LAMA

'Compassion is the deep awareness of your suffering and that of others, linked to the desire and commitment to relieve it.' This is the definition of compassion by Paul Gilbert, a professor in clinical psychology at the University of Derby and the founder of compassionate mind training (CMT). In other words: compassion means confronting the difficulties of life without being swept away by them, and with the intention of decreasing others' and your own suffering.

An elderly Tibetan is sitting by a campfire with his grandson. The grandson asks: 'Grandfather, are people good by nature?' The man replies: 'Inside me, there is a fight between two wolves. The grey wolf is bad; it consists of anger, jealousy, resentment, greed, conceit, self-pity, inferiority, lies, false pride, superiority and ego. The brown wolf is good and represents joy, contentment, love, hope, calmness, humility, kindness, sympathy, generosity, truth and compassion. This battle rages in every human being. In you, too.' The grandson gazes into the fire and then asks: 'Which wolf will win the fight?' The old man smiles and answers: 'The wolf you feed.'

SIT-UP	Take note today which activities, thoughts and emotions you feed to your grey wolf, and which to your brown wolf. Which wolf has gobbled up the most?

In Part 2 of *The 12 Week Mind Workout* we will build on the attention training we looked at in Part 1. You have learned that a strong attention muscle gives a lot of benefits: to be less stressed, have stronger impulse control, achieve more effective communication and let your emotions be. Now you're in good enough shape to start working on increasing the power of your compassion. Compassion gives you a constructive approach to difficult phases and moments, and subsequent emotions.

By training your compassion you develop a deep realization that we are all connected and that we are all responsible for making the world a little bit better. A compassionate attitude towards yourself and others leads to resilience and wellbeing.

With compassion you give conscious focus on pain and suffering. You may think this isn't a very uplifting activity, but the following experiment proves the opposite. The subjects were asked to exercise compassion for strangers shown in portrait photographs. After a break, the subjects were shown photographs of modern artworks and were asked to comment on them. Some of the artwork slides were preceded by the portrait slides previously shown, but so quickly that the subjects did not consciously notice them (this method is called 'priming'). And the outcome? The subjects gave a higher evaluation to the artworks shown after a portrait slide than to works shown on their own.[39]

✖ WATCH OUT!

Before you proceed, a word of warning: in the next four weeks you will see the word 'compassion' exactly 6,234 times. Yes, that's rather a lot, I admit, but I'm afraid it can't be helped. These training weeks are about the C word, and there's no other word that captures precisely its meaning. So while reading, remember to take a short break from time to time so you don't suffer from compassion fatigue. Have a cup of tea or coffee and scream: 'This compassion thing is driving me crazy!' – or some other, stronger phrase – and then, when you're ready, continue.

WHAT COMPASSION IS

During attention training you learned to separate your observation from your thoughts and interpretations. You now notice this split in your mind, and you will not follow any old random direction but consciously choose to follow a left or a right turn. By stopping to think and keeping your distance, you can monitor helpful thoughts and let go of the unhelpful ones. But there's also a third way. You create it yourself by generating your own thoughts: this is the route of self-created compassion.

There are three steps to compassion,[40] which I will clarify using the example of a homeless person begging on the street. The first step of compassion is to see the person's pain. You don't pass by, but you really notice the person, giving him or her open and judgement-free *attention*. The second step is that you realize that it could also have happened to you: you experience *shared humanity* (every person suffers, and this suffering connects us).

In the third step, you have a desire to mitigate the person's situation and you might act and do something constructive. You show *kindness*, for example by giving attention, a smile or something tangible, such as money or a sandwich.

WHAT COMPASSION IS NOT

Compassion and empathy are not the same. Whereas compassion focuses on suffering and its alleviation, empathy is focused on every kind of feeling or situation: the homeless person's pain, a friend's new love affair, the joy of a toddler celebrating his or her birthday. Compassion always focuses on alleviating suffering, which does not necessarily apply to empathy.

Compassion isn't the same as pity either. Pity is born out of self-interest. Pity means: *me* first; compassion means: *we* first. Pity is: 'Oh, how terrible, I hope this will not happen to me.' Or: 'How awful for me to have to feel this way when I see a starving woman.' Sometimes pity involves a rather gleeful putting things into perspective: 'She's a size 18, so I shouldn't complain about my size 14.' Pity often includes distance and an aversion to suffering, devoid of any desire to actually do anything about it.

What compassion is certainly not is the pursuit of pleasant emotions. Feeling loving emotions is not a condition for being able to show compassion. Compassion is not at all related to a specific emotion at all. Feelings come and go, while compassion is always there. Sincere compassion is the *intention* to alleviate suffering. Compassion often feels satisfying; it can feel good if you offer the homeless person a cup of coffee or shed a tear with another at a funeral. However, it's not true that we only show compassion because we expect a feel-good reward – an objection we sometimes hear. Feeling good about compassion is merely a pleasant side effect.

What are your feelings and thoughts when you hear the word 'compassion'? What do you think of when you hear the word? Do you think it is the preserve of a particular group of people or those who have a specific profession?

SIT-UP

PREJUDICES

Chances are that you have prejudices about (self-)compassion. These can be quite persistent.

↔ Compassion is a soft skill and (therefore) is of little use.
↔ Compassion is mainly needed in the healthcare professions.
↔ Self-compassion is selfish and makes you lazy.
↔ Compassion can sometimes be unjust: some people just happen to be jerks; they don't deserve compassion.

In short, chances are that when you think of compassion you think that it's tantamount to indulging others and yourself in your behaviours and that it's the opposite of 'tough love': skipping the gym to indulge yourself, for example, or not giving someone feedback because you feel sorry for them. But compassion does not mean being content with doing nothing, or just pampering others or standing up for the weak in society almost as a reflex action. Compassion is a strong driver for growth and development. You can give someone else negative feedback with compassion, or treat yourself with compassion if you have made wrong choices. According to research. it's not a sense of humour, nice pecs or shared interests, but the extent to which he or she shows compassion, that is one of the most important traits in a (potential) partner.[41]

BENEFITS

Prejudices about compassion as being soft, ineffective and selfish are contradicted by science. Compassion training appears to yield more strength, effectiveness, happiness and health.[42] The following results of compassion training are based on findings in 200 articles and studies published since 2003:

↔ Resilience in difficult times
↔ Greater efficiency and proactivity
↔ More positive emotions
↔ Reduced fear of rejection or making mistakes
↔ Greater self-respect
↔ Improved personal care and a healthier diet
↔ Higher emotional intelligence
↔ More social connection, less loneliness
↔ An improved immune system
↔ Taking more responsibility for your own behaviour
↔ More sense of purpose
↔ Better performance levels.

EYE-OPENER

Participants in compassion training showed significantly more brainwaves in gamma frequencies, which indicates that all parts of the brain are connected. The outcome is an increased state of consciousness, being quick to respond and finding it easier to deliver excellent performance.[43]

You do not have to be a scientist to understand the importance of compassion. As people we are very dependent on one other. Dozens of individuals from at least 35 countries were involved in the creation of the page you are currently reading.[44] This printed piece of paper would not exist without the writer, the editors, the salespeople, the plantation workers, the woodcutters, the printers and so on.

Compassion fatigue? Then it's high time for a coffee, a walk or a cat video!

SIT-UP

COMPASSION TRAINING

If you saw a toddler fall into a pond, what would you do? You don't want to get your shoes and socks wet? You'd rather continue your journey to that important appointment? Of course not. Instinctive compassion would make you jump into the water to rescue the child without a second thought, let alone a first one. In addition to the fight–flight–freeze response, the threat system also includes a fourth response: *tend-and-befriend*. In the event of (shared) danger, we become allies and we want to take care of each other.

Whereas fight, flight and freeze are mainly associated with self-interest, tend-and-befriend focuses primarily on the interest of others: you sacrifice yourself.[45] This instinctive response is the short cut to compassion. Instinctive compassion cannot be trained, but fortunately it's inherent in most people. It's present even at a young age. Behavioural researchers assembled 30 hours of film material about a group of playing toddlers and came to exactly this conclusion. They registered no fewer than 1,200 forms of collaboration, sharing and/or consolation.[46]

Monkeys instinctively show compassion, too. When a mother monkey loses her infant, she often continues caring for it for several days. She de-fleas and strokes the animal, and other monkeys around her make noises to show they feel her pain. It's a sound we all know: 'Ahhh.' The sound is a shared legacy of our communal ancestors, and we also make it when we see a child trip and fall or when a friend tells you that they've failed their driving test.

The capacity for both compassion and selfishness is embedded in our DNA. But the more intelligent animals have become through evolution, the stronger the soothing system and (consequently) the tendency to compassion. The greatest step in human evolution is not fire, the spear or the cave drawing; it's compassion. Charles Darwin drew this conclusion in his book *The Descent of Man* (1871): 'Sympathy will have been increased through natural selection, for those communities which include the greatest number of the most sympathetic members, would flourish best, and rear the greatest number of offspring.' A foetus evolves and grows in the womb until it's ready to be born; yet human babies are still completely dependent on a caregiver in order to survive. To raise their children, humans have taught themselves compassion, in other words the capacity to nurture and educate. This is in contrast to, say, snakes and turtles, which produce a lot of offspring in the hope that some will survive. They then desert their offspring and leave them to survive (or not). Compassion has become human beings' strongest instinct, and it is precisely this instinct that ensures humans survive as a species. Darwin's supposed phrase 'the survival of the fittest' – in fact coined by his contemporary and follower Herbert Spencer – should there-fore have been 'survival of the most compassionate'. Whoever shows compassion will survive.

In addition to instinctive compassion, there is conscious, non-instinctive compassion. This is mainly driven by our soothing system. This compassion is what you will be training over the coming weeks. You have already done some of the basic training: attention training helps you notice suffering, which is the first step of compassion. The next two steps – shared humanity and showing kindness – will be covered in the compassion training over the next four weeks.

> *'If you teach me something, I will forget;*
> *If you show me something, I may remember;*
> *If you make me do something, I will own it.'*

CONFUCIUS

In the first two weeks (Weeks 5 and 6), the focus is on self-compassion. Then, in the third week (Week 7), you will start on compassion for others and in the final week (Week 8) you will integrate compassion into your daily life. If you feel the need to spend more time on Week 5 or Week 6, please do so. Compassion for yourself is the foundation here; once you have mastered it, you are ready to extend this to your environment. Compassion training can be challenging because some difficult patterns and (deep) suffering will surface. If you are extremely strict with yourself or have previously suffered trauma, a coach or trainer can give you additional support. Another possibility would be to attend an organized compassion training course for extra support and insight. A third option is to train with a group of your friends over these four weeks.

Compassion training takes courage: you must face pain and suffering instead of turning away from them. Fortunately, compassion works as a virtuous circle: compassion strengthens courage, which gradually makes training easier, which enriches compassion...

Remember: compassion training isn't an organized package tour; it's an adventure tour. On the former, you know exactly where you're going; on the adventure of compassion training you need to be fully open to whatever it brings and wherever it leads.

So compassion and selfishness are embedded in our DNA. The more intelligent animals become through evolution, the bigger and stronger the soothing system and thus the tendency to practise compassion. Hopefully, the next layer of the human brain, which will be piled on top of our old 'new brain', will make it easier for us to see and work towards the bigger picture, rather than to see only our little insignificant self. For now, the question is not how compassionate you are, but how compassionate you want to be. As a little human being, bet big on compassion. Replace the idea of 'It's just a drop in the ocean' with 'Every little bit helps'. You may not care about the bigger picture and you may not care at all whether humanity will survive. Then ask yourself: What is important to you? Would you rather live in a society where violence predominates, rather than kindness?

WEEK

05

SELF-COMPASSION: THE BASICS

'The best place to find a helping hand,
is at the end of your own arm.'
SWEDISH PROVERB

In the coming weeks you are going to learn how to exercise compassion, and how to act from within the soothing system. This will give you the strength and courage you need to keep yourself going when faced with pain or grief, either your own or that of others – not by suppressing it or by drowning in it, but by dealing constructively with it – with compassion. Self-compassion is at the core of compassion. This week you will learn why 'Look at me!' – in other words, self-esteem – is not a form of self-compassion, and you will use tools to enhance your self-compassion – moving from self-esteem to self-compassion.

WARM-UP

Have you ever seen a boot camp trainer with a beer belly and a fag hanging from his lips? It's preposterous. The same applies to compassion: having no compassion for yourself means having no compassion for others. If you treat yourself with compassion, you'll also find it easier to treat others with compassion, and likewise, others are more likely to treat you with compassion. Because a good example tends to be followed.

Self-compassion is also important for your self-development. Without any compassion for yourself, you will find it difficult to develop the inner motivation you need to make a go of life. A manager who cares about her employees cares about their happiness. And who do you manage? Exactly, yourself. Without self-compassion you may not accept that responsibility, because you do not care enough about yourself.

It's important to remember that self-compassion isn't a tool to become a 'better' (slimmer, smarter, richer) human being. It's a tool to accept yourself unconditionally (as slightly overweight, averagely intelligent Joe or Joan Blogs with an average income). Reconsider the difference between self-compassion and self-pity. The latter means 'me first', allowing you to wallow in a victim role; self-compassion means 'we first'.

> Take a pen and paper and think back to a time when a good friend was struggling, stressed, had failed or didn't feel they could face a challenge. How did you respond? Write down the words you used and the words that come to mind about him/her and that situation now. Now think of a situation in which you were struggling, stressed, had failed, or didn't feel you could face a challenge. What words come to mind now? Write them down. What have you noticed? Are the words you use for yourself and the other person the same? If not, consider why there's a difference.

SIT-UP

A LACK OF SELF-COMPASSION

It appears that in practice people show themselves little self-compassion.[47] And yet there is every reason to treat yourself with self-compassion: you didn't choose to be born, choose an optimum bundle of genes out of a catalogue, or choose suitable parents and a prosperous home country out of a shop window. Making your way through life isn't easy, in a world in which you struggle with all kinds of things that are not of your making or as you would have chosen. Why don't you reward yourself with a little self-compassion?

> *'Be careful how you talk to yourself, because someone is listening.'*
>
> ANONYMOUS

THE 12 WEEK MIND WORKOUT

BELONGING

We need to go back in time to find the answer to this question –
back to the good old ancient times, I mean. One of primeval humans' main life necessities was to belong. Exclusion was a death
sentence: there was no food, no safety and no offspring without a
group. Although today we have become much more independent
of each other, the wish to belong has remained just as strong. Each
emotion regulation system (the ancient threat system, followed by
the drive system, and finally the soothing system) offers its own
method of belonging. Your soothing system manages to do so by
connecting with other group members. The system uses compassion, including self-compassion, to achieve this; you have an accepting attitude towards yourself. Unfortunately, this new system often
loses out to its two older siblings.

Your threat system and drive system certainly do not use (self-)
compassion as a 'belonging' method.

THE INNER CRITIC AND COMPETITION

Our ancient threat system focuses mainly on preventing exclusion
from the group by avoiding feedback from others, by adapting to a
group with a shame-based ethos, pointing with an accusing finger to
the situation or by internal criticism. In short, your inner critic de-
grades your self-image. You may imagine yourself safe by not raising
your head above the parapet. Your drive system uses competition as
a 'belonging' method; education, business, the whole of society does
the same. If you are stronger/more beautiful/smarter, you will be first
in the line at mealtime or maybe receive an extra portion; you will be
popular or even 'indispensable' to the group, and so on. You compare
yourself with others and hunt for more self-esteem; this is how you
try to enhance your self-image.

CANCELLING THE IMBALANCE

Your emotion regulation system can be out of balance in two different ways. If your threat system is overactive, your inner critic will

be too loud and your self-esteem extremely low. If your drive system is overactive, you'll conceal excessive self-criticism because your hunt for self-esteem is most important. This drive system gives a lot of energy, but after several years, months or even weeks, depending on how hard it has to work, it will flag up a big ERROR message. The system is overworked and exhausted; you can no longer fool yourself or continue keeping up appearances. And then the threat system comes into action. It sounds the alarm: 'I've messed it up! It's all my fault. I'm hopeless!'

However, it's not your fault that your brain is programmed for (avoiding) danger. Only you, though, can balance the three systems. However, it takes compassion to move the soothing system into the foreground. You will learn how you can control the threat system next week, but this week we will discuss the drive system. You will see how self-esteem can get out of hand, and you will learn how self-compassion helps you prevent this from happening.

FOCUS ON SELF-ESTEEM

The drive system causes you to constantly measure yourself against others. If you want to belong, you need to know where you stand compared to colleagues, family and neighbours. It probably makes sense that people with low self-esteem are passive, unsuccessful and more often lonely. And their opposites, people with high self-esteem, are often active and cheerful and more successful, with more friends. It's a fairly accurate picture.

But a common fallacy is that self-esteem is therefore a prerequisite for success. On the contrary, it's a consequence: success makes you feel good and appreciate yourself. Over 15,000 articles on self-esteem have been published showing that high self-esteem does not lead to improved job performance, better management skills, better communication skills or a healthier lifestyle, nor does it lead to more happiness or better impulse control, such as staying off the bottle.[48]

Despite all this evidence, we continue to believe in self-esteem as the great panacea. In Western society improving our self-esteem has become almost an obsession, evident in everything from TV makeover programmes (from ugly duckling to swan) and our up-bringing, to 'be wonderful'-advertising, self-help books, business leadership programs and the desperate hankering after friends on Facebook.

DISADVANTAGES

Unfortunately, this focus on self-esteem does more harm than good. First, it is utterly exhausting to try to create your self-image based on self-esteem. It is as if you are stuck in a never-ending talent show trying to show the jury how good and fantastic you are – with your inner critic, belonging to the threat system, watching you from the wings. Only when someone else gives you a positive assessment does it make you happy about yourself, whereas a negative assessment makes you feel worthless.

Another disadvantage is that you disregard the talents and successes of others, fearing that your own positive self-image will suffer in comparison. You only appreciate things that are important to you and you can do well, ignoring other people's achievements. A polyglot couldn't care less about the best drawing techniques and a violinist places no importance on good ball control. It's in your interests to makes others feel somehow less by gossip, so that you can move up the pecking order: 'That humourless oaf has been given a promotion!'

The focus on self-esteem also encourages escapist behaviour. You can no longer handle posts tagged #happylife and #always-successful, so you delete your Instagram. As an escapist you avoid people who make you feel uncomfortable due to their success. You avoid meeting them both digitally and face to face. Escapism is the perfect recipe for loneliness and resentment. It also misses its mark: there will always be someone you esteem better than yourself.

Another disadvantage of the focus on self-esteem is that it creates a limited and defective sense of togetherness. Human beings have a herd instinct – in less than a quarter of a second you have made up your mind whether or not someone is a member of 'your group'[49] – and this instinct makes an individual's self-esteem depend on their 'membership'. If Argentina scores more goals than England, their success also belongs to each Argentina supporter. Although this sounds positive, the downside is that the group members do *not* feel connected with 99 per cent of the rest of society. What's more, there's a good chance that a feeling of superiority will emerge – a phenomenon open to exploitation by dictators and cult leaders.

The obsessive hankering after self-esteem also leads us to overestimate ourselves. In general, people think that they are better-looking, smarter, more sensitive and just plain better than average. For example, 90 per cent of all motorists think they are above-average drivers.[50] Most people think that they are above average in terms of their capacity to self-reflect and their self-understanding. But it stands to reason that we can't all be above average. (Undoubtedly even now you're thinking – yes you – that you are well above average at something or other. Am I right? Admit it!) That said, a modest form of self-overestimation – for example, being a bit thick-skinned – can be useful. Without being completely blind to your flaws, it may give you just that little bit of additional self-confidence. However, it all goes pear-shaped when overestimation becomes structural, so to speak – when you acquire skin as thick as an elephant's. If you Photoshop reality so rigorously, you will overlook your flaws and won't correct the mistakes you made, because you'll deny making them in the first place.

Finally, here's the greatest disadvantage: self-esteem is as unstable and transient as a house of cards. Of course, you should enjoy your success, be proud of your achievements, be happy that you are popular. However, you're on the wrong track if you can only feel comfortable if you're successful. If your self-esteem depends entirely on your job performance, your posh car and your large house, then the lightest criticism from a friend, or an unexpectedly downturn at work (you've been outperformed by a competitor, say), can be enough to make you feel lousy.

An even bigger blow might completely knock you off balance. Think of the celebrated cyclist or hockey player who falls into a deep depression after their sports career has ended; their self-esteem was determined entirely by that red jersey or gold medal.

FROM SELF-ESTEEM TO SELF-COMPASSION

Whereas self-esteem revolves around that first in your degree and your thousands of Facebook friends, self-compassion focuses only on the fact that you exist. Isn't that wonderful and simple?! Self-compassion refuses to damn yourself because of your skinny body or your chronic shyness, but insists that you embrace these things or even laugh about them. Self-compassion allows you to admit that the retail job you're doing just doesn't suit you, instead of going into a breakdown. Self-compassion helps you embrace your strengths, your average performance and your weaknesses without you feeling the need to photoshop them. You realize profoundly that nothing is wrong with you and that you can be at peace with yourself without having to meet certain conditions.

EYE-OPENER

Mark Leary, a professor in psychology at Duke University, investigated the impact of self-esteem versus self-compassion on self-reflection.[51] His subjects were asked to make a short film in which they introduced themselves. The group was then randomly split into two: one half received a positive rating for their video, while the other half was given a neutral rating. What was the outcome? The subjects who practised self-compassion were relatively unaffected when they heard the feedback and could better value the worth of the comments – whether positive or neutral. By contrast, the subjects with a remarkably high level of self-esteem were angry about the neutral assessment or considered the assessor incompetent. Leary showed that, whereas self-esteem can prevent people from seeing their not-so-great qualities, self-compassion creates an open, accepting mind.

ADVANTAGES OF SELF-COMPASSION

Before I give you two tools to enhance self-compassion, I will first lay out the advantages of compassion. Research shows that self-compassion helps you perform better. While self-esteem paralyses you and sooner or later burns itself out, self-compassion has a motivating effect. You dare to make mistakes and have enough resilience to rectify them.[52] After receiving negative criticism, you calm yourself down instead of making things worse by punishing yourself with self-reproach.

> *'What is oxygen to our lungs is kindness to our brains.'*
>
> DANIEL SIEGEL

Another advantage of self-compassion is that it saves your energy. You're less inclined to want to airbrush yourself or to be the hippest thing on the planet. You no longer need to tell your friends that you're always being headhunted because you are perfectly satisfied with your office job, where a cheese and pickle sandwich is the highlight of your day. The energy you used to invest in enhancing your self-image can now be used for things that really matter to you.

Finally, self-compassion gives a sense of connectedness – not with that elite group of high-scoring students, top-level bridge players or advanced kite surfers, but with everybody. After all, most people are average; everybody performs above average in some areas and less well in others, but otherwise we are remarkably similar to our neighbours. 'Embrace the average' isn't a clarion call for the pursuit of mediocrity, but for a culture in which everybody does their best for themselves and others, without frills or façades.

SIT-UP	Write down five competencies or skills in which you consider yourself better than others, five in which you would have an average score and five in which you think you are – or have been shown to be – below average. In short, what are your strengths, weaknesses, your mediocrities? Can you be at peace with all the aspects of your personality, including the 'not-so-good' ones? Are you prepared to acknowledge that you will be average in many traits? Self-compassion assumes an honest, kind encounter with yourself; it is about not being afraid to look in the mirror.

TOOLS FOR SELF-COMPASSION

Later in the training course I will give you several exercises to help you reinforce the power of self-compassion. Imagination and touch will play a central part. Before you begin practising, however, there is some more background information on why these are such effective tools for self-compassion.

SIT-UP	Vividly think of a trait that makes you feel ashamed or annoys you. Pause a moment and then think of a pleasant location or activity, a friend or a loved one. What is the effect on your mood and body? Did you notice the difference in the way you felt before and after the pause?

Your imagination is powerful. It can excite you, move you, make you shiver, make you drool. Think of sex, a good conversation, that hot curry you made or the embarrassing comment you made recently, and one or more of the above (physical) responses follow. The more senses you use when imagining these things, the more powerful your image will be. For example, visualizing your partner's breasts or buttocks will be pleasant, of course, but add to this their smell, their voice and the feel of their skin and immediately your fantasy is much stronger, more vivid and tangible in your body.

The imagination helps with impulse control,[53] but also has an anaesthetising effect. In the United States, imagination therapy is included in treatments in more than 3,000 hospitals.[54] Encouraging patients to 'travel' to nice places makes them feel less anxiety and less pain and therefore leads to a reduction in the use of painkillers.[55]

EYE-OPENER

SELF-CALMING IMAGINATION

Unfortunately, your imagination is programmed to recognize danger: you would rather mistake a branch for a snake than vice versa. Although we may not come across many snakes in our daily lives, we are still champions at sensing danger. Before you know it, you have spent half the night worrying about a presentation or meeting your prospective parents-in-law.

A study at the University of Florence found that 44 per cent of the men who were given a hair growth drug and were told that impotence might be a possible side effect went on to experience exactly that. Among the men who were not informed of the side-effect (but who took the same drug), only 15 per cent developed impotence problems.[56]

EYE-OPENER

Maybe you don't make enough use of the positive side either, the self-comforting and self-calming side of the imagination, as described in the example of the American patients.

Chances are – even if it lasted only a short time – you felt more comfortable after the pause, after you used your imagination. Or maybe the exercise triggered resistance in you, and you just found it childish or woolly or a cheap trick. If that's the case, bear in mind that, although everything you imagine is just a figment of your mind, the effects are real. Moreover, you are using your imagination all day long: you're thinking about the argument you had with your partner this morning, about how your mother will respond to the surprise party you've laid on for her, or how you're going to have to run to catch that train.

Imagination can also make you 'smarter'. In a controlled experiment, one group of subjects were asked to think of university professors for five minutes, while another were asked to think about football hooligans. Afterwards, the participants were asked difficult Trivial Pursuit-style questions. You may have guessed the outcome: those who imagined the professors answered more questions correctly than those who imagined hooligans.[57] So if you are going to play Trivial Pursuit, don't think of football hooligans but of Stephen Hawking.

TOUCH

Before humans learned to speak, touch was the best way to communicate. Playfighting and caressing helped us discover who we could work with and who was not to be trusted. But even today touch plays an important role in communication: the handshake, the pat on the shoulder, the arm around the neck. Touch is a social connector between friends, partners, parents and children.

At the beginning of the twentieth century, the protocol in (European) orphanages was for the people who worked in them to touch children as little as possible. The mortality rate in orphanages – partly due to the abominable conditions such as the lack of nutritious food and exercise – averaged a shocking 75 per cent.

By contrast, one forward-thinking orphanage had different ideas about childcare, with employees encouraged to cuddle the children, sooth them at bedtime and give them a hug if they fell over. It is no coincidence that the mortality rate in this orphanage was many times lower.[58, 59]

Our need for touch is just as important when we are adults, as shown in a survey focused on touch in NBA basketball teams. In brief, teams whose members gave each other an occasional friendly tap or embrace were more successful than teams with a less 'giving' ethos.[60] The effect of improved performance due to touch can be extended to any kind of organization or team.[61]

SELF-CALMING TOUCH

Touch is indispensable and offers support. Whether it is a friendly squeeze, a high five, a hug or a light caress, touch is the most effective way of comforting somebody.[62] Touch gives your soothing system a boost[63] and activates and develops more (self-)compassion. The addition of 'self' is deliberate here. Because if no one else is around to give you a hug, you can simply do it yourself!

If you are tense or find yourself overwhelmed by self-criticism, try touching your heart lovingly or give yourself a hug. If it feels a little strange at first, even embarrassing, switch on your imagination. Pretend that you're not touching your own arm, but the arm of a brother or sister or a close friend.

Try to reassure yourself through touch – for example, by placing a hand on your heart or on your stomach, caressing your cheek, squeezing your arm lightly, rubbing your tummy or chest, or taking hold of the other hand. We all have our own preferences; just see what feels best for you.

SIT-UP

Self-touch may be a new thing for you. And you might find it embarrassing or strange. That's fine, but when you start practising it, you'll find that your skin doesn't judge. Your skin will respond as if your mother had stroked your cheek, as when you were a child. Research shows that touch with the right intention will help your blood pressure to go down and beneficial chemicals are released (including the hormone oxytocin, which triggers empathy and compassion). All in all, you will feel calmer. Make sure you imbue the touch with friendliness and warmth, as though you're embracing a good friend who has suffered a broken heart, or a toddler who has lost his or her cuddly toy.[64]

TOUCHY-FEELY BUSINESS

Tycho, an ambitious entrepreneur, attended compassion training. At first, he was rather hesitant: 'I am a down-to-earth kind of guy, I can't stand all this touch-feely stuff.' But he attended the training sessions all the same knowing that something had to change. Although he was successful, Tycho was never satisfied with himself. His drive system continually played games with him; he believed that his performance needed to be at 200 per cent before he could feel satisfied with himself. During compassion training he learned about the comforting effect of self-touch. He remained sceptical, however: 'Come on, I've got better things to do than stroking myself.' Eventually he was convinced to start trying it out; it couldn't hurt him after all. Initially, Tycho experienced no positive effects, but when he applied himself to the practice wholeheartedly, he started to feel the benefits. Six months after training, he is still amazed at the power of something so simple. Thanks to these moments of self-touching, he has been able to let go of his conviction that 'I must work even harder, my performance must be perfect'. He generally experiences more gratitude for what life gives him. And he now finds a calming touch an easy thing to do; intensive training has made it second nature.

TRAINING

When you undertake compassion training, bear in mind that you should do so from within the soothing system. This is important. If you find that you're using expressions like 'I have to practise. I can't skip it, it's mandatory', you'll know that the threat system is in operation. Often these expressions are mixed with worry, fear, doubt or anger. You'll recognize the drive system (using competition as a tool for belonging) when you notice that what you want is reward and a good feeling, and you're using terms such as 'want', 'aim' and 'long for'. This focus on pleasure can be an obstruction if you want to deal compassionately with something unpleasant. Compassion training starts with acknowledging the existence of pain and difficulties.

Plan to practise compassion from within the caring and calming system. You will need to use sentences like 'I grant myself compassion', 'There's nothing I need to achieve or to escape from', 'Let me treat myself with compassion' and 'I wish myself happiness', or any others that work for you. Be aware of potential resistance (such as irritation, doubt, criticism of yourself or the exercises, the tendency to give up) and don't judge. Accept the resistance and use it as practice material for compassion. Paradoxically, acceptance brings more relief and pleasant emotions. Once again, choose the training level that suits you at this moment. Give the exercises a fair chance. Try not to see them as homework, but as suggestions for ways to get more out of life.

▮▯ LIGHT

In this first week of Part 2 about compassion power, choose one of the following four exercises each day. Alternate them.

EXERCISE 1: CALMING BREATHER

This exercise builds on the exercise in Part 1, in which you learned to register your breath without wanting to influence it. Using this you can consciously control your breathing, though obviously without driving yourself to the point of hyperventilation. How? By exhaling a little longer than inhaling. When you inhale your heart rate increases and when you exhale your heartbeat decreases. So, if you want to relax, you lengthen your exhalation a few seconds compared to your inhalation. Note that we're not suggesting here that you can 'exhale' your feelings to get rid of them.

Remember DANC(E)? Breathing helps to accept your thoughts and feelings (DAN) and helps you calm yourself (C).

TRAINER'S TIP

Be careful not to feel you're short of air or become more stressed. If you do, maybe you are trying too hard. Definitely don't see this exercise as a competition to see how long you can exhale.

EXERCISE 2: SELF-COMPASSION PAUSE

Kristin Neff, a compassion scientist, has developed the self-compassion pause, which is a powerful exercise you can practise whenever you feel you are having a hard time. The exercise is based on the three steps of compassion: open attention, shared humanity, and the desire and commitment to alleviate that suffering.

Try to imagine vividly when you experienced a difficult time or problem in your life: it must be suitable for practising with. Try to connect with the discomfort in your body. If you don't feel anything, then choose a more serious problem. Tell yourself internally or even whisper: 'This hurts.' This is an aspect of open attention: registering that there is suffering. Variations that might work better for you are 'Ouch!' or 'This is painful.' Then you tell yourself internally or whisper: 'Everybody struggles.' This is an aspect of shared humanity. Variations on this might be: 'We are all in the same boat', 'Suffering is part of life' or 'I'm not the only one.' Now reassure yourself with a touch, perhaps a hand on your heart or stomach. Conclude by wishing yourself something supportive: 'Let me be kind to myself.'* This is an aspect of the wish and commitment to relieve suffering. Some variations of this include: 'Let me accept myself', 'I deserve to be strong', 'Let me forgive myself' or 'My wish is to learn how to be kind to myself.' Words that move you are the most effective. 'Let me accept myself' may suit one person, while may sound too new-agey to another or like a sermon. 'Hey, I'm fine!' is also OK. Before the exercise, write down 'your' words; it will make them come faster during the compassion pause and more naturally.

EXERCISE 3: THE POWER OF THE IMAGINATION

Choose a moment to consciously use your imagination to strengthen your sense of security and peace of mind. Interrupt your activity. Then practise several deeper inhalations and exhalations and take up a relaxed sitting or standing posture. Next spend a couple of minutes thinking of a place or person that gives you support, in whatever way. This could be a beauty spot (a beach, forest, a holiday cottage, possibly even a busy city) or it could be a compassionate person (a good friend, a parent, trainer, or an inspiring role model like your favourite teacher), as long as you feel safe and supported. Your imagination is infinite; you yourself control the picture in your head. So, if you like the idea of reading a Tintin comic strip with your feet in the Trevi Fountain, then get yourself to Rome – in your head. There are no rules. Use the senses that work for you in that moment (the smell of fresh bread, the sound of crashing waves, etc.).

---

* If you are more used to treating yourself with ruthlessness than compassion, try considering what a loved one, a close friend or some other kind person in your life would say to you.

TRAINER'S TIP

Are you concerned you might not have enough imagination for this exercise? Then start with something as simple as imagining a banana. Try to imagine: the sweet smell, the squidgy texture, the mottled yellow and brown of the peel. It's not that difficult, right?

Experiment at different times: when you're feeling great, uncomfortable or neutral. The more often you do the exercise, the easier it will become to automatically call up these imaginary situations.

EXERCISE 4: THE POWER OF TOUCH

Experiment with touch. You can do this in unpleasant situations (after that unpleasant phone call with a customer) but also at neutral moments, for instance while you are cooking dinner. Remember the intention behind this: you allow yourself it. Don't do this from within the drive system ('I want to feel good') or the threat system ('I want to get rid of this horrible feeling'), but from within the soothing system. It is like touching a child to comfort them when he or she's sick: it won't cure the flu, but it will soothe him/her.

Continue this investigation in the sit-up earlier in this chapter. See which kinds of touch work for you. You may not feel comfortable hugging yourself or stroking your cheek in front of a colleague or in a queue at the checkout – that's quite understandable – so just find a quiet, private space or try doing it secretly so nobody will notice. For example touching one hand with the other. You could even practise the exercise in your mind, using the power of your imagination.

EXERCISE 5: ENERGY BARS FOR YOUR SOOTHING SYSTEM

In addition to the previous four exercises you could also nurture your soothing system by using external boosts:

↔ Music. What kind of music comforts or supports you? It doesn't have to be a powerful requiem mass or a tear-jerking ballad. If a simple tune by Justin Bieber touches and comforts you, that's fine! Listen, sing along or maybe even dance.

↔ Scent or taste. Freshly mown grass, eucalyptus leaves, pine needles, your granny's apple pie or even the earthy odour of a stable: smells have a particular power to arouse our imaginations and memories and go straight to the heart. If you can't think of a particular smell, then imagine one.

↔ Objects. A photograph of your child, a soft toy, an inspiring quotation, a keyring: use anything that gives you a feeling of peace and warmth. Just looking at something like this can help you exercise your self-compassion.

Is your mood buoyant or are you having a particularly bad day? Either way, take a moment every day to activate your soothing system. You could also try combinations of exercises. For example, start with a breathing exercise, then listen to a comforting song and conclude by bring your hand to your heart. It doesn't matter which exercises you choose and in which order you do them. Even if you only take one minute a day, it's a win for your wellbeing. Continue practising this all week.

EXERCISE 6: EMBRACE YOUR GREY MOUSE

This week pay attention to the moments when you are trying to enhance your image. This might range from using an extra filter for a selfie posted on Instagram, overstating your salary or your sports performance to exaggerating how good that so-so holiday in Majorca was. Don't judge yourself for doing this. Try, instead, to embrace your boring average and accept who you are in all your facets. You could do this by means of the self-compassion pause.

ⅢMEDIUM

EXTENSION TO LIGHT This week, the following audio track can be used for some extra daily training:

🎧 Audio track 7. Calming imagination

✖WATCH OUT!

It may be that travelling to that place where you feel secure is a way of shielding yourself from present danger. This motivation comes from within the threat system: the secure spot is a kind of bunker that gives you shelter. That's certainly not the intention of this exercise. By imagining, primarily, a hideout, you're strengthening your threat system, not the soothing system. Try to spot when you're making these hideouts of the imagination. If you catch yourself doing this, experiment by imagining a different comfortable spot, a haven where you can be yourself but without escaping from a potential danger.

💪 TRAINER'S TIP

Because we are focusing on (self-)compassion in this part of the book, we move towards suffering. The risk is then that you'll be focusing on misery all day long. That's certainly not the intention behind these exercises. The idea is not for you to deliberately cultivate suffering, but just to register when a difficulty arises.

Now that your attention muscle is stronger, you can now also focus your attention on things that give you joy too. For resilience in your approach to difficulties, it's important that you remain actively aware of all the pleasant moments in your life. So why not make time for some fun activities in the next few weeks (and beyond!): a relaxing walk, listening to your favourite music, reminding yourself of your important achievements – yes, you can enjoy success as long as your self-esteem doesn't depend on it – or a night out with a good friend.

ⅲ INTENSE

EXTENSION TO LIGHT + MEDIUM You can train your compassion more intensively by keeping a diary of your experiences. What has helped you, what were your insights, and what were your obstacles? Which exercises did you find difficult, and which ones were rewarding? Write playfully and with self-compassion. Don't try to write a piece of literature; no one but you will ever read it. If you like, throw your writing in the bin immediately afterwards.

🎧 You can download the audio tracks from 12weekmindworkout.com.

COOL DOWN

How did this first week in Part 2 go? Your goal of the exercises was to strengthen your soothing system, and perhaps you've already noticed this is working: you remain calm in stressful situations or you are acting less impulsively. But it's also possible that you haven't noticed much difference yet, or that you even feel irritated or uncomfortable. This is quite normal: your drive and threat systems (which we will focus on next week) may be protesting against the strengthening of the soothing system.

Ask yourself if you have achieved any of the following in Week 5:

↔ Are you aware of the danger of social comparison and the moments you fall for it?
↔ Can you apply the self-compassion pause at difficult moments?
↔ Can you activate your soothing system through touch, your breathing or your imagination?

06

TAME YOUR INNER CRITICS

> *'Life is so hard. How can we be anything but kind?'*
>
> JACK KORNFIELD

Being criticized by your boss, parent or partner takes its toll. However, the greatest critic is none other than you yourself. The inner critic (the threat system) – like self-esteem (the drive system) – is an obstacle on the way to more compassion power. But you can train yourself to overcome those obstacles! This is Week 6, and during it you will read how that inner critic arises and learn how to give a kind answer to that extremely strict voice: by activating your soothing system using your choice of words and your voice, moving from self-criticism to self-compassion.

WARM-UP

Matt is almost four, so it's time for his parents to choose a school. His parents attend the open day of the Four-Star School, where the policy is to push your child to amazing levels. In her welcome speech, the director holds forth on 'the value of hard work', 'the highest achievements' and 'child prodigies'. This school does not accept weakness, she says, she believes in punishment and reward – 'and the latter only for exceptional performance!' Matt's parents are shocked and leave the Four-Star School to visit The Duffer, the school on the opposite side of the street. There the director shows them all the classrooms and enthusiastically tells the parents about her philosophy, using terms such as 'play', 'asking for help', 'working together' and 'development'. She emphasizes that children are encouraged to make mistakes, because it's the best way to learn. Pleased and surprised, Matt's parents walk home. In their mind they have already ticked The Duffer.

Which school would you choose for Matt? This may sound like a rhetorical question. But it isn't. Think about the kind of school you run in your head, and you'll probably find it's as strict as the Four Star School. People tend to be quite hard on themselves. Even those who seem to have everything sorted, like your successful colleague who has the nickname 'Mr Promotion' (often subconsciously) put themselves down. Research shows that 80 per cent of people are more lenient towards others than themselves.[64] This is quite strange.

If a good friend said to you things like 'You're a failure', 'You'll never get a job' or 'Your face looks hideous!', how long would you remain friends?

While you're doing a daily activity like cooking, sports or tidying up, just tick off mentally how many self-judgemental thoughts you have, ranging from the minor ('Hey, I am stupid') to the major ('I'm a complete failure!'). If you can, use a timer to see how many such thoughts you have in 15 minutes. Don't become too engrossed in the content of the judgements, notice them without judgement and just keep counting. How many times did you put yourself down, condemn yourself or criticize yourself? Do you think this number a lot or quite small? Does the number shock you?

SIT-UP

The overcritical voice often does its work in a whisper, which makes it all the more dangerous because it prevents you from consciously noticing what's going on. In reality, the voice is chattering away much more often than you realize.

BELONGING THROUGH SELF-CRITICISM

I explained in Week 5 that your overactive inner critic operates under the aegis of the threat system and arises from the desire to belong. When we're threatened with exclusion, we may resort to extreme self-criticism or criticism of others (the psychological equivalent of a physical fight), isolate ourselves (flight) or become fixated on our suffering (freeze).

An adolescent girl tells herself 'You're too fat – you must lose weight', in the hope that if she does she will be included in the popular group. She uses self-criticism as a (counterproductive) method to belong, and to prevent exclusion. Her self-criticism is a fight–flight–freeze response, not focused on external threats like an approaching tram, but on herself. Hence, she calls herself 'fatso' (fight), isolates herself so that she can('t) secretly eat on her own (flight) and focuses obsessively on her own body (freeze).

An overactive threat system might be caused by an exhausted drive system (by trying too hard to achieve self-esteem) or because the threat system has been working hard from the start. In the latter case, there may well be an internalized critical voice from the past. Sometimes that inner voice really sounds like your strict grandpa, your demanding piano teacher, or your critical mother. This is exactly what happened to Jacob, a man now in his thirties. His father has always been extremely judgemental about his below-average intelligence. He has internalized his father's remarks, such as 'You don't have the brain for that'. Consequently, Jacob's father is always in the background – not necessarily physically present – as an inner critic. The words 'You are stupid' are like an uninvited guest who knocks on your front door or sneaks in through the back door, unannounced at any time.

No matter how much Jacob – or you – would like to put in earplugs or hate the inner critical voice, it won't go away. Dealing with your inner critic through your inner critic has a snowball effect: the voice will just get louder. Your challenge is to understand that the inner critic is really trying to help you, albeit in a clumsy way. It's like a panicking, overprotective mother who would really prefer to make her child wear gloves, knee protectors and a helmet all the time, all the while chiding: 'Be careful!' The critic has good intentions, but it's best to ignore it in a kind manner.

NEED FOR STABILITY

The need for security and stability can also strengthen the critical voice, or at least keep it jabbering away. Jeffrey works as a kitchen porter but has never been able to climb the social ladder. He has low self-esteem. Secretly, he dreams of a career as a lawyer, but he would rather be trodden on by his boss and his colleagues than risk trying to achieve his dreams and taking a fall. At least his job in the kitchen is predictable and he knows what treatment to expect, even if it's bad, since that suits the image he has of himself.

> Depressed people seem to prefer partners and friends who treat them badly, according to a study at the University of Texas. During the research they also preferred interaction with the (intentionally) negative researchers, giving them a more positive rating than the intentionally positive researchers.[65]

EYE-OPENER

Jeffrey subconsciously fulfils the self-verification theory:[66] no matter whether his self-image is that of a hero or a failure, he prefers to have it confirmed again and again rather than challenging it. Consequently, Jeffrey looks for behaviours in himself and from others that support his self-image. You may think that negative self-verification applies only to people like Jeffrey – the wallflower in your class at school, the guy at your evening class who trembled simply at the teacher's gaze – but in fact it applies to all of us, to a greater or lesser extent.

HOW DOES SELF-CRITICISM WORK?

There are two points of view in self-criticism: the critic and the criticized. From the perspective of the critic you are in control of the self
you are criticizing. You are annoyed with your own failings and give
yourself a psychological beating 'I'm such a moron.' The fact that you
realize that you are an idiot/jerk/scaredy cat may give you a temporary sense of wellbeing, a high: 'I'm not so bad after all.' By doing this
you distance yourself from your weaknesses instead of addressing
or reconciling yourself to them. And then you return to the role of
the criticized dumbo for a longer period, which only increases your
feeling of worthlessness.

The best description is taken from a book by Timothy Gallwey,
The Inner Games of Tennis, first published in 1974. Every person has
a 'sayer' and a 'doer' in them. Problems arise when the sayer does not
direct the doer but tells them off and hounds them. It can make the
doer a petulant rebel or a nervous child.

ANTI-BOOST

SIT-UP	Imagine that your inner critic vanishes into thin air. You are no longer ashamed, you no longer tell yourself off, you are no longer angry with yourself. What do you feel? Chances are you won't feel relief, but fear. And a common fear is that you will no longer be able to perform without a critical voice.

In Western society the belief that we cannot move forward or realize
our dreams without a strong self-critical voice is deeply entrenched.
However, the opposite is true: countless studies show that this whip
of self-criticism (just like the carrot offered to us by self-esteem) is in
fact detrimental to our performance.[67]

Self-criticism demotivates us, and excessive self-criticism weakens our trust in our own talents and our belief that you can do something (*self-efficacy*),[68] all of which are prerequisites to achievement.[69]

It has been scientifically proven that self-critical people are less motivated, and they quickly give up in the event of a setback.[70] Phrases like 'I've missed sports again/only played for half an hour – I'm hopeless!' are a kind of masochistic drug. They give you an addictive anti-boost and make you turn your back on sports for the rest of the month. Or you try to be ahead of the self-castigation by pre-empting and paving the way for failure. This is the self-handicapping solution: you make yourself look more stupid, lazier or weaker than you are. 'I have undoubtedly failed that exam; I didn't start studying until two days before.' By not doing your utmost or by postponing work, you can blame your failure on a lack of effort or time constraints instead of personal ineptitude.

HARDENING

The key motivator for your inner critic is fear. On the one hand you're afraid you won't achieve your life goals and are therefore worthless; on the other hand you are afraid of being selfish and vain, which would make others no longer like you. You don't achieve your dreams. The truth is, though, that it's the excessive self-critic in you who's disliked, because it's usually harsh and critical towards others, too. People tend to avoid a critic, and this makes you vulnerable to the very loneliness you were trying to avoid. Subsequently, this loneliness becomes a strong incentive for further self-criticism.[71] If this vicious circle continues for a long time and becomes engrained, it can lead to depression.

Today, practise receiving positive feedback, compassion and attention, or think back to an occasion when you received such feedback. What were your feelings? What were your emotions (embarrassment, pride, joy)? How did you respond to the compliment? Did you find it difficult to receive feedback? If so, why? If you find it difficult to accept compliments such as 'Nice job!' and 'Well done!', it's probably because they don't match your (negative) self-image.

SIT-UP

Don't get me wrong: I don't object to wholesome self-reflection and self-correction when you're assessing your own role in an argument or failed collaborative project. In such cases you need to do this and you learn from it, as long as it is coming from within the soothing system.

FROM SELF-CRITICISM TO SELF-COMPASSION

Self-criticism makes you ask yourself whether you are good enough; self-compassion makes you ask yourself what's good for you and whether you make the best of it. This was first pointed out by compassion scientist Kristin Neff. The research she conducted using failed students as her subjects underlined her thesis: the cohort that approached themselves with compassion saw their own failure as an opportunity for growth. Among the self-critical students, their failed exams undermined their self-esteem and they were less optimistic about the future.[72]

In contrast to self-criticism, self-compassion has a positive effect on self-efficacy and your intrinsic motivation. Self-compassion makes you feel calmer, safer and happier even in stressful circumstances. This attitude makes it easier to move forwards. Your actions are based on the will to grow, not on avoidance behaviour or the fear of damaging your image. You dare to be vulnerable and your potential fear of messing things up can even be liberating. And if you do fall flat on your face, you accept the fall, and then get up again with courage and resilience. The following example contrasts two students, one of whom is compassionate and the other is self-critical. Both tend to procrastinate. The former manages to keep going through self-compassion.

Table 6.1   Self-compassion versus inner critic: a student experiences procrastinating behaviour

SELF-CORRECTION FROM WITHIN THE COMPASSION MODE	SELF-CRITICISM FROM WITHIN THE INNER CRITIC MODE
Focus on growth and improvement: 'How can I make sure I do open that book?'	Focus on mistakes and punishment: 'This is one of my poor characteristics.'
Focus on the future ('What are the possibilities?'): 'What will I achieve if I do open my book?'	Focus on the past ('What went wrong?'): 'What was the reason I started so late?'
His/her manner is kind, supportive and encouraging.	His/her manner is strict, impatient and disparaging.
Builds on what has gone well ('The glass is half full').	*Attacks what is wrong ('the glass is half empty').*
Focuses on qualities: 'Fortunately, I'm a speed reader.'	Focus on weaknesses: 'I am easily distracted.'
Focuses on hope and success: 'If I work hard, I'm sure I will manage.'	Focuses on risk of failure: 'I am not going to manage.'
If all goes wrong (failed exam)...	*If all goes wrong (failed exam)...*
Looks at his/her own contribution to the failure: 'I'm sure I could have passed, but I started too late.'	Feels shame and fears rejection: 'I am so ashamed; my fellow students must think I'm stupid.'
Feels regret and is concerned about consequences for others and him/herself: 'I've had enough of being like that, and I'll reassure my parents. Next time I'll start sooner.'	Collapses and worries about the consequences for himself: 'My parents will be furious. I'm sure it will happen again next time.'
Metaphor: kind, patient teacher who helps and supports a child with learning difficulties.	*Metaphor: critical, impatient teacher who chastises and punishes a child with learning difficulties.*

Source: Modified version of a self-compassion model developed by Frits Koster and Erik van den Brink, *Mindfulness-based compassionate living*. Routledge, 2015.

SIT-UP

On which aspects of yourself are you critical? Think of something that is fundamentally changeable, so not your height or heritage, but your weight, an addiction, or a trait such as moodiness or poor organization. Connect with the associated painful feelings by using the DANC(E) method. Connect with your compassionate voice using the techniques we looked at in Week 5. How would a supportive friend encourage you? Would he or she say that your criticism helps or discourages? Would he or she suggest that there are other solutions? Allow the words that are in line with your wish to be happy and are wholesome sink in. If your inner critic tries to shout over you, simply take notice of it and return to your compassionate voice.

YOUR COMPASSIONATE SELF

'Be true to yourself' has long been a popular piece of advice given by a parent to a child or by a trainer to a client. But what is the 'self'?

The way you talk to an employee is probably different from the way you talk to a client. At work you may be a wallflower, whereas among friends you're happy to dance on the table. You have different personalities that change in different situations, encounters and stages of life. And even in the same situation, different selves can pop up – think of the alternating shy and seductive self that turn up when you are flirting.

SIT-UP

Take a look at the room you're sitting in. First, take on the part of a firefighter – what's your focus? Next take on the part of a child – what things do you notice? And now take on your own perspective. From within which role are you observing? As a father, a woman, a client? As an offended person, as a successful businesswoman, as a competitive human being? Depending on the role you adopt, you interpret and select your facts differently. The firefighter in you probably saw things quite differently (possible escape routes, fire extinguishers and fire blankets) from the child (suitable hiding places and materials you could use to make a wigwam).

'Properly speaking, a man has as many social selves as there are individuals who recognize him and carry an image of him in their mind.'

WILLIAM JAMES

You may also be inclined to hold on to just one self or one self-image (such as dishwashing Jeffrey did); your self-image is your lifebuoy. But the buoy will not take you anywhere. It might be ever such a good idea to cling on to it if you're drowning, but it's unwise to continue doing so if it means missing a passing vessel. 'Releasing yourself from holding on' begins with open attention: you register that you are doing it. Then you try to let go of the unhelpful thoughts like 'I'm slow/pessimistic/overbearing' and concentrate on the encouraging thoughts that will help you. Compassion training teaches you, in addition to releasing unhelpful thoughts, to connect with one of your many selves: noticing the self that is already compassionate.

Take a piece of paper and divide it into quarters. Label each quarter as follows: 'Thoughts', 'Emotions', 'Physical sensations' and 'Behaviour'. Leave some space to add your own words. Wait a moment and allow a calming breathing pattern to emerge. Then think of a an argument you've had with someone you love. Imagine the argument vividly. Then focus on your angry self. If necessary, adjust your posture and/or facial expressions. Next, write down, without letting go of the image you have conjured up, what your angry self thinks, and what thoughts and emotions arise. Notice if any memories pop up and, if so, which ones. For example, the argument at primary school which you 'carry with you' in this conflict (memories drive the present). Also write down what you feel physically. Then imagine your anger increasing: how does that feel? The angry self has taken control of your behaviour and takes no account of consequences. What would happen now? Write this down under 'Behaviour'. Once again focus on a calming breathing pattern and allow your angry self to leave the stage. Don't forget to thank it or even give a little applause. Repeat the exercise with your fearful self and your sad self.[73]

SIT-UP

You will notice that your different selves do not think, feel or respond in the same way, and that different types of behaviour emerge: your angry self wants to fight, your sad self withdraws and your anxious self worries. All the selves respond to the autopilot, often conflicting with each other. They try to keep each other under control, but usually one of them is dominant. So how do you counter-balance this anxious, sad or perhaps angry self? Give space to your compassionate self.

SIT-UP	Take some time to call to mind the argument in the previous sit-up. Then try to summon your compassionate self. Remind yourself of your own wisdom, warmth, calmness, courage and your urge to be helpful, to others as well as to yourself. Write down how this feels in your body. What are your compassionate thoughts? Don't think too much; just see what comes to mind. What do you feel when you imagine your compassion intensifying? How would you like to respond? What's new about this sit-up is that the imagined wisdom comes from within your compassionate self. You're not practising through the representation of a compassionate friend or a nice place, but you yourself embody compassion in your mind.

The anxious, angry and sad selves are self-centred. Your compassionate self is kind and empathetic, like the wise big brother who helps his younger siblings resolve their argument – not (only) by soothing frayed tempers, but by taking a constructive approach. And maybe more importantly: your compassionate self doesn't start a fight with the other selves but looks at them from a distance and tries to understand. It asks questions such as: 'What motivates the anxious/angry/sad self?' In this week's training section, you will use a technique that allows you to start a conversation with your other selves from within your compassionate self, using this week's tool: carefully chosen words.

THE POWER OF WORDS

In the film *Arrival*, a linguist tries to unravel the language of aliens. In her attempt, the Sapir–Whorf hypothesis[74] comes to the fore: the idea that each language has its own world view and that language therefore has other functions than simply transferring information. You can also apply this hypothesis globally. For example, Westerners experience time horizontally, while the Chinese, who read vertically, see time as an ascending motion. Likewise, the Russian language has more words for blue than English. Research shows that Russian speakers are therefore better and quicker at distinguishing shades of this colour than English speakers.[75]

The power of words also applies at a micro level. Have you ever been at the receiving end of a harsh bit of criticism? Or maybe you have been verbally abused for no reason at all? Even if it happened years ago, you can still feel something of the shock, anger or hurt when you think back to that moment.

Words are powerful, and they can hurt and sting more than any slap in the face.

MORE COMPASSION IN YOUR CHOICE OF LANGUAGE

No matter how damaging language can be, it can also be healing, for others as well as yourself. Your use of words says much about how you deal with yourself and it also influences your own feelings; you become the words you use. If you want to encourage compassion, it is therefore worth using words that encourage compassion, both in your thoughts and speech.

A useful tool is to look at how certain words tend to cluster around the three emotion regulation systems we discussed in Week 1. This will make it easier to notice when you have unconsciously switched on the drive or threat system, and it will help you switch to the soothing system: from must to may, from avoidance to caring, from striving to giving. The following verbs reveal which emotion regulation system is in play:

↔ Must, have got to, should, serve, demand, avoid, stop, threaten: *threat system*

↔ Want, achieve, expect, aim, long, crave, perform, consume: *drive system*

↔ Acknowledge, grant, allow, give, offer, rest, care, help, accept, permit: *soothing system*

SIT-UP	Today, pay close attention to the verbs you use. Did you notice that the language of the threat or drive system was to the fore? If so, replace them and use words from the soothing system. Focus on the intention and meaning behind your words/thoughts and adjust accordingly. Don't think, 'I've got to call my grandmother', but, 'I'll call my grandmother shortly', or even: 'My granny will be happy if I ring her.'

PUT MORE COMPASSION INTO YOUR TONE OF VOICE

C'est le ton qui fait la musique: your tone of voice and the volume you use also determine the effect of your words. 'Come here' may sound threatening, alluring or just plain neutral, depending how (loudly) you say it. You'll be more aware of this in your communications with others, but it applies to your internal dialogue as well. So please take account of the potentially powerful impact of tone of your internal dialogue on your own mood.

SIT-UP	Produce an aah sound while clenching your jaws and tightening your facial muscles. Now make an aah sound while releasing your facial muscles, as if breathing a sigh of relief after a long day at work. The emotional tone belonging to your compassionate self is that of the second aah. Try to notice the tone of your inner monologue today. Notice without judgement whether it sounds harsh, cold and strict, or neutral. Then experiment with adopting a warmer, kinder, more supportive tone towards yourself.

ASKING QUESTIONS

Questions linger in your mind, while answers evaporate. For this reason, questions tend to influence your subconscious much more than answers. This in turn drives your behaviour. One way to create compassion is to ask compassionate questions. The more often you ask such questions, the greater the impact will be.

> *'Some questions are so good that it would be a shame to spoil them by providing an answer.'*
>
> HARRY MULISCH

Compassionate questions you could ask yourself include:

↔ What do I need now?
↔ What will kindness give me?
↔ What would it be like if I could fully accept my pain?
↔ What if I am good enough without having to overachieve?
↔ What if I already have what I think I need?
↔ What would it be like to accept myself?
↔ What would it be like if I don't feel I have to understand everything?

EYE-OPENER

MEDITATING WITH WORDS

Language is also a powerful tool for meditation. Intention training or loving-kindness training is a suitable format here, involving the repetition of wishes for yourself or someone else. Standard wishes are 'May I be happy', 'May I be healthy', 'May I be free from pain and suffering', 'May I accept life/myself as it is/as I am', but do try using your own words, too – as long as they generate compassion!

Examples might include: 'My wish is that I have trust', 'I grant myself acceptance' and so on.

> **SIT-UP**
>
> Try out a kindness meditation. For a minute, notice your breathing, then, for several minutes, repeat a phrase you've chosen: it might be 'May I be happy' or 'I wish that I will have enough strength.' Or choose a single word like 'trust' or 'health'. Avoid using unfamiliar or formal language; choose a message and words that suit you at this moment.

The exercise seems simple, but appearances are deceiving. Maybe you found it difficult to wish yourself something? Or to feel something? If so, start by focusing your meditation on a loved one. It can be easier to say or think kindness phrases when they're directed at a loved one, because you naturally wish them the best. Then move on to focusing on yourself (and eventually on people who are not so close to you; we'll cover that in Weeks 7 and 8).

✖ WATCH OUT!

Intention training is not a technique for getting rid of your pain or only to feel good; its goal is to strengthen your benevolent intentions towards yourself (and others). As we saw in Part 1, resistance, suppression or avoidance cause even more suffering. It's important to let go of your expectations during these kinds of exercises.

So don't confuse these kindness meditations with the positive affirmations or pats on the back you give yourself when you're out on a date, say, or at a job interview or a 'meet the parents' evening – and tell yourself 'I'm the best/nicest/smartest!' in the hope of making you feel like that and seem that way to another person.

Positive affirmations only work if you feel good about yourself. If you feel unsure of yourself and you repeat 'I am self-confident' over and over, it may even backfire. Deep down, you know only too well you don't feel that way, and the discrepancy makes you feel even more uncomfortable and so even less self-confident. So affirmations like this can cause more harm than relief.[76] A possible compassion variant would be: 'May I accept myself as I am, although I may not manage right now.' In short, you wish for something without demanding a result.

Intention training also helps when you are in physical pain, according to a study undertaken at Duke University School of Medicine in Durham, North Carolina. A group of patients with severe back problems underwent treatment in part based on intention training. Compared to the control group, the pain level of these patients was significantly lower after eight weeks. Moreover, these subjects were less affected by frustrating emotions such as anger and fear.[77]

Sometimes feelings of doubt can arise during intention training sessions: you feel the words are simply meaningless, or you feel irritated or restless. Be non-judgemental about such feelings and take note of them, but keep going. You could remind yourself of the following story.

A Zen student asks his master: 'Why does your poem ask us to put loving words on our hearts, and not in our hearts?' The master replies: 'As we are now, our hearts are closed and we simply can't put loving words inside our hearts. That's why we lay them on our hearts – until the days comes when our hearts break open and the words fall into them.'

EYE-OPENER

WRITTEN WORDS

Writing appeals to different parts of the brain compared to speech and internal reflection. For this reason, I have incorporated many writing exercises into the sit-ups and training sessions. A study conducted at the University of Missouri found that after three consecutive days of (only) 20 minutes of writing on an emotional subject, an individual's mood was affected so positively that it was still noticeable after three months. By contrast, the control group writing about trivial things didn't notice any difference. In addition, 'emo-writers' also scored better on clinical measurements, such as lower blood pressure.[78] Even in a follow-up experiment involving just two days of two-minute writing sessions still had an impact after six weeks.

The study was nicknamed 'The Two-Minute Miracle'.[79] Other studies have confirmed that writing about your feelings, strengths, weaknesses and difficulties has a positive effect. Are you having an argument with your mother? Start writing. Are you insecure about your body? Type these insecurities away. You don't know what you want to achieve in your job, in your love life, or life itself? Pick up your pen.

TRAINING

If you've experienced little (self-)compassion flowing in your direction for quite some time, or if you lacked warmth and compassion in your youth, compassion training can potentially trigger resistance. Compassion scientist Christopher Germer called this 'backdraft', a term borrowed from the fire department. It means that if the door in a room in a burning house is opened suddenly, a huge burst of oxygen will enter and the room will be ablaze in a matter of seconds. It may be that the fickle behaviour of, say, a carer or a teacher in the past – kind one moment, unkind the next – makes you distrust compassion. The threat system sounds the alert when compassion shows itself, like an abused dog reacts aggressively when you approach it kindly. Another possible reason for resistance is that you are finally allowing pain in.

If the resistance you are feeling becomes too strong, you may want to stop compassion training. Remember, though, that this resistance is positive because it creates movement. Like growing pains, it's annoying but one day it will end and is a sign of development. Open attention is the best medicine for resistance and doubt. Notice your thoughts and emotions with kindness. If the resistance gets too strong, then focus your attention on some neutral or pleasant anchorhold, or distract yourself by eating something nice, going for a short walk, visiting a museum, or reading a good book. Go back to the training later.

ᵢ◍ LIGHT

This week you will start to use new exercises to increase your compassion, but you'll also do exercises you already know. Keep your own pace and choose the exercises that suit you best.

EXERCISE 1: CALMING BREATHER

Practise the breather in Week 5, once or several times a day.

EXERCISE 2: BEAR WITNESS TO YOUR COMPASSIONATE SELF

Note the times when you give or receive compassion.

EXERCISE 3: CATCH YOUR CRITIC

Note the times when you criticize yourself. Remind yourself that your inner critic is trying to help you (if clumsily) and don't fight it.

Use DANC(E) to connect with your painful emotion(s) and try to evoke a compassionate voice.

EXERCISE 4: LANGUAGE TOOLS

Experiment actively with the following tools:

↔ Instead of using language from your drive and threat systems, substitute words from the soothing system.
↔ Practise intention training: 'Let me...' or 'I wish for myself...' (see Week 5).
↔ Keep a notebook handy for when strong emotions arise: do you feel cheerful or annoyed, jealous or touched? Write to connect and understand the emotion, if only for two minutes.
↔ Stand in front of the mirror and imagine invoking your compassion. Don't forget your body language; try smiling gently, for example. Address your mirror image with supportive thoughts (aloud, in a whisper or internally). If you don't like the mirror exercise, feel free to skip it.

💪 TRAINER'S TIP

Pay close attention to the exercises that work for you. One person thinks in pictures and will be keen to use their imagination during compassion training; another person is more excited by touch, and yet another finds writing or intention training more effective. You will also notice that the skills support each other: if the power of your imagination seems weaker for whatever reason, try adding words or touch to enhance its impact. Switching from skill to skill will help maintain the vibrancy of your compassion.

ıl MEDIUM

EXTENSION TO LIGHT If you would like to do more training this week, there are various options.

EXERCISE 1: KIND INTENTION TRAINING

Each day carry out the following intention training session, focusing on a loved one and yourself.

🎧 Audio track 8. Intention training for a loved one and yourself*

EXERCISE 2: A COMPASSIONATE LETTER

Write two compassionate letters to yourself this week. Connect with your compassionate self. Use one or more of the four tools from the light training or exercises from Week 5 (touch, imagining an inspiring place or a compassionate friend/inspiring person). Then think of a difficult situation, something you blame yourself for and which you want to change. You can then choose between two options:

↤ You envisage yourself as a wise, kind friend, someone who supports and encourages you unconditionally. Write an encouraging letter to yourself from their perspective.

↤ Write a letter from the part of you that is wise, courageous, warm and kind to the part of yourself that is having a hard time. The 'you' in the letter is your suffering self and the 'I' gives the perspective of your compassionate self.

Don't try to win the Nobel Prize in Literature; write playfully and open-mindedly. It doesn't have to be pages long, but try to write more than half a page, which is too short to get to the heart of the

---

* Audio tracks 8, 9 and 10 are based on lyrics by Frits Koster and Erik van den Brink.

matter. Do you sense resistance while you are writing? State this in your letter. If your resistance is too strong, take a break and try again later.

Once you're done, read the letter carefully. Is it full of compassion? Note how you've used words and tone. Does the letter feel warm or cold? Do subtle self-reproaches, or pointing fingers, emerge from between the lines? By rereading your letters, you will begin to recognize your self-critical voice.

Revise the letter by replacing self-critical words with supportive ones. You can also practise your tone by reading the letter out loud. Observe unfriendly or strict tones without judgement and continue to practise using a more understanding tone.

▮ INTENSE

EXTENSION TO LIGHT + MEDIUM If you would like to train intensively this week, then write *four* letters of compassion to yourself.

🎧 You can download the audio tracks from 12weekmindworkout.com.

COOL DOWN

Have you noticed the power of your compassion increasing? Or do you still lack aptitude? This was a full week in which you learned a lot of new ways to strengthen your compassion. Maybe that's why you occasionally lost track and couldn't find compassion immediately. Don't worry! Don't try to remember and apply everything at once. You need time and practice to strengthen compassion. Words, intention training and compassion training become meaningful through repetition. Only then do you understand compassion and experience it. Remember that you don't have to do all this on your own. Allow yourself to find support and guidance from others, perhaps a coach or a friend, a psychologist or a compassion trainer.

Ask yourself if you have achieved any of the following in Week 6:

↔ Do you notice your inner critic compassionately?
↔ Have you figured out which threat system strategy you use?
↔ Can you manage to motivate and correct yourself from within self-compassion instead of from within self-criticism?
↔ Can you activate self-compassion through language?

07

COMPASSION FOR HEALTHY RELATIONSHIPS

In the past two weeks you have started practising self-compassion to train your compassion power. This week you will extend this foundation to compassion from yourself to others – not only towards your loved ones but also towards people with whom you have neutral, varying, or downright difficult relationships. You will consider the inevitable pain that relationships bring and how you can effectively deal with it – with compassion. The common thread: compassion underpins healthy relationships.

WARM-UP

An Orthodox rabbi allegedly lost his youngest daughter and wrote a letter to Albert Einstein. In addition to his own pain, he was distressed by his eldest daughter's grief; she was devastated by the death of her younger sister. He tried to help her and support her as much as he could, but the girl seemed inconsolable. Devastated by this double whammy, he asked Einstein what to do. The scientist's reply was fascinating. He asked the father to consider a human's place in the word, in what we understand as our 'universe' and widen our sense of connection and compassion beyond our immediate peers. We tend to experience emotions – our sense of self, our thoughts and feelings – he explained, from within a prison of delusion which leads us to believe that the few persons nearest to us are those of most value. To embrace all people and all living things, Einstein suggested, was a goal which might liberate us from that grief and provide a foundation for inner security.

Does this explanation move you? Maybe you even nodded in agreement while taking in the meaning? This doesn't mean you will be able to immediately put this shared connectedness into practice. It's likely to seem somewhat abstract. In the coming two weeks, your goal is to focus on making this abstraction concrete and realizing Einstein's 'widened circle of compassion'.

RELATIONSHIPS - A LIFE ESSENTIAL

'Hell is other people.' This terrifying quote is taken from one of the greatest thinkers of the twentieth century: Jean-Paul Sartre. Although your own ideas might be slightly more nuanced, you may frequently have experienced something of what Sartre means: 'That stupid mother of mine and her eternal criticism'; 'I don't understand how my friend could forget my birthday'; 'My colleague's endless whining drives me crazy.'

To avoid these kinds of feeling towards others, you could of course choose to live like a hermit. There would be all sorts of practical problems, such as getting your hair cut or having root canal treatment, but at least you would have excised all those intimate relationships that caused you so much trouble. The problem is, instead of suffering 'the pain of relationships', you would experience the opposite: the pain of loneliness.

Unfortunately, many people are lonely (involuntarily). According to the UK's Campaign to End Loneliness, five per cent of adults (aged 16 years and over) in England reporting feeling lonely 'often/always'; 45 per cent feel occasionally, sometimes or often lonely.[80] Loneliness in turn leads to all kinds of mental and physical problems and can even lead to premature death.[81] Like oxygen for your brain, human connection is essential to human flourishing. From this we can conclude that the pain of loneliness is far greater than the pain of relationships. There's no heaven without hell; no pleasure without pain. The challenge in relationships is to stay close to yourself and at the same time open up to others. The neuropsychologist and meditation trainer Rick Hanson puts it like this: how you can create a secure base of 'I' inside yourself to be more able to explore 'we' out in the world.

CONNECTING WITH OTHERS

A moving video first broadcast on Danish television[82] shows how you can feel connected with everyone. In the film, groups of people from a diversity of backgrounds, professions and subcultures – including healthcare workers, farmers, Muslims, football supporters and people with tattoos – meet in a large hall.

Each group is assigned to a specific square; one square is left empty. Then the film producer gives an order: 'If you were the clown in your year group, then go to the empty square.' In each group, someone steps forward, hesitantly and sniggering. The composition of this new group – the school clowns – turns out to be pretty diverse. Muslims, businessmen, people with tattoos and so on are all jumbled together. The following questions have similar results: 'Which of you like dancing?', 'Which of you is a stepparent?' and 'Who used to be bullied?' This is a wonderful illustration of how we all have something in common with each other. And probably even more with those with whom we see-mingly do not share anything.

If you want to remain 'me' amid the 'us', you need to experience the 'us', the connection with others. You will always have some-thing in common with another person, no matter how minor (a hammer toe) or major (neglect in childhood). Even being randomly assigned to the same study group (A or B) seems to strengthen feelings of connection.[83] We often tend to stress differences and group together with those who are clearly and superficially like us: blondes, eighties babies, surf enthusiasts, organic foodies, football players, Londoners, gourmets, and so on. But being human is en-ough to feel a connection. Just 'being' there may suffice, extended compassion (see Week 8) could even make you feel connected to an earthworm.

THE KNOCK-ON EFFECT

Somebody else's cheerfulness can be infectious, just like someone's grumpiness. This is more than just an interesting fact; it should make us feel seriously responsible for others' moods. The way you look at somebody in the street can have a huge knock-on effect. If you give someone a nice smile, they'll be pleasant towards the overworked cashier in the supermarket, who returns home in a better mood to his partner, who's a police officer and who leaves in a good mood to start her late shift. That night the officer pulls over a driver going slightly over the speed limit – you – but because she's in a good mood, she lets you off the hook without a ticket. Not a bad result for one smile!

Even if you don't reap any direct positive results yourself, the example makes clear how infinitely catching your attitude and behaviour can be. That is a reward in itself. However, connecting with others isn't always easy. Before you start practising compassion towards others, let's first discuss the two different types of pain you can feel in relationships: the pain that comes from feeling connected (the feeling of being 'us' – empathic pain) and the pain that arises because you don't feel connected ((in)voluntary isolation, a lack of the communal 'us' feeling).

THE PAIN OF CONNECTION

On screen James Bond punches a villain in the face, in the street a toddler falls off her bike, a friend yawns during a dinner party; none of these will not leave you untouched. Why is this? Our mirror neurons enable us to learn from others' experiences – 'apparently I shouldn't touch that scalding heater' – and to care for them. You can sense what someone else needs, whether it's a plaster, something to drink or a hug. It is how you identify with someone else's thoughts (cognitive empathy) and emotions (emotional empathy). However, as I've mentioned before, empathy isn't the same as compassion. Compassion focuses on pain and the desire to alleviate that pain; empathy focuses on any kind of emotion or mood but does necessarily entail the wish for alleviating suffering. Think of the empathic executioner, or the news agent who says different things to the hipster and the man in the suit.

The difference between empathy and compassion is visible in the brain. Matthieu Ricard, molecular biologist and practitioner of intensive meditation (dubbed 'the happiest man in the world'), performed an fMRI scan of his own brain while inciting empathy in himself by thinking of a heart-breaking documentary about neglected orphans. The scan showed that the active parts of his brain were like those of the average person who imagined the plight of others with empathy, and he described his state of mind as unpleasant and emotionally exhausting. Subsequently when he accessed his compassion, which involved similar thoughts but accompanied by a deep desire to alleviate the pain, different parts of his brain lit up. This time, he described his feelings as warm and pleasant.[84]

More than 30 studies have confirmed that repetitive empathy for other people's pain can exhaust us emotionally and lead to burnout.[85] This often affects stereotypically caring individuals (such as overconcerned mothers or professional carers): every day they face pain and suffering and eventually they can no longer cope. If you feel the pain of others without listening compassionately to your own needs, it will exhaust you and you'll end up shutting yourself off from other people. Just think of the family doctor who seems cold and remote because he or she can no longer open themselves to others' suffering. The good news is that you can arm yourself against empathic fatigue through (self-)compassion: by supporting yourself and the desire to alleviate your own suffering (and of others) you build a buffer.

This will prevent exhaustion and create space where you can be ready for others.[86]

> Picture a difficult relationship (with a colleague, member of the family, friend) in which you often take on a caring role. Use the DANC(E) technique to connect with any unpleasant emotions that arise. As you breathe in, wish yourself compassion in relation to your discomfort and show compassion for the other person when you breathe out (though only if you feel you can).
>
> **SIT-UP**

COMPASSION = EMPATHY + LOVE

Paradoxically, being open to other people's pain, including friends and loved ones as well as strangers, brings more health and happiness. The sense that you are having the same experiences and (therefore) see more similarities between you gives you a greater sense of connection. During the day, it will help you experience more interactions that refresh and boost you than experiences that irritate and drain you. The stronger sense of connection increases the ease with which you evoke compassion: the virtuous circle is born.

PAIN THROUGH LACK OF CONNECTION

YouTube shows an experiment by the developmental psychologist Edward Tronick[87] in which he examines the bond between mother and child. After several minutes of happily playing with her baby, a mother is instructed to stop responding to the child. As expected, the baby then tries to elicit some response from the mother by laughing or making chirping noises. When this does not work, the child switches to another tactic: uncontrolled crying and screaming. In vain. The mother remains neutral (as instructed) and unperturbed. As a result, the baby eventually becomes passive, staring ahead, and becoming apathetic and withdrawn.[88]

If parents – unlike the mothers in the experiment – structurally ignore their children (emotional neglect), children will experience the attachment as insecure and carry this with them on their journey towards adulthood.

They will fall seriously behind in establishing healthy relationships,[89] and this can manifest itself in all kinds of destructive behaviour, from drug addiction to craving love and recognition: the feeling that they cannot be complete without being noticed. Alternatively, it may express itself in relationship avoidance, trying the utmost not to be heard and to feel 'secure'.

Fortunately, training can help reverse insecure attachment disorders. You may have guessed: we are once again dealing with the C-word. Practising compassion builds a secure foundation for healthy relationships. Research has shown that just reading and hearing words that are related to intimacy, such as 'love' and 'friendship', can promote a sense of secure attachment.[90]

SIT-UP

Write down words associated with connection and intimacy, such as 'love', 'friendship', 'warmth', 'cuddling', 'contact'... whatever comes to mind.

Even if you are unaffected by an insecure attachment, you can sometimes be involved in a relationship that lacks a strong sense of connection or one in which the sense of one has completely vanished. It nearly always leads to a sense of disappointment and frustration because of unfulfilled expectations. You do not feel seen or heard by your partner, you do not feel respected, you feel distant from others, their expectations of you oppress you, and so on. And then comes the finger pointing – 'It's your fault that I feel so worthless!' – or self-criticism – 'I'm such a fool that I have allowed them to do this to me!'

EYE-OPENER

Did you know that difficult people in your life are your best teachers? Difficult people wouldn't annoy us so much if they didn't say something about our own needs, strengths and weaknesses. You, as an executive, are irritated by that one colleague who doesn't pull his weight. What can you learn from him? Let go – and the lazy worker can actually say something about your own management skills. Or take someone who gets to you because they're overly shy and meek. Maybe that's because your own mouth is sometimes working overtime. You can learn from them to stay in the background more often.

The good news is that even difficult relationships provide opportunities to discover more about your own deeper needs. In this way you can replace blaming others with self-management and being mindful of the needs of others. This means you must engage in the kind battle with two emotions prevalent in poor relationships: shame (associated with self-criticism) and anger (associated with finger-pointing).

EMOTIONS IN RELATIONSHIPS

Shame and (embittered) anger are the emotions that hinder us most when trying to live compassionately. Again, this doesn't mean that you shouldn't feel these emotions, or that it would be preferable to suppress them or push them aside. Unfortunately, however, if you are caught up in these emotions, there is a significant risk that they will work against you. Below we discuss how to deal constructively with shame and anger, so that they may even help you as you learn to exercise compassion.

SHAME

Have you ever screamed at the top of your voice at a very boring meeting: 'I am fed up!' Probably not. Shame makes you behave considerately; it keeps you aligned with group behaviour and thereby increases your chances of survival. However, shame is also your critic's favourite emotion, so you don't always need it and it can be dysfunctional – for example, if you are ashamed that you did not complete secondary education, every day try to cover up your bum with a baggy sweater or are unhappy in spite of your wealth and success. In such instances, shame will give you a strong sense of 'not belonging'. If that inner critic goes to the extreme, your drive to protect yourself can go into overdrive and you will be less inclined to make connections that make you potentially vulnerable. The feeling of not being good enough is a hole that neither your partner nor your friends can ever fill. It gets in the way of any real connection with others because you are only concerned with yourself.

A major negative event, such as job loss, can send you spiralling into a negative downward spiral of shame. If a feeling of shame becomes too strong, it can turn into the conviction that you are a bad person or inferior. You condemn yourself, which makes you feel even more ashamed, and so forth and so on.

GUILT

There's a significant difference between being ashamed and feeling the potentially useful emotion of guilt. Shame focuses on 'being', while guilt focuses on 'doing'. Along with guilt comes remorse, which calls on you to amend a behaviour; shame makes you think you've done something wrong but leaves you feeling a sense of paralysis and confusion. You do not need empathy and compassion when you have a feeling of shame, but you do when you feel guilt.[91] The latter makes you take (positive) action, as you find ways to do better next time. On the other hand, you should not allow yourself to become too absorbed in your feelings of guilt, which can totally overwhelm you.

Imagine you are having an affair. Your feeling of guilt will say to your partner, 'I am sorry: it hurts me that I hurt you. What can I do to ease your suffering?' Shame tells you, 'It's terrible, I am such an awful person' and/or, 'What will people think of me?' Shame can also be more aggressive: it will say to your partner, for example, 'It's because of your low libido that I cheated.'

SPOTTING SHAME

It is not always easy to recognize shame. Shame causes you to reject yourself and to literally turn your gaze away from yourself, ending any chance of self-reflection. We are often ashamed of our shame and mask it with other emotions that are more tolerable, such as anger or jealousy. A bit of analysis will help you spot shame. The physical element of shame is expressed for example in a feeling of emptiness, a knot in your stomach, muscle tension, pressure on the chest, blood rising to your head, feeling flushed, and hot red cheeks. The mental aspect of shame can be recognized by negative thoughts in your head: I cannot be trusted, I am no good, I do not deserve to be loved. Or maybe by the finger-pointing variants: he is no good, she cannot be trusted, you are hopeless. Excessive shame often gives a sense of isolation. This is rather surprising because shame affects us all, and everybody will recognize the negative core beliefs associated with it. Shame ought to be a connector because we are all in the same boat of shame.

Try to imagine as vividly as possible a moment when you felt a superficial, fleeting shame: the time you did not recognize your neighbour, tripped over in the street where everybody could see you, or were unable to string together a simple sentence when ordering food in a posh French restaurant. As you imagine the situation, remember to include both the physical and mental aspects of your shame and embarrassment and then take note of the negative core beliefs you recognize in relation to that feeling of shame. Address these core beliefs and your shame compassionately. For this use the DANC(E) technique and apply the compassion techniques in your final calming step. The techniques you use could include the self-compassion pause, the power of touch, or other exercises in Weeks 5 and 6 that work well for you.

SIT-UP

The compassion techniques will comfort and calm you, so you can relate to your rising sense of shame without judgement. You should not disallow the associated pain because it is how the emotion will eventually lose power. The desire to push shame aside and hide it will disappear. Whether you missed that decisive penalty, whether you accidentally mistook the baby's mother for the grandmother, or you feel ashamed about your number of sexual partners, try to practise registering shame in your daily life as often as possible. It provides the perfect opportunity to practise compassion.

'I'm sorry', 'forgive me', 'sorry': words that many of us state profusely. The feeling of shame is almost unbearable. One Chinese businessman saw this ignorance as his goldmine: he founded an excuse company. People pay him and his business to say sorry on their behalf and have gifts or flowers delivered to others. Those who do so think the price is reasonable: avoiding having to apologise in person.

EMBITTERED ANGER

The Pakistani activist Malala Yousafzai is famous for her righteous anger, indignation and fighting spirit. As a young girl she first expressed her anger on a BBC Urdu blog about the exclusion of girls from education and other areas of life in her region of Pakistan, a policy imposed by the Taliban who had seized control there. Partly thanks to this blog and the brutal attempt on her life the following year, the school ban and wider educational inequalities received worldwide attention. On 12 July 2013 – Yousafzai's birthday – the United Nations instituted Malala Day to draw attention to the 32 million girls and 29 million boys across the globe who do not have access to primary education.

Malala's anger was a useful force, and your anger, too, can also have a positive role in your daily life. Anger stems from the threat system. It alerts you and focuses your brain on protection and security.

This does not mean, however, that you should simply follow wherever your anger is leading you. If you feel your anger rising, then step back, so you can allow yourself to understand your deeper needs and feelings, before blind anger can take over. Non-constructive anger can stand in the way of you developing your power of compassion.

Anger is often like grasping a hot coal to quickly throw at someone else (yet you are the one who gets burned). However, like many difficult emotions, anger can stay with you. The more often you feel anger, the easier it becomes for it to take hold. Anger can become second nature, just as bitterness and resentment have become entrenched in Scrooge in *A Christmas Carol*. Prolonged anger embitters; it will become part of you even when you don't need it. Science shows that long-term anger is not only very unpleasant, but also extremely unhealthy.

> Anger affects the heart, where it is stored. In a study, 785 selected adults, men and women, were followed for ten years. Male subjects who could express their anger constructively – in other words, who used their emotion to change something for the better – were less likely to develop heart failure. It made no difference in women, but both women and men were significantly more likely to develop heart disease if they expressed their anger in the form of blame and self-justification.[92]

EYE-OPENER

EMBITTERED ANGER AND SOFT EMOTIONS

Embittered anger is like a steel suit of armour hiding softer feelings such as sadness and fear. The soft emotions flow: they are not static; they arise and disappear and change quickly. Harsh emotions such as anger, resentment and grievance take root, which makes them increase in strength. The armour of anger creates an illusion of control. You think you are invulnerable and shield yourself from blame by others (or from yourself!).

In reality, embittered anger tragically makes you more vulnerable: you are easily hurt and you have less control over your life goals and more often you are lonely (think back to the circle of loneliness we discussed in Week 6). Getting angry is an easy way out; it's much less challenging than daring to express soft emotions like sadness and fear. By expressing soft emotions, you drop your guard. Soft emotions help you shine a light on your unmet needs. There are roughly three kinds of such needs and they are linked to the emotion regulation systems:

↔ The need for security (wanting to feel safe): the threat system.
↔ The need for recognition (wanting to be recognized and heard): the drive system.
↔ The need for connection (wanting to feel loved): the soothing system.

In short – and this is the topic of millions of songs, novels, films and poems – the need to be loved often hides behind anger. If you allow those needs to be known, there is the chance they can be met by someone, though they may also be ignored or rejected. Showing your softer side can be painful.

FIVE STEPS TO DEAL WITH ANGER

How to identify the real need that is hiding behind your anger. The first thing you have to do is to pause immediately when you feel anger rising (this is comparable with the magic quarter-second we looked at in Week 4). You may find it easier to do this with people who are not too close to you – it's easier to deal with a complaint from a client than a snappy remark from your partner. Once you've pushed pause, follow the following five steps:

1. Experience and acknowledge your hard feelings (anger, inflexibility, withdrawal, condemnation).
2. Use the self-compassion pause to calm yourself and to prevent yourself from following your impulse (snapping, ending a call, making a deliberately hurtful remark).
3. Examine the soft feelings behind your anger (sadness, disappointment, fear, worry).
4. Name your unmet needs (security, recognition, development, love).
5. Make your need clear to others and/or address the need yourself (then meet the need through one of the self-compassion exercises in Weeks 5 and 6).

Think back to an argument in the past. Can you still feel the anger? What were and are the unmet needs hiding behind the anger? Are you ready to do something constructive with those unmet needs? Follow the steps above. What was it like to acknowledge the anger? Did you notice soft feelings and the underlying unmet needs? What self-compassion exercises did you use? Did you manage to feel compassion for yourself and others?

SIT-UP

Let's look at a case study. The main conflict between Gaby and her husband Chris is that he does not do any DIY around the house, even though he keeps promising to do so. Gaby's real need, however, is not an immaculately painted and decorated house. Her underlying, deepest desire is for her husband to notice her, for Chris to listen to her and love her. The fact that he does not care about the peeling paint on the window frames Gaby sees as a confirmation that he doesn't care much about her. Chris, in turn, feels snubbed and not recognized for the man he is: it is as if picking up the paintbrush is the only way for him to 'deserve' Gaby's love. Chris and Gaby are like two islands without a footbridge. Both crave each other's love, but in all those years of built-up anger and resentment they have not given their needs much consideration. Their arguments are a string of never-ending reproaches and defences centred around one specific time bomb, the house.

Just as hours of massage cannot provide a long-term resolution for the knot in your back when stress is the underlying cause, likewise real expectations and deeper needs will remain hidden if you do not move beyond addressing and 'resolving' a particular situation or conflict. Both Gaby and Chris cling to the surface of their conflict, where they feel safer.

Instead of Gaby asking for a hug, she says reproachfully: 'You're never nice to me.' This is how she stays in control. An anticipated rejection seems to hurt less and is often preferred to a show of vulnerability, whereas that vulnerability is precisely the sweet spot where we can feel connected. If Gaby were to show her sweet spot to Chris, she would increase the chances of him embracing her lovingly (and of him also daring to express his real needs). And if she fails to declare her needs to Chris, or Chris fails to meet them, she can still, by connecting with the pain that she is not acknowledged by Chris, meet her own need with saying to herself: 'I see you, I acknowledge you.'

> *'In the middle of difficulty lies opportunity.'*
>
> ALBERT EINSTEIN

These five steps apply to any difficult (hard) emotion. Self-compassion will give you what you had been hoping to receive from others. It makes you less dependent on recognition and love from others. You can then have healthy relationships without setting conditions, such as only paying a compliment if you want to be liked. Making yourself less dependent on recognition by others keeps your 'me' among the 'we'. And only then will you become neither passive nor aggressive but assertive.

�֎ WATCH OUT!
It's important to note that there's a difference between men and women (often acquired) when it comes to anger. Whereas boys learn that 'real men don't cry' and are expected to express their anger, the stereotypical expectation of girls is that they are 'sweet and compliant'. Moreover, young girls often learn to get their way by showing tears, and a feisty woman will soon be called a 'bitch'. Each time they feel anger, girls learn to automatically switch to another soft emotion that is tolerated and effective, such as fear or sorrow. It is important for anyone (irrespective of gender) who has not learned to connect with their anger to fully experience anger without any sense of guilt.

WEEK 07: COMPASSION FOR HEALTHY RELATIONSHIPS

COMPASSION WITH OTHERS

The Babemba tribe of South Africa has its own very individual way of trying criminals. The criminal is made to stand naked in the centre of the village. Everyone in the village stands round the criminal in a circle, and one by one individuals address the offender, not about their offender's misconduct but their good deeds and qualities. This African people believes that everyone is born good and sets out to pursue only happiness and love, making mistakes along the way in their quest. The ceremony lasts several days and ends in a large party in which the criminal is welcomed back into the group. A rebirth has taken place.

Western culture is quite the opposite to that of the African tribe: if someone has done something wrong, if we do not like someone, we exclude them. Imagine, though, how different things would be if we had warm feelings for every person. What if we were to expand our circle of compassion from our loved ones only to people for whom our feelings are neutral (the administrator at the other end of the phone line, the man standing next to you in the bus queue) and even to people who rouse angry, irritated or other kinds of negative feelings in you? If you were to manage this, it would benefit not only those who come into contact with you – partly because your behaviour is kinder – but you, too. Being compassionate to the grumpy waiter, the arrogant girl, the introverted cashier or the person who jumps the queue can give you a good feeling and make you feel connected. And that's great, because you may not always have the people you love around you, so it's wise to expand your circle of connection.

Of course, this doesn't mean that you should always embrace and hug difficult or irritating people or never address annoying or antisocial behaviour. However, by showing your compassion more widely, you are less likely to fall prey to your own judgements and will experience less stress and discomfort, so you can explain with more clarity and respect what bothers you or, if necessary, keep a healthy distance.

EXPANDING THE CIRCLE OF COMPASSION

Here are four techniques of compassion that may help you expand your circle of connection and compassion. You will use them to practise during this week's training.

TECHNIQUE 1: JUST LIKE ME

You are out for a walk in the woods and meet a dog. The dog barks ferociously and bares its teeth. You think, crikey, what a horrible animal. But then you notice that the animal is caught in a trap. Your attitude to the dog changes immediately from 'That's a monster – I need to steer clear' to 'Poor thing, how can I help?' Our behaviour is related to tens of thousands of factors – not only our genes, environment and upbringing, but also daily occurrences such as headaches, an empty stomach, an unpleasant phone call... Often you do not really understand a person until you know their background. That's when you realize that the other person is just like you and only wants to be happy and avoid suffering. Everybody makes their own mistakes, often unintentionally, in their quest for happiness. There is always a reason for bad choices or behaviours, and while this will not always excuse a behaviour, it can offer an explanation.

The realization that someone like you is looking for happiness (even though their quest may be quite different from yours) gives another side of the picture. Just like that African people, you should condemn only the behaviour and show compassion to the person who committed the crime.

SIT-UP

Try to see whether you can remind yourself that random passers-by are just like you. A simple phrase that you could repeat during the day is: 'Just like me he/she is...', completing the phrase as appropriate ('on their way to...', 'looking for...', 'in a hurry', 'sad', etc.).

TECHNIQUE 2: EXTENSIVE KIND INTENTIONS

In Week 6 you were introduced to intention training: positive words for yourself and for loved ones. This week, we extend this training to other people, those for whom you have neutral feelings – whom you tend to see primarily in terms of their role, rather than their full humanity: the teacher you don't particularly (dis)like or your sister's boyfriend whom you don't relate to – or someone you really don't like at all or whom you think demonstrates annoying behaviour – ranging from your authoritarian sports coach, a megalomaniac actress to the slow guy from the post office.

Good intentions towards such people do not mean that you want to justify their behaviour, but that you realize that we humans are not perfect. You also realize that if the other person is (un)happy, there's an even greater chance that you will be (un)happy, too (remember, your behaviour and your attitude to life are infectious!).

You may experience difficulties in this area of intention training, because neutral people can intrinsically be boring (you just don't know them), which causes your attention to drift, or because difficult people in your life give rise to feelings of annoyance, fear, sadness or maybe even hatred. Don't worry, it's all part of the training. Recognize the feelings, name them and approach them with compassion – after all, you're the one suffering at that moment. So by training your extensive intentions you are also training your self-compassion.

TECHNIQUE 3: THE POWER OF ACTIVE COMPASSION

Active compassion is also known as *tonglen* (Tibetan for 'giving and taking').[93] In this technique, you visualize your own or others suffering and absorb it when you inhale, and then wish yourself or others love, happiness and wellbeing when you exhale. The art is to accept the undesirable with an accepting attitude, and on the exhalation to practise generosity in relation to all the things you would prefer to keep to yourself.

Active compassion works to defuse automatic behaviours such as pushing aside unpleasant and clinging on to the pleasant, and to create new automatic behaviours that will make you happier and more resilient. Compare the voluntary suffering you experience during your inhalation with a vaccination: the injection hurts, it might even make you feel slightly unwell, but the goal is to prevent future suffering. Whether this technique will help the other at this moment, or whether the positive energy will enter them, is irrelevant, and it is not our goal. The point is that you will feel stronger amidst pain and suffering and be more open to joy.

TECHNIQUE 4: THE COMPREHENSIVE TECHNIQUE: FORGIVENESS

In 1993, the US teenager Oshea Israel shot dead fellow student Laramiun Byrd at a party. For the first few years after, Laramiun's mother, Mary Johnson, was filled with an intense hatred for Oshea. Because the hatred ruined her life, she had the intention to forgive him. Finally, after 12 years, she had the courage to visit Oshea in prison. It was an emotional meeting. Oshea expressed regret and was repentant, and Mary Johnson forgave him on the spot. The two embraced each other in an expression of deep sadness. Later, Mary described how her hatred had suddenly evaporated. After their meeting, she kept in touch with Oshea, and they formed a strong friendship, so strong in fact that Oshea went to live next door to Mary after his release; she now treats him like an adopted son.

This is an extreme example and it may sound almost like a modern fable or a horror movie: why would you want to forgive your son's killer? Even when offences or behaviours are much less serious (stealing, lying, having an extramarital affair), people often ask themselves what the point of forgiveness is for them. There are numerous studies showing that forgiving people are less angry, depressed, hostile, anxious or neurotic. They experience greater wellbeing, happiness and health and they are more compassionate.[94] It also appears that men tend to hold on to their feelings of resentment and revenge longer.[95] Male readers: this means more training practice for you!

'To forgive is the best form of self-interest.'

DESMOND TUTU

The following three reasons or excuses are often used to avoid forgiving someone (or yourself); the objection to each reason is printed in italics:

1. The other does not deserve to be forgiven: your hatred is part of their punishment. *Hating is like shouting in the wind: it doesn't reach the other; it only makes your voice hoarse.*
2. If I forgive someone, it implicitly means that I condone their behaviour. *Herein lies a major misunderstanding of forgiveness, because you forgive the person, not their behaviour.*
3. If I forgive another person, it means that we are reconciled and I have allowed them to enter my life. *If you think that ongoing contact with someone else might not be desirable, forgiveness and keeping one's distance can be compatible. You keep your distance while harbouring no resentment for and having goodwill towards the other person.*

Nelson Mandela remains a model for the power of forgiveness. He practised the African humanist concept of *ubuntu*: 'I am because we are.' Mandela believed that we owe our existence to interconnectedness. After almost 30 years of imprisonment, he chose forgiveness over revenge, taking the first steps on the road from apartheid to a society of solidarity.

If you find yourself overwhelmed by Nelson Mandela's extraordinary sense of forgiveness (how can I possibly live up to that?), treat him as a source of inspiration to forgive the driver tailgating you or the client who's let you down on a job. If we want to flourish as a society, forgiveness must be part of our society, institutions and laws. But it starts with yourself, in your own real world.

> **SIT-UP**
>
> Read the newspaper (or your tablet) and scan the headlines that make you angry. Connect with your anger. Check whether there are any other underlying emotions, for example fear that the world is coming to an end, or sadness about all the suffering in the world. Then connect with your compassionate self and the desire to ease the pain and act. How does it feel?

FORGIVING YOURSELF

After a snidey remark or a silly action, you may wish to hide behind an excuse such as 'Sorry, but I wasn't myself' or 'I don't know what came over me', which means that you are not allowing yourself self-forgiveness. You are denying the self, which had its own reasons for speaking or acting in this way. And the longer you deny your guilty self, the louder it will scream for attention. Denial is a form of resistance and makes your guilty self grow, instead of disappearing. Self-compassion helps you forgive and completely accept yourself.

FORGIVING OTHERS

Self-compassion is the first step towards forgiving others. Thus, you let go of the anger that no longer serves you. Then use the previous techniques to put yourself in the place of the other person: 'just like me', seeing good things in others (what can I learn) and wishing others the best (intention training). How do you know that you have forgiven someone? 'Forgiving' somebody without emotion often is a suppressive strategy. Do you still feel as if you are hanging on to feelings of revenge and hatred, or are the soft emotions of the soothing system (such as calmness, warmth, sadness, disappointment, contentment) slowly gaining the upper hand? Forgiveness cannot be forced, take your time.

'Forgiveness means giving up all hope of a better past.'

VARIOUS

All (self-)compassion techniques come together in forgiveness. Connect with your anger, the underlying pain, and unmet need(s) to forgive others or yourself. Thus begins the process of releasing resentment or anger that you no longer wish to serve. Forgiveness is not just good for your own wellbeing – as has been scientifically proven – but also forces you to think in terms of 'we'. Without identifying with the perspective of the other person it is impossible to let go of the coldness you feel towards the person, the 'perpetrator' you should forgive. Often their damaging behaviour is caused by ignorance and unconsciousness. Only if you understand and empathize with this realization, then forgiveness has a chance.

TRAINING

This week, pain in relationships takes centre stage. As in earlier weeks, you practise light training whenever appropriate situations occur during the day. No matter how you practise, it takes courage to circumvent the automatism of pain avoidance. 'I don't feel like it' often means: 'Oh no, that's scary.' Don't give up, but hold on to the idea that, in Part 3, which focuses on happiness, you will be working on how to let your relationships thrive. Remember the platitudes 'No pain, no gain', 'Rain after sunshine' and 'You don't get something for nothing', and so on... They are platitudes for a reason!

ılı LIGHT

This week choose one or two of the following five exercises. Choose the ones that appeal to you most, those that suit you (or your situation).

EXERCISE 1: FROM EMPATHY TO COMPASSION

During the day take note of situations when you empathically focus on somebody's pain. Then make a conscious switch to giving compassion. First recognize compassionately the pain you experience yourself by seeing the other person's pain; then focus your compassion on the other person. Use the techniques you learned in Weeks 5 and 6 and in the Sit-Up earlier in this chapter, practising extending compassion towards difficult people.

EXERCISE 2: SPOTTING SHAME

During the day look out for feelings of shame or think of an embarrassing moment in your past. Then focus on your physical experience and register your negative core principle ('I am hopeless', 'I can be so tactless', 'He must think me very stupid', or something like that). Then approach the pain that arises compassionately, by activating the

174

soothing system. Remind yourself that shame is a universal emotion that connects us all.

EXERCISE 3: SPOTTING ANGER

During the day, notice moments when you feel anger. You might also be able to recall a situation in your past. Focus on the pain with compassion and practise the five steps to deal with anger earlier in this chapter.

EXERCISE 4: OPENING UP TO NEUTRAL AND DIFFICULT PEOPLE

Be aware of distancing yourself from others or condemning them. Make a conscious decision to see the whole person. What makes them a wonderful person? What do you appreciate in them? What warm memories do you have about them? What do you respect about the person? Then try to stretch the circle of compassion by using the techniques in the warm-up:

↔ What can you learn from them?
↔ The 'just like me' technique.
↔ The kind intentions technique.

EXERCISE 5: ACTIVE SELF-COMPASSION

Use active compassion when faced with somebody else's suffering – if you see a homeless person sleeping on a bench, a distressed friend talks about his or her sick father, a friend tells you about his or her divorce... Breathe in the pain and send them positive energy when you exhale. Use your (sensory) imagination: breathe in cold pain and breathe out warm reassurance. Or if your sense of pain is warm, then breathe in the warm pain and breathe out cooling reassurance. Breathe in polluted air, breathe out clean air; breathe in nails, breathe out feathers. It doesn't matter which metaphor you choose – just as long as it works for you. This is how you practise allowing and accepting the undesirable to enter and sharing what is valuable with others.

ı||MEDIUM (EXTENSION TO LIGHT)

Would you like some additional exercise to help you hone your power of compassion this week? If so, practice the Intention training for a neutral and a difficult person every day. Only start this intention training if you have fully processed the Intention training for a loved one and yourself. If this hasn't quite worked yet, then keep working on your intention training from Weeks 5 and 6.

🎧 Audio track 9. Intention training for a neutral and a difficult person

ı||INTENSE

EXTENSION TO LIGHT + MEDIUM If you feel like doing some intensive training, then follow up the Intention training for a loved one and yourself with the Intention training for a neutral and a difficult person each day.

🎧 Audio track 8. Intention training for a loved one and yourself

🎧 Audio track 9. Intention training for a neutral and a difficult person

You can download the audio tracks from 12weekmindworkout.com.

COOL DOWN

How are you doing? Maybe you are well on your way with your compassion training: you have a better understanding of others, you are more courageous in showing your vulnerability and it looks as if loved ones are more receptive to your needs. You may have experienced the relief of letting go of pointless anger and have seen how a cheerful manner can be infectious. But you may also have noticed how difficult and frustrating compassion training can be. As with any training (e.g. an art or tennis course), the third lesson (or week) often presents the biggest hump. The initial enthusiasm for something new has somewhat died down, including your self-tolerance if you haven't quite yet caught on. You are annoyed with your messy approach on the canvas or impatient because you cannot serve properly yet. In compassion training, it irritates you that you can 'only' manage self-compassion at the moment – and you think therefore that you must be selfish. In other words, you are 'consciously incompetent'.

You may still accidentally return to former 'inappropriate' behaviours: you have noticed your tendency to judge or condemn or distance yourself from others. You may find that, however hard you try, you still cling on to some resentment, fear or bitterness. If these thoughts and feelings are still around, you need to realize that they have appeared because you are working on your own vulnerability. Your protection mechanisms are trying to help you survive, however clumsily, by shouting: 'Stick to the old! Change is scary!'

Do you still remember the discussion about the 'backdraft'? If you have not granted yourself enough compassion all your life, compassion may initially feel quite unpleasant: your threat system goes haywire due to this sudden and unknown gesture of warmth. Moreover, compassion training can open you up to pain that you had previously been hiding.

All in all, you might feel like giving up compassion training. If so, remember that all these forms of resistance – frustration, anger, the inclination to give up – are part of the process. There's movement and it's unpleasant, like those aching muscles after the tennis lesson, but the pain won't last. Moreover, it's a sign of healing and strengthening. Welcome your signs of resistance and notice them without judgement. And, above all, keep practising.

Ask yourself if you have achieved any of the following in week 7:

↔ Are you aware when you respond with empathy to pain when connecting with others?
↔ Can you take the step to respond with compassion?
↔ Can you spot your shame compassionately?
↔ Are you capable of discovering unmet need(s) sheltering behind difficult emotions (anger) and of recognizing that maybe you can now meet them yourself?
↔ Have you managed to extend your circle of sympathy to neutral and difficult people, through 'just like me', kind intention training, with active compassion and forgiveness?

'Have compassion for everyone you meet, even if they don't want it. What appears bad manners, an ill temper or cynicism is always a sign of things no ears have heard, no eyes have seen. You do not know what wars are going on down there where the spirit meets the bone.'

MILLER WILLIAMS

WEEK

08

COMPASSIONATE
COMMUNICATION

'If you think you're too small to make a difference, you haven't spent a night with a mosquito.'

ANONYMOUS

This final week of compassion training is all about conveying and consolidating. Last week we saw how the way in which you present yourself, behave and relate to other people has a direct and indirect impact on the people around. Your smile this morning could have an impact of a week, a month or even a year. Your compassionate approach could potentially be taken on by your neighbours, relatives, colleagues and even people beyond your own circle. Therefore, one of your main tools is the way in which you communicate.

WARM-UP

A young man is walking along the beach. As he walks towards the sea, he is shocked to see hundreds, maybe thousands, of starfish washed up on the shore. The creatures are slowly dying out in the scorching sun. The young man picks one up. He has a quick look at the creature and throws it back into the sea. He picks up a second starfish and flings it, too, back into the water. An old man stops and observes the scene in amazement. He walks up to the young man and asks him: 'What are you doing?' The young man replies: 'When I see a starfish that's still living, I throw it back into the sea.' The old man responds: 'What's got into you? Why on earth would you do that? There are thousands of them.' The young man keeps on searching and finds yet another live starfish. He says: 'It might not make any difference to all the other starfish. But it does for this one.' The young man stretches back his arm and flings the sea creature as far out to sea as he can.

Compassion is a powerful tool. Not only does it have the capacity to change your life, it can particularly change others' lives. Compassion starts with the individual but can potentially reach much further. But then your next step should be action. Because only thinking about compassion is like doing sports in your mind only: it doesn't improve your physical fitness.

It is not until you turn your compassionate intention into action, that it becomes integrated into your daily activities. And what's your main activity, the tool you deploy every day, no matter how? It's communication.

COMPASSIONATE COMMUNICATION

We have already looked the power of language and communication in previous weeks, including communicating with attention; using the magic quarter-second to stop yourself from making too hasty a judgement; THINK; generative listening; the power of language and voice, and using words such as 'allow', 'grant' and 'help' instead of 'demand', 'must' and 'expect'. This week you are going to take the next step in compassionate communication, the kind that aims to relieve pain in relationships. Communication has two sides: the sending and receiving of messages. What are the catches here and how can you avoid them with compassion?

SENDING COMPASSIONATELY

It is great talking to others, but chatter can also shatter: sometimes your communication can cause others hurt. Often, this happens inadvertently (a clumsy choice of words), sometimes maliciously, such as a snidey remark to your partner, the passing on of a juicy piece of gossip, or a jealous remark made to a friend. Chattering – mostly harmless small talk – can turn into blathering (the indiscriminate passing on of others' business) – especially when we have to convey bad or difficult news.

LYING AND GLOSSING OVER

We do not like being the bearer of bad news. We often use one of two techniques: we tell a white lie or we gloss over what we say.

EYE-OPENER

On average we lie one to three times a day,[96] men doing so more often than women. 'Yes,' we say, 'that dress really suits you', all the while thinking, 'It's hideous!' 'My exam went really well, Mum!' (It didn't). Or to your partner, 'No way would I have an affair,' when you are just about to send a sexy message to your lover.

If we do choose to pass on the unpleasant message, we often gloss over it, as a manager might do if someone has missed out on a promotion: 'I am sure you are next on the list,' says the manager, even though he or she knows that the chances are minimal. Lying and glossing over are certainly not the right way to give bad news or negative feedback. They are short-term solutions. Either the truth comes out in some other way, or you will have to tell the truth later down the line. Moreover, lying feels unpleasant.

It may be easy to twist words, but your body often reveals the true message anyway (you look away, blush, tap your fingers). Communication is largely non-verbal, encompassing facial expression, voice and body posture. If your body language isn't consistent with your words, something won't feel right either to you or the other party: without being able to put their finger on it, they will sense that something is amiss. And what about you? You feel guilty and your stomach feels tight; you condemn yourself for telling a lie.

SHIRAZ'S TRICK

If you want to stop yourself gossiping, lying, speaking ill of others, or glossing over the truth, then try the following trick developed by communication trainer Shiraz Khan. Imagine your conversations being recorded on camera to be shown at a party with all your loved ones and people you respect, ranging from your favourite nursery teacher to Gandhi, from your mother to Elon Musk. By imagining an audience you think highly of and who will judge you on your short-falls, it becomes easier for you to communicate as honestly, objectively and fairly as you can. You are less likely to be derogatory and more likely to be kind and truthful.

> Think of situations in which you often tend to lie, temporarily forget about your integrity, or simply overstep the mark. And then imagine that the conversation is being recorded on hidden cameras to be shown to people who are important to you. What are your feelings? What is in your mind? Shame, confusion, pain? If this situation recurs, think of Shiraz's trick.

SIT-UP

SPEAKING COMPASSIONATELY

You have just thought of the situations in which you habitually speak ill of others or lie. Now you want to change your approach. How will you go about it (other than applying Shiraz's trick)? How are you going to tell the truth in a kind way?

You've guessed it...by speaking compassionately. It is how you deliver a message, not blurting it out. Speaking compassionately means speaking the truth (in this case your truth) and doing this in a harmless and constructive manner, even if the message is not pleasant. Imagine you are a manager and you must dismiss some employees. If you do this compassionately, you act from within the soothing system. You are mindful of the pain your dismissed employees may be feeling, including your own pain. Your focus is on how to meet their needs and how to support them through this painful time.

ROSENBERG'S FORMULA

As you have already read in Week 6, one and the same message can be conveyed in dozens of ways, depending on the words you choose and your tone of voice. So how do you make sure that a difficult message is understood in the intended way? The American psychologist Marshall Rosenberg, the creator of the process known as Nonviolent Communication, posited that an appropriate response to this situation can be articulated using the following formula.

'When X happens, I feel Y because I need Z'.

To give an example, when something (X) happens which I witness objectively, I respond with emotions such as anger, anxiety or fear of rejection (Y), because I need whatever deeper need motivates that emotional response (Z). For example – to be criticised less, or valued more highly.

This ability to explain your reaction will provoke less defensive behaviour in others, you make it easier for others to be receptive to your wishes, and at the same time you give yourself a clearer picture of what you are trying to achieve.

I will give you a concrete example. Jim enjoyed a good social status, he was quite outgoing and was very good at his job. His boss, Linda, continuously praised him. That was great, but it made it more difficult for Jim to tell her the truth: he no longer enjoyed his work and wanted to resign. Once he had gathered courage to tell Linda, she physically distanced herself from him. Both her facial expressions and her demeanour expressed the anger she felt towards him.

Jim immediately felt inclined to mitigate the situation and thought, 'Maybe I could work part-time – it's not *that* bad!' But he reminded himself that short-term relief (a pleasant conversation) would have little impact in contrast to the optimal effect of long-term relief (enjoying a new job). So he stuck to his guns.

Rosenberg's formula came in handy here: 'When I told you just now that I wanted to leave my job, I saw you distance yourself from me by turning away. I am not used to the curt way in which you spoke to me (X). It made me feel unsure and it gave me a sense of guilt (Y), because I really want you to support me in my decision (Z).'

At first, Linda was taken aback by his observations and feelings, but she appreciated his honest and self-contained message. She explained that she was indeed disappointed because he had been such a good employee. But she also explained to him that she therefore wished him the very best. In the end, Linda and Jim parted on good terms, and Jim started mediator training. He now supports others in conducting difficult conversations.

BODY LANGUAGE

If you need to have a difficult conversation, like Jim, then let your feelings and your underlying needs speak. Let your body help you. So, if you want to say something with compassion, do not cross your arms but maintain an open posture. Relax your facial muscles. And if you want to be more assertive, gently throw back your shoulders. Your mind will then invariably follow your body.[97]

What makes a message difficult for you to convey? What is the fear that stops you from giving the message? And if you went ahead how would it benefit you? Be kind and do not force yourself to take the plunge immediately but allow yourself to feel motivated by your compassionate intention.

SIT-UP

TIMING

In addition to the delivery method, timing is also essential. The first day after maternity leave, it might not be wise to stand at your manager's desk asking for a pay rise. Timing is an intuitive process, but sometimes fear plays havoc and you impulsively choose the wrong moment, like you tell your parents at your grandma's funeral that you want to quit your studies, because you can't take any more. This is when attention (training) comes into play. It helps you pay less attention to these impulses and to listen to your own wisdom first.

In conclusion: the things that are hardest to say, are often the most valuable. And that does not only apply to unpleasant or difficult messages, positive messages can also make you vulnerable, so it takes courage to convey them. A simple phrase like 'I love you' is often only said on a deathbed. Or even worse: only verbalised at a funeral.

RECEIVING COMPASSIONATELY

Communication training often touches on feedback rules. Interestingly, these are often only focused on giving feedback and not how to receive. This is no more useful than a tennis trainer teaching you only how to serve, but not how to receive, the ball. Not only is it hard to deliver difficult messages, but receiving them can be challenging, too. Both are essential if two or more people want to interact constructively with each other.

DEALING WITH FEEDBACK

If your partner tells you that you flare up easily, it's hard not to respond by protesting, 'I DON'T SHOUT!' In Part I you learned to register your thoughts and feelings with open attention and not to follow your first impulse immediately. Compassion training helps you soothe yourself when you feel pain and makes you receptive to the suffering of others. You notice your partner biting their nails because of your (negligent) behaviour, and you are doing all you can to alleviate the situation, regardless of whether you think their criticism justified. Only when your eyes are fixed on the server, will you be able to return that hard serve. Only if you are prepared to receive negative criticism, can you determine its value and how to deal with it. By practising compassion, you develop enough strength to deal with incoming pain and discomfort. Only when you admit that you are imperfect, will you be open to feedback, improvement and development instead of merely protecting your self-image.

> Think of the most recent occasion on which you received a difficult message. What was your first impulse? Did you immediately tell the other person to get lost? If so, how did that feel? What was the impact on your relationship? Or were you prepared to really receive the feedback? How did that feel? What was the impact of that on your relationship?
>
> SIT-UP

Next time you receive feedback (this could be not only work-related, but in more personal situations including a remark like 'I thought you were rude/unkind/antisocial') you could ask questions like 'How could you tell that from my behaviour?', 'How did it affect you?' and 'Could you suggest a better way to respond?' If you notice painful feelings and thoughts arising, deal with them compassionately (e.g. by using the self-compassion pause). Also focus on your physical sensations. Meanwhile, be receptive to the message from the other person, even if it's delivered rather clumsily. It's a pity if a message is lost due to the delivery, or because you're not prepared to accept feedback, or because you think: 'Who do they think they are? How dare they!'

> Look in your diary to check when you might be expecting a formal piece of criticism (e.g. an appraisal interview, or feedback on an assessed project or a presentation). What kind of in-depth questions could you ask to explore the criticism?
>
> SIT-UP

In conclusion, it might make accepting feedback less frightening if you remember that you are the boss. Of course, you can always decide to accept the criticism with a thank you and then, after careful consideration, put it aside.

AVOID THE ADVICE ROUTE

It can be great to revel in other people's misery. At least, when we can consume it indirectly – in a piece of gossip, in a movie or newspaper article – and we are stretched out comfortably on the sofa with a bowl of popcorn. But, generally, if it's a question of real, immediate contact, we prefer to avoid other people's pain. Maybe you recognize this: faced with other people's misery, you are liable to small talk about other things or even avoid coming into contact with them at all. To hide behind a parked car, when your terminally ill neighbour is walking down the street.

Another well-known coping style to reject such empathic pain is the 'advice route'. If you tend to give advice to actively support others, it can of course be extremely useful, but be aware that usually it's rooted in a desire to minimize your own feelings of discomfort. It takes courage and stamina to listen compassionately to someone's pain without immediately taking the easy route out: 'Well, if I were you...'

The American psychologist Carl Rogers described his approach to patients evolving over the years – where once he asked himself how he might treat and heal them, he later pondered how he might build a relationship with them which would aid their personal growth.

People really want to be understood. Sometimes it can be enough just to be present listening silently, without offering 'helpful advice'. If you can tolerate the pain and the empathic discomfort compassionately, you will have a stronger listening capacity. It makes the other person feel heard and recognized. And the result is that the person will then come up with their own advice to themselves. Usually, they already have the answer and it only needs to be heard and experienced by a listening ear.

THE FOUR LIFELONG FRIENDS

In addition to compassion, there are three other forces you can use that are just as important: kindness, sympathetic joy and equanimity. These four 'lifeguards' balance each other. You can use your compassion, kindness, equanimity and sympathetic joy by deciding what is needed in each situation and for each individual. Each 'type of weather' requires a different approach: compassion in sub-zero temperatures and storms, sympathetic joy when it's bright and sunny, kindness when there are a few clouds dotted around, and equanimity as the seasons pass.

Table 8.1   The four lifeguards

LIFEGUARD	CHARAC-TERISTIC	DIRECT CAUSE	BENEFICIAL EFFECT IN THE CASE OF...	TRAP
Friendliness (light clouds and a weak sun)	The desire and willingness to promote wellbeing	An awareness of the good, and the desire to be happy	Hatred, dislike	Sentimentality and attachment
Compassion (when there's a storm)	The desire and willingness to relieve suffering	The sense of suffering and pain	Cruelty, glee	Pity, over-involvement, moodiness
Sympathetic joy (when the sun is shining)	Rejoicing in success and happiness	The sense of prosperity	Jealousy, envy	Pretence, affectation or excessive euphoria
Equanimity (during a change in the weather)	Bringing inner balance	The sense of imbalance	Excessive involvement, pride or inferiority, excessive preference or aversion, fanaticism	Indifference

Source: 'De vier levensvrienden' [Four life guards] in Frits Koster and Erik van den Brink, *Compassie in je leven* [*Compassion in Your Life*] (Boom, 2019)

Each situation requires a different type of strength. If you don't apply the right one, or switch in time, you may well fall into one of the traps in column four. The trap associated with kindness is having too much focus on the pleasant things in life. For example, to your partner who has nothing to worry about but wants to have a good moan, you say, 'Cheer up, after all you've such a wonderful home /

a really good income / your mother is still in good health', and so on, and in doing so don't allow her space for the clouds in her life, however light they may seem to you.

The trap associated with compassion is veering towards feelings of pity and melancholy, which makes you lose sight of real compassion. Then it's time to switch to one of the other life guards, for example equanimity – 'It is what it is' – and allow yourself to recharge. The trap of sympathetic joy is too much involvement in other people's happiness. This occurs, for example, with the obsessive 'soccer mom' who plans her whole life around her son or daughter, a talented football player, cheering them from the side-lines in all kinds of weather.

In this instance, too, a transition to equanimity might be wise, allowing you to realize that everything is transient and your influence is limited. This is exactly what loving parents do when a child leaves the nest. They know that their daughter will make painful mistakes, but she is responsible for her own choices. However, if they take this too far, their equanimity becomes indifference. It may then be time to switch to one of the other three life guards – and the right choice depends on the 'weather forecast': their daughter's situation.

SIT-UP

This is an exercise in equanimity. Think of a loved one, someone you have been wanting to change for a while for their own good, but without success. Connect with your emotions and potential pain. Then repeat the following sentences to yourself: 'Everybody creates their own life history. I am not the cause of suffering. I can help, but I can't make choices for them. May he/she and I maintain a balance through the highs and lows of life.' If there are other words that work better for you, use them – provided they bring calmness and acceptance in the face of life's vicissitudes.

There is another way in which you can ask the four life guards for assistance. The destructive internal processes where kindness, compassion, sympathetic joy and equanimity may help are listed in column three of the table. Does your colleague really bother you? Then focus on what you appreciate in them: be kind and wish them the best. If you find yourself gloating about the business failure of your ever-successful brother-in-law, realize that he is suffering and wish him relief: this is the wholesome effect of compassion. The third life guard, sympathetic joy, can be applied when you notice that you feel jealous about a friend's new love. Just be happy for them and share in their success and happiness. Finally, if you're fed up that your holiday is nearly over, wish yourself equanimity.

COMPASSIONATE SOCIETY

Let's return to the nub of the matter, to our wish to live a compassionate life, the theme of this second part. As I mentioned before, showing compassion to others doesn't mean having compassion only for those you love. It also applies to your neighbours, your colleagues, the gardener, the call centre employee, the police officer, people you really don't like and, finally, people you don't know or will never meet. It applies 'even' to nature and animals, from the elephant to the ant.

Climate champion and actor Leonardo DiCaprio agrees. In his documentary about climate change *Before the Flood* he uses the Early Netherlandish painting *The Garden of Earthly Delights* by Hieronymus Bosch – a triptych depicting Paradise, the Seven Deadly Sins and Hell in fantastic detail – as a metaphor for how humans related, relate and will relate to their environment. Humanity has now entered stage two, the Seven Deadly Sins, and if we don't stop our destructive tendencies, our addiction to self-indulgence and materialism, DiCaprio (and science!) says that we are well on the way to stage three, Hell.

SLIPPING

Scarcity of resources – which we have not known in Western society for centuries – has programmed us to be gatherers. This 'have have have' mentality is in our blood, part of our survival mechanism. Technology is the bogeyman that facilitates our tendency to stockpile.

Take the fast fashion industry, which produces 1.5 billion items of clothing annually, much of which will be thrown out the following season – because, of course, it's already out of fashion. Adults and their clothes are just like children with their toys. Every day, we throw out more than we think: for every bin you fill each week, you could fill another 70 with all the resources needed to produce these items.[98]

Human greed has disastrous consequences. First, there is an increasing gap between rich and poor: one per cent of the world's population owns more than the rest of the world's population put together, and this division, due to all our greed, is becoming increasingly skewed.[99] One and a half billion people live in extreme poverty;[100] every day one billion people do not have enough to eat.[101] And we should not forget to mention the indirect impact on health and education (or lack of).

But Mother Nature also suffers: 90 per cent of major fish species are extinct, by the end of the 21st century one-third of all mammals and amphibians will be in danger of extinction.[102] Humans have cut down more than half of all forests, and the prediction is that in 30 years' time, if we continue in the same way, we will only know about the rainforest from pictures and stories.[103]

Due to our reckless consumption of fossil fuels and fertilizers, extensive livestock farming and excessive meat consumption, the Earth is warming up. Before you say, 'It can't be that bad', you should know that 97 per cent of all (climate) scientists say that humanity must change its lifestyle quickly or the damage will be irreversible (the three per cent in denial are often commissioned by conglomerates who have invested interests in 'It can't be that bad'). And even technology won't save us from such a disaster.

WHAT CAN I DO ABOUT IT?

Why this sudden rant? Just to illustrate how bad things really are – and what's worse – that most of us are dulled to the reality of the situation (that is, without compassion). *Yes, yes, yes, I know. It's terrible, but what can I do about it?* And then they go and stock up at a cheap clothing store and then buy some plastic toy or other for their daughter or nephew. Perhaps you're not in the mood for all that worry and guilt feelings either, or would rather look the other way. But sooner or later...

'Why should I care about future generations? What have they ever done for me?' Groucho Marx asked. It's a joke, but it contains a solid grain of truth. 'The free-rider phenomenon' is precisely why the climate and environmental emergency has happened. It's just like the argument that you changing your behaviour will be just like a drop in the ocean, so what's the point? Even if you are that one drop, it's the only drop for which you are 100 per cent accountable.

Rosa Parks accepted her responsibility. In 1955 this African American activist refused to give up her seat to a white man on the bus in Montgomery, Alabama. Her personal act of defiance triggered a major rebellion against racial segregation in the USA. Half a century after Rosa's heroic campaign, her country had its first black president, Barack Obama. Rosa Parks showed how thousands of drops could become a cooling waterfall, and she made the first step towards dousing the hotbed of racism.

EYE-OPENER

MUCH HAS BEEN ACHIEVED

We do not want to fall into the evolutionary trap of focusing on misery: humankind has not only wreaked destruction, but has also achieved much in the past 500 years and especially in the last five decades. In 1970, 29 per cent of the world's population was undernourished, now it is 'only' 11 per cent. Poverty has reduced more in the past 50 years than in the previous 500. Over the past 25 years the number of people who have access to safe water has increased by 285,000 every day, and global violence has decreased spectacularly: 30 years ago four to five people out of every 100,000 died as a result of war atrocities, now it is only 1.5.

In his book *Progress*, the Swedish author and activist Johan Norberg describes these improvements.[104] In addition to its polluting, destructive aspect, technology also has a clear ameliorative and progressive side. 'All' we need to do is to take care that we deploy it correctly. Currently, technology could potentially solve all global food shortages and save the climate. If we all were to stop eating meat today, everybody would have something to eat and it would save millions of tons of carbon dioxide emissions.[105] If we had the will to do so, almost all energy could be generated sustainably. There are some wonderful technologies that have the capacity to turn deserts into jungles. It's not a question of whether we can do it, but when: when will winnings be defined as the wellbeing and sustainability of our planet instead of as a few figures on a balance sheet.

EYE-OPENER

The US documentary *Alive Inside: A Story of Music and Memory* (2014) shows social worker Dan Cohen visiting Alzheimer patients in nursing homes and playing their favourite childhood music. This has amazing results for patients' wellbeing: the music brings back precious memories, and their lost zest for life is regenerated. A video on YouTube[106] about one of the revived patients not only moved millions of spectators, but inspired many people, ranging from nursing staff to relatives, to follow Cohen's example, and to return joy to the lives of Alzheimer patients.

A COMPASSIONATE LIFE

The greed that stems from an overactive drive system is not your fault. But it's your responsibility to make sure you aren't getting hooked. You will need a moral compass. Unfortunately, 'Practise what you preach' is not a piece of wisdom we tend to apply. Many studies show that there is no connection between moral reasoning (chatting) and proactive moral behaviour (doing).[107] However, compassion training has been shown to nurture social action and increased altruism.[108]

It's not a matter of how compassionate you are, but rather whether you take the responsibility to train your compassion. Compassion does not happen to you; it requires a conscious choice to be kind to others and to yourself – to realize that doing nothing, and saying nothing, can sometimes be the best answer; to help people in need, close by and far away; to look beyond your own little comfort zone; to help restore our planet's ecology; to seek support if you are in trouble yourself; to embrace the wisdom that you cannot save the world, but you can do what is possible, without losing self-compassion. Let us do our best to be compassionate to our fellow human beings, to animals and to our environment, not to enter the hell of the *Garden of Earthly Delights*, but to work hard and compassionately to preserve that 'Paradise' stage – together.

TRAINING

▮▯▯ LIGHT

EXERCISE 1: FOUR LIFE GUARDS

Make sure you have a break each day (e.g. a breather) to determine whether you want to enter the situation and meet the person with kindness, equanimity, compassion or sympathetic joy.

EXERCISE 2

Practise a compassionate conversation at least once a day:

↔ *Sending.* Do not avoid difficulties, but use the Marshall Rosenberg method: 'When X happens (something you have seen and which you describe without judgement) I feel Y (especially softer emotions) because I need Z (your unfulfilled deeper needs).'

↔ *Receiving.* Practise receiving criticism from within your soothing system. Experiment with listening compassionately to other people's suffering. Try to resist the tendency to take the advice route. Important: approach your own discomfort during the conversation with compassion.

▮▮▯ MEDIUM

EXTENSION TO LIGHT

EXERCISE 1

🎧 Audio track 10. Intention training for the whole world

EXERCISE 2

Would you like some extra training? If so, each day choose one of the audio tracks from the previous three weeks. Find out which one suits your needs best at the time. You could also try practising without using the recordings (if so, set a timer).

EXERCISE 3

This week, spend one half-hour on a compassionate activity. If possible, schedule the activity into your diary. The activity can be focused on yourself or on somebody else. Phone a good friend who is having a hard time, search for a good cause on the Internet, have a massage, allow yourself to spend half an hour doing nothing.

ıll INTENSE

EXTENSION TO LIGHT + MEDIUM

EXERCISE 1: DRAW YOUR COMPASSION CARD

It wouldn't be a good idea to sew your parachute while you are plummeting down to the ground. The same applies to compassion: if you have come a cropper, it's difficult to continue training. By mastering the compassion skills now (and during the past three weeks), you will be well prepared if you make another nose-dive. Even then, it can be difficult to call on your acquired compassion and put it into practice at crucial moments. Therefore, compose your own compassion card including reminders to help you in difficult circumstances.

Include the following on your compassion card:

↔ **Situations** in which you are at your most vulnerable. Do they arise when you receive feedback from colleagues, or during holidays, or particularly on Monday mornings? Do they occur when you are with friends, or having a row with your partner? Describe the circumstances.

↔ **Signs** that warn you that you are rapidly heading towards the bitterness trap. Break these down into mental (you feel confused or judgemental, or have gone into worry mode), emotional (you are listless, irritable, anxious), physical (you feel a headache coming on, your jaws are clenched, you are breathing shallowly) and behaviour (you are fractious, sleeping badly, isolating yourself, going out more than usual, slipping back into your smoking addiction).

↔ What is **helpful** to you? One person will seek distraction, another will try to accommodate the situation, a third may prefer to be alone, and a fourth needs company. What activities, objects and/or compassion exercises feed you? What people support you in such situations?

↔ What is **counterproductive** for you? What are your typical traps? Very often they are behaviours that give you short-term relief but which you regret afterwards (e.g. resorting to addictions – smoking, shopping, drinking, sex, sugar; putting others down; energy-sapping activities such as surfing on the Internet).

You should realize that drawing the compassion card always requires effort. If you feel down, stressed or exhausted, self-reflection may not be the first thing you are looking to do. Attention (training) will increasingly help you to be quicker at registering signs. And the quicker you register the signs, the easier it will be to adjust to them using your compassion card.

🎧 You can download the audio tracks from 12weekmindworkout.com.

COOL DOWN

After four weeks of compassion training you may have become a fan of its positive effects, but perhaps the word 'compassion' is now making you feel nauseous? Training (self-) compassion often goes through a number of typical stages that might be compared to the process of falling in love.[109]

In the first phase, you are head over heels. Your new love is wonderful, and you cannot see any imperfection. Compassion feels the same, it's like a revelation and the perfect solution for everything. You notice the effects and feel happy.

But then you arrive at the next stage: disillusion. You're starting to notice that your new love doesn't let you finish your sentences, that your new love's values don't seem to be yours or that they are sickeningly close to their mother. You start to feel annoyed. This is the point that you realize that compassion training isn't an everlasting aspirin for pain, but only a tool to help you better endure pain. 'I can't believe it, I've done all those compassion exercises, and I still feel $%^#*^$#.' You are beginning to doubt whether compassion training is the right thing for you. This is a crucial stage and you have to persist. Your resistance is a sign that you are closing yourself off, but it's also an invitation to be receptive to what is happening.

After disillusion comes the third and final phase: real love and acceptance. You accept your partner's carelessness or their endless WhatsApp calls; you realize that compassion isn't about pain relief but a way to build a different relationship with pain and suffering. (Sometimes suffering does disappear into the background, and this will take you back to the first phase where you fall in love with this effect all over again.) The third phase means that we accept our struggles and thereby need comfort and support.

So, are you in the disillusion phase? If so, there's no reason to feel stress. Remember, practice makes perfect. Focus mainly on intention, not on results. It is not about mastering compassion in a few weeks; compassion training is the work of a lifetime. Like fitness, it's something you will have to keep on doing. The power of your compassion, like your attention muscle, will weaken if you stop exercising. At the end of Week 4, advice was given how to keep up training. Go back to those pieces of advice because they also apply to compassion training.

When you are practising compassion, you may need to ask for support. An eight-week compassion training course provides a solid foundation for the integration of compassion into your daily life.

Ask yourself whether you have achieved any of the following in Week 8:

↔ Can you now speak with compassion? Has it become easier for you to convey a difficult message in a kind and constructive manner?

↔ Can you listen compassionately without immediately offering advice?

↔ In addition to compassion, have you been able to apply kindness, equanimity and sympathetic joy?

↔ Can you see the bigger picture of compassion? Have you fully taken on board how, when using compassion, you can influence not only your immediate environment but the whole of society?

IN CONCLUSION

Two monks are on a journey. When they arrive at the river, they see a woman on the bank. She appears to be afraid of the current and asks the monks to help her cross. The older monk hesitates. The youngest monk, however, lifts the woman on his shoulders, walks through the water and puts her down on the other side. The woman thanks him and continues her journey. The monks continue their journey in silence. The younger monk enjoys the beautiful landscape, but the older monk seems introverted. After two hours of walking, the youngest breaks the silence and asks him what the matter was. The old monk irritably tells him what is bothering him: 'We have learned not to have any contact with women, but you carried the woman on your shoulders!' The youngest monk replies: 'I only took the woman across the river; you, on the other hand, are still carrying her!'

PART 3
HAPPINESS SKILLS

'The ultimate goal of human life is, simply, happiness, the ultimate purpose in order to realize your potential.'

ARISTOTLE

Many seek happiness in status, power and success. Others understand happiness as something more abstract, something that cannot easily be added to a to-do list. And if something is intangible or vague, you tend to forget about it, or have the wrong ideas about it. What is happiness for you? In these four weeks you will try to gain a clear picture of your answer. What makes you happy and how do you achieve happiness? After all, it's ultimately only your own experience that counts.

Money can buy you a lot, but not everything, such as a good laugh, an enjoyable conversation with a friend or relative, or a moving encounter with a stranger. In short, you cannot buy moments of happiness. But suppose it were possible, how much would you pay for such a moment of happiness? One pound, ten pounds, or all your monthly salary? On average, most would pay 75 pounds.[110] It might sound a bargain, but at that price lasting happiness would be unaffordable. Fortunately, you don't have to raid your bank account, because in Part 3 of *The 12 Week Mind Workout* you will try to build your happiness skills. A variety of techniques taken from positive psychology will teach you how to lead a meaningful and happier life.

'You first need to know what happiness is to be happy.'

JEAN-JACQUES ROUSSEAU

WHAT = HAPPINESS?

Up until 2000 we had a good understanding of why we feel bad but we were bad at understanding why we feel good.[111] There were 17 studies on depression, mental disorders and illnesses for each study on happiness.[112] Luckily, this has changed in recent years. Happiness is no longer restricted to the 'Mind, Body and Spirit' corner in the bookshop; thanks to an increasing amount of scientific research, happiness now has a lot more substance as well as airtime.

It appears from studies that happy people are healthier, kinder to themselves and others, have a better idea how to manage conflicts, are more resilient to life problems, and are more creative, successful and effective in their work.[113]

Happiness even appears to affect lifespan. Scientists investigated the relationship between the feeling of happiness and the age of nuns. The setting of this longitudinal study (research over an extended period, in this case 60 years) was highly suitable because the lives of 180 women in the convent were quite similar. The researchers made an important finding in that nuns who regarded monastic life as positive when they were young (they used words like 'happiness' or 'joy') lived on average nine years longer than 'negative' nuns, who used words like 'fate', 'serve' and 'doing my best'.[114]

EYE-OPENER

What does happiness mean? Dictionaries and Wikipedia more or less agree that it is 'contentment with one's circumstances' (*Oxford English Dictionary*). Related emotions are joy, relaxation, contentment and cheerfulness. Maybe you associate (the quest for) happiness with soppy romance magazines or intuitive 'follow-your-heart' coaches. You may even be repelled by the word 'happiness'. But imagine you had a magic wand and you could wish for anything you wanted, what would it be? A million pounds? Fame? The love of your life? Success? Why would you want any of these? Be an inquisitive toddler and repeat the 'why' question after each answer. You may end up with the same answers: 'Because I want to be happy.'

SIT-UP

Now write down what you mean by happiness. Which words work best for you? Here are some suggestions of words that might appeal to you rather than 'happiness': quality of life, wellbeing, wisdom, energy, vitality, positivity, success, fortune, health, contentment, good standard of living, prosperity, affluence. Reflect on the meaning of the words that affect you.

CAN HAPPINESS BE LEARNED?

You can philosophize about the beauty of a piano until the cows come home, but all the philosophy in the world will not make beautiful music. You have to practise those scales. This also applies to happiness. You can increase your happiness skills through practice.

You might be thinking: well, that easy to say, but is it really possible to provide training in happiness skills? Isn't it just a matter of bad luck if you're not happy?

A Harvard study shows that only 10 per cent of long-term happiness can be derived from circumstances. It means that you are responsible for the other 90 per cent. Sonja Lyubomirsky, one of the best-known happiness scientists, came up with this 90:10 ratio. She also found that about 50 per cent of your happiness is fixed at birth and that up to 40 per cent is determined by your *internal state of mind*.

Even in the most extreme circumstances, it's your outlook that determines your degree of happiness. In his book *Man's Search for Meaning* (first published in German in 1946), the neurologist, psychiatrist and concentration camp survivor Viktor Frankl wrote about the different ways in which his fellow prisoners dealt with deplorable circumstances: one thing that cannot be taken away from a person is their freedom to choose one's own way, to choose one's attitude in any given set of circumstances. It is the first and last of human freedoms.

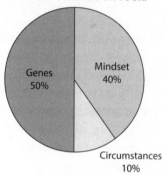

HAPPINESS DEPENDS ON YOUR:

Genes 50%

Mindset 40%

Circumstances 10%

Figure 8.1
Source: 'What determines your happiness?', Sonja Lyubomirsky, *The How of Happiness* (Piatkus, 2010)

Training can boost your basic level of happiness. And although it might not always be easy to find happiness and contentment in yourself, you cannot find it elsewhere.[115]

'Happiness is an inside job'[116] or, as John Milton writes in *Paradise Lost*: 'The mind is its own place and in itself, can make a Heaven of Hell, a Hell of Heaven.'[117]

WHAT DO WE TRAIN?

We train the right mindset. Tal Ben-Shahar, a professor of positive psychology at Harvard, distinguishes four mindsets, or archetypes, in relation to our attitude to life and quest for happiness. Probably unconsciously, each of us prefers one of the four archetypes of this 'hamburger model'.

THE HEDONIST

The hedonist chooses a greasy double hamburger dripping with cheddar cheese. Their objective is to 'feel good' with the least possible effort. In the long run, the hedonist tends to be unhappier. The quest for pleasure leaves them with a sense of emptiness, and any potential consequences (weight gain, poor health) eventually become today's realities.

THE RAT-RACER

The rat-racer opts for the healthy, tasteless specimen and consumes the dry quinoa burger without enjoying it. The objective is to grow old in good health. The rat-racer is the 'if...then' type: 'If I pay off my mortgage, I will be happy.' It is the objective that matters and not the journey. The rat-racer does not really enjoy achieved success. The rat-racer does not feel happy, but feels relief when an objective has been achieved. The problem is they immediately need a fresh objective to fill their sense of emptiness.

THE NIHILIST

The nihilist orders an unhealthy and yucky hamburger that is greasy and in a soggy bun. The nihilist believes that they are no longer in control of their own happiness and have become a victim of circumstances. The self-fulfilling prophecy means that the nihilist assumes that their current state of unhappiness will continue in the future.

THE HAPPY INDIVIDUAL

Fortunately, there are also tasty and healthy/healthier hamburgers: fresh burgers with plenty of vegetables in wholegrain bread rolls. The happy individual believes and proves that pleasure in the now can yield profit in the future.

It is not a matter of 'either...or' but 'and...and'. A student who enjoys studying will find it easy to obtain good exam results. They stay focused on their destination and also enjoy the journey.

> Which archetype (currently) dominates you? Are you happy with that? What advice would you like to give yourself? Write down your answers.
>
> **SIT-UP**

You may think that a healthy, tasty burger isn't a very realistic proposition. To some degree you're right: often present and future happiness are in conflict, as with the cheering drink that becomes a nasty hangover (the hedonist has popped their head round the corner). But in the flow of the struggle between these two poles there is a sense of happiness that rises from our own capacity for resilience (the basis of compassion training!). Happy individuals find that many moments of happiness in the now and in the future are closely linked.

BUT HOW DO YOU BEGIN?

The first step to happiness is knowing what happiness means to you. Step two is to explicitly put those experiences and activities at the top of your to-do list. It's as simple as that.

Reminding yourself to be happy will make you happier. This was the conclusion reached by research conducted in seven different Fortune 500 companies. Half of the employees were given a weekly reminder to put happiness at the top of their priority list; the control group was not reminded. After several months it appeared that the former group experienced more happiness. They were more satisfied about the choices they made, such as not working overtime but going to see their daughter performing in a gymnastics competition, or not doing menial jobs but relaxing instead.[118]

> Repeat this question from waking up to going to sleep during as many activities and as many different moments as possible: 'What makes me happier right now?' It does not matter whether you are cycling, talking to colleagues or reading a/this book. Find out what doing the activity gives you. How does it influence your current experience? Does it affect the situation and/or your stance? Does it change your mood?
>
> **SIT-UP**

The big 'but' while defining any quest for happiness is that the pursuit of *continuous* pleasant emotions (hedonism) is a recipe for unhappiness and even depression.[119] The answer is to make happiness a priority without trying to achieve it relentlessly with blinkers on. There's a delicate balance here, but it is possible. Think of a romantic dinner date: you can't force it (insisting that it will be romantic will probably be counterproductive), but you can set the right conditions (Barry White, nibbles, candles).

Happiness is wanting what you already have – combined with a relaxed wish to grow and develop.

RESISTANCE

Talking about 'happiness' and particularly the quest for happiness may make some people positively 'thrilled'. Some consider the quest for happiness superficial; happiness is either silly or un-achievable. Others think that happiness makes you lazy. The latter prejudice has been disproved. Success does not lead to more happiness, whereas happiness leads to more success. You get more done in less time. Shawn Achor, a professor at Harvard, calls this 'the happiness advantage'. He claims that your IQ predicts 25 per cent of your work success and your feelings of happiness predict 75 per cent. According to Achor, a positive happy brain is on average 31 per cent more productive than a negative or even a neutral brain. In addition, a happy individual has a 37 per cent higher success rate in sales. If a doctor is happy, they will be 19 per cent quicker and more accurate in their diagnosis. In short, happiness makes your brain work harder, quicker and more intelligently, which in turn leads to more success.[120]

The most often voiced criticism of the quest for happiness is that it is selfish. We live in a world of so much misery, ranging from famine to war, what right have we wealthy Westerners to focus on our own happiness? The world needs us to act, not navel-gaze!

However, research shows that happy people find it easier to share, are readier to help, do more voluntary work and spend more money on others than unhappy people.[121] Think of how you feel when you are miserable: is your focus on yourself or on others? When are you most effective, creative and energetic? When you are feeling depressed and listless or when you are feeling good?

TRAINING OBJECTIVE

You do not learn to ride a bicycle by reading a book about it. No, you get on the bike, however unsteady (perhaps first with stabilizers) and start to pedal. And then you fall. Inevitably. Often. The most challenging but also most effective way of learning is through practice. This final part of *The 12 Week Mind Workout* contains your passport to becoming a happier person. In the preceding parts you learned to let go of destructive patterns; well, you are now going to strengthen patterns to help you boost your basic level of happiness.

The essence of every form of training is perseverance, even when you experience setbacks. You might still be walking instead of taking your bike if you had given up after the first fall off your bicycle. So, keep practising your happiness skills, especially if you feel resistance (often in the form of sadness). If you allow this resistance to enter (remember your compassion training), it creates more space for you to be happier.

In Week 9 we will train ourselves in activating our positive emotions. In Week 10 the focus is on relationships, one of the main sources of happiness. Week 11 concentrates on how to achieve a balanced, pleasant, committed and meaningful life. Week 12 is about perseverance: how will you build on, even after you have read this book, attention, compassion and – in short – happiness?

09

THE BASICS

'Happiness consists more in the small conveniences of pleasures that occur every day than in great pieces of good fortune that happen but seldom.'

BENJAMIN FRANKLIN

Moments of happiness are exactly that: they are moments. No matter how short they are, they have great value in your quest for lasting happiness. After highlighting the difficult aspects in the previous four weeks, from now on you will start training your happiness skills. In Week 9 we'll begin with a focus on how to increase and deepen positive emotions, gratitude and optimism. You will learn to notice them, but also how to evoke these emotions and stay connected for longer.

WARM-UP

Researchers at the University of California analysed the smiles in 140 passport-type photographs in a school yearbook: which were real and which fake. It is quite easy to distinguish a real smile (also called a Duchenne smile) from a fake one. If you see little crinkles around the eyes, the smile is probably genuine. It is difficult, if not impossible, to consciously tense the small muscles at the corners of your mouth. Thirty years later the researchers compared the fake smilers to the genuine grinners. The latter appeared to be much happier than those who forced a smile. Even the divorce rate was significantly higher among those with fake smiles.[122]

POSITIVE EMOTIONS

I already mentioned that, during the past 200,000 years, fear, sadness, anger and disgust have helped humans to survive, which is what we are programmed for. But what is the benefit of positive emotions such as joy, inspiration and delight? Science has struggled with this question for years, but we now have a consensus. Positive emotions motivate us to be (in)active; we will do something (exciting) or nothing at all (satisfaction).[123] Barbara Fredrickson was the first to explore this 'discovery' in her broaden-and-build theory.

The following sit-up helps us understand the theory.

Go to a news website of your choice and read a few bad-news items on topics that affect you. Let the message really sink in. Now take a few minutes to produce a list of solutions to the problem of traffic jams. There is no need to address them to the Department of Transport; your ideas can be as wacky and impractical as you like. Then take a short break. Spend a few minutes thinking of a pleasant moment in your life, something that makes you smile, such as the birth of your child, the first weekend away with your loved one or a good conversation with your granny. Enjoy the emerging feeling. Now have a look at your list of traffic jam solutions and see if you can think of more.

SIT-UP

BROADEN-AND-BUILD

Did new ideas arise after the sit-up? Yes? – I thought so. I will explain why. Negative emotions constrict attention like a waterlily closing in the dark. They narrow your mindset – the drive or threat systems are at work. When the waterlily opens up to the sun, this is a positive emotion: the soothing system creates space for your attention and allows you to broaden your mindset.[124] A sourpuss sees only the brushstrokes, the happy bunny will also see the whole picture. The happy-go-lucky see the details and have an overview.

Here is an example of the 'build' aspect: your eight-year-old niece or nephew plays with their dolls every day and every day he or she gives the dolls new roles, ranging from action hero to film star to parent. It is the 'broaden' aspect of the child's cheerful nature that makes him or her imagine new scenarios. At the same time, the child is building his or her long-term creativity and social skills (the 'build' aspect). Replace 'playing happily with dolls' with 'working with colleagues in a relaxed manner' and the same applies to adults: a good mood makes you receptive to new ideas and helps you build resources (competencies and qualities such as sensitivity and perseverance) for the future.

EYE-OPENER

Even at micro level there is a build aspect: cells grow in a positive environment, while negative emotions generally slow down cell growth.[125]

You can use these resources when things go wrong. In the long run, they will help you be more flexible in difficult situations. Because the more positive the emotions you experience, the broader your attention becomes, the more new ideas and activities you develop, the more resources you build, the better it is for your health and satisfaction...all of which in turn bring you more positive emotions, which broadens your attention... In short, you 'cheer up' your brain; it is the positive spiral of positive emotions.

POSITIVITY RATIO

This week is not intended to be a one-sided plea for positivity. Negativity plays a role, too. Let's use a sailing analogy: if you have your eyes fixed on the horizon, the foresail of your boat is your optimism; it catches the wind and gives you energy. The keel, by contrast, is negative – it keeps you on course.[126] Negative emotions keep you alert (you probably remember the example I used earlier in the book that you would rather mistake a branch for a snake than vice versa) and keep your feet on the ground. If you fall in love with a house, you are blind to its poor foundations and the mould on walls. A touch of negativity helps you look critically at your potential new home. But how do you keep negativity in perspective? By boosting your positivity ratio.

Positive emotions reduce or prevent the harmful effects of negative emotions; this is the so-called *undoing* effect.[127] For example training in positive emotions can be beneficial for people with depressive complaints.[128] Not only the absolute number of positive emotions you experience is important, but also the ratio of positive to negative emotions: your positivity ratio. The higher the ratio – the more *uppers* compared to *downers* – the more you feel you are thriving.

FUNCTION OR BLOSSOM

On average, people have a positivity ratio of 2:1 (two positive emotions compared to one negative emotion).[129] This produces a 'relaxed' state of mind in which you can function normally. At 3:1, you are thriving.[130] In relationships, you need a high positivity ratio, 5:1 (five fun, happy or connected moments versus one negative moment), to experience it as successful. In teams, the ratio might even be 6:1.[131, 132]

TOPPING UP

How do you increase your positivity ratio? By mitigating (the impact of) negative feelings on the one hand (see Part 2: Compassion) and by experiencing positive emotions for longer on the other. What is important is the kind of emotions you need now. If your body craves protein, it's useless eating an extra orange. The same applies to emotions. A missing sense of togetherness cannot be filled with more pride; the feeling that you are being appreciated does not connect with your longing for more enthusiasm.

All the needs you feel belong to one of the three core needs: security, satisfaction and connectedness – the three emotion regulation systems are back again! You can only start topping up when you know what you're short of.

Attention helps you recognize negative feelings. You can then decide which counterpart is needed to complement them (see Table 9.1). How can you do this? By taking conscious action, actively evoking them through your imagination (see Part 2) and/or by noticing when you do experience the required positive feeling.

Table 9.1

	Core need: security	Core need: satisfaction	Core need: connectedness
Positive	Trust, peace, strength, calm, relaxation, rest, power, efficiency	Adequacy, satisfaction, satisfied, **gratitude**, happy, enthusiastic, fulfilled, successful	Togetherness, love, recognized, loved, appreciated, invaluable, cherished, special
Negative	Insecure, anxious, angry, paralysed, defeated, weak, overwhelmed, helpless	Frustration, disappointed, failed, sorrowful, sad, regretful, stressed	Hurt, rejected, abandoned, lonely, abused, annoyed, envious, disadvantaged, jealous, ashamed, inadequate, unworthy

Source: Rick Hanson, *Hardwiring Happiness* (Harmony, 2013)

Are you feeling rather lonely? Think back to a happy moment when you felt loved, phone an acquaintance or an old friend, and try to be thankful for the brief moments of connection you have felt: a chat about spring at the florist's, exchanging a look of understanding with a stranger in the restaurant, and a wave from the three-year-old girl next door.

GRATITUDE

Gratitude is one of the most effective and powerful strategies for happiness, because it evokes a huge amount of positive emotions. Robert Emmons, the well-known researcher into gratitude, defines gratitude as follows: 'A feeling of surprise, recognition and appreciation for life.'[133] The emboldened text in Table 9.1 has a point. According to Sonja

Lyubomirsky, a professor of happiness (what a great job!), gratitude is a meta-strategy because it promotes happiness in so many ways:

↔ Gratitude helps you really appreciate lovely moments, but it also brightens up humdrum routines.
↔ Gratitude motivates and empowers action in yourself and in others.
↔ Gratitude energizes and stimulates positive emotions.
↔ Gratitude increases your coping skills in difficult situations.
↔ Grateful people do not ignore life's difficulties, but always highlight the positive aspects.
↔ Gratitude stimulates prosocial behaviour, like giving and showing compassion.
↔ Gratitude is the perfect antidote to social comparison and the associated destructive emotions, such as jealousy.[134]
↔ Finally, gratitude reduces the chances of depression, loneliness or anxiety.[135]

What makes you grateful in life? Look at your hand and for each finger think of something minor or major that gives you a feeling of gratitude. 'A handful of gratitude' can be performed at any time of day, for example while daydreaming on the train or waiting in a queue.

SIT-UP

'Boredom is simply a lack of attention.'

FRITZ PERLS

MINDSET

Did you find something you were grateful for? Or did you mainly think of things that you would like but do not have? This would mean that your mindset is one of scarcity. The good news is that you

THE 12 WEEK MIND WORKOUT

can train yourself to switch to the mindset of abundance, where you assume that there is enough for everybody and you are satisfied with what you have.

In her book *Attitudes of Gratitude*, Mary Jane Ryan describes the abundance mindset as follows: 'It lights up what is already there. You don't necessarily have anything more or different, but suddenly you can actually see what is. And because you can see, you no longer take it for granted.'[136] And now the torch of attention is back, shining in your face. If you practise enough attention in your life and can switch between the different forms of attention, you can step out of your autopilot and count your blessings, even at moments that you find boring or challenging.

SIT-UP

If you find yourself complaining or grumbling, then add 'and' to your thought, followed by something you are grateful for. For example: 'What a pity it's raining now...*and* aren't we lucky that we can shelter in the car?' Or 'My presentation wasn't a great success...*and* I am happy that I was not afraid to deliver it.' Look for the gain. If you find that you are doing well, focus on that feeling. It can be fun to do this sit-up with somebody else, for example with a friend who is a bit of a moaner or an Eeyore.

RELATIONAL GRATITUDE

It is important that you express your gratitude when you feel it. This will increase your own sense of gratitude, but it will also strengthen your relationships.[137] Both you and the recipient of the thank will experience positive feelings, such as emotion, hope, pride and – once again – gratitude.

Whom are you grateful for? Think small – he took you out to the cinema, she helped you move – but also think deep – because she supported you during a great loss or because he always believed in you. Try to verbalize why you are grateful to that person, what you like about them and what that means to you. Take your phone and send a WhatsApp message (or a text or an email) expressing your thanks. Without waiting for the reply, consider what this exercise means to you. Focus on that feeling in your head, heart or body. And if you receive a reply, once again focus on the emotion it evokes in you.

SIT-UP

Also thank someone outside your immediate circle, think of people you have a neutral relationship with, people in the background, or people you just take for granted. Thank the helpdesk operator, the canteen assistant, the roadworker... Shine the spotlight on the lighting technician instead of the actor. Make the thank you specific, verbalize what you like about the person, what their actions or personality have meant to you, or why you were touched by them.

Look around you (today) and identify people who receive little recognition or gratitude. Get in touch and tell them specifically what you appreciate about them.

SIT-UP

GRATITUDE 2.0

Gratitude training for more advanced students consists of expressing gratitude in situations when you don't feel particularly grateful. In fact, you might even be 'ungrateful'. Think of the flickering fluorescent light in your office, a bout of poor health, your unhygienic colleague, or a leaky gutter. It can be helpful to think of other aspects that are positive (the colleague with poor hygiene is also extremely helpful) or the other side of the coin (you could have no roof or light

THE 12 WEEK MIND WORKOUT

over your head at all). All this will work on one condition: you must believe in this exercise.

SIT-UP

Be unusually grateful for usual and unusual things today: from your big toe to your satchel, for the unexpectedly high bill from the physiotherapist, for the heavy rain shower you got caught in...

'What doesn't kill you makes you stronger' is an awful cliché, but it's (often) true. People who have been through a lot, such as illness and loss, often feel great joie de vivre and enjoy small things.[138] Note: this doesn't apply to people who cling to their victimhood or others who wallow in sadness or anger; they will learn little or nothing from unpleasant events. Only those who realize the value of their suffering (as you learned in Part 2 about compassion) and feel gratitude will learn from their painful past.

SIT-UP

Take a pen and paper and reflect on something in the past you really struggled with, but the cloud eventually had a silver lining. How did the silver lining come about? Did you sit back and wait for the matter to pass? Or did you address it immediately? What have you learned from it? Now reflect on a major challenge, a struggle or dilemma that is bugging you now. What is the hidden value behind this suffering? Which life lessons can you learn? Write down your answers.

It's not easy to feel and express gratitude towards the difficult people around you. Irritation and annoyance blinker you to the better sides of those individuals. You cannot see (clearly) what they have meant (or still mean) to you, others or the world – for example, the domineering manager whose behaviour has taught you to stand up for yourself.

> Think of an individual you find annoying or irritating, somebody who makes you feel uncomfortable or simply miserable. Now think of any aspects or characteristics you appreciate in them and for which you are grateful. There is no need to express your gratitude to them but do try to really *feel* grateful.

SIT-UP

A large-scale study into practising gratitude showed that committed and intrinsically motivated participants experienced a stronger positive outcome from their expressions of gratitude.[139] Therefore, it is not happiness that makes you grateful. It is gratitude that makes you happy. All that is needed is your willingness to train gratefulness.

OPTIMISM

Optimism is the third tool on the road to happiness. It yields so many benefits that it's a bit boring me enumerating them here again, but if you have forgotten, here are some: better health, improved performance and more wellbeing. And consider this: a study of nearly 1,000 elderly people who were observed over a period of nine years showed that an optimistic disposition was the best medicine for a longer lifespan.[140]

There's a pessimist and an optimist hidden in every person, and they become stronger the more you nurture them. For example, lawyers reinforce the pessimist in them, because their attention is generally focused on negativity. Consequently, the profession is 3.6 times more susceptible to depression than the average.[141] You may also unconsciously strengthen your pessimist side: just think of all the shocking negative news reports you are subjected to in our digital era. Just check, who do you feed most, the optimist or the pessimist in you?

<table>
<tr>
<td>SIT-UP</td>
<td>What if you did not give yourself breaking news, but a news-break instead: don't watch the news for a day or – preferably – for a week and don't read (online) newspapers. Instead, pay special attention to things around you that make you feel optimistic, such as an acquaintance who has recovered from an illness, the clever guide dog on the bus, and the girl on the pavement juggling and collecting for charity.</td>
</tr>
</table>

OPTIMISM ABOUT THE IMMEDIATE FUTURE

Your outlook on the future appears to have a strong impact on your current life satisfaction. Having a rosy view of the future has a positive effect that is almost three times greater than a happy marriage.[142] I am not suggesting that we should always have positive thoughts or that we should be dreaming of a wonderful land of milk and honey, flowery dresses and fluffy bunnies. Indeed, a touch of friction and particularly a sense of reality are indispensable. A study of students from poorer socioeconomic backgrounds in New York by Gabrielle Oettingen, a social psychologist, showed that those who were encouraged to pursue the American Dream performed worse than those with a more realistic vision of the future. So should we all be downbeat about our future? Certainly not – what's most effective is 'mental contrasting': you imagine a positive outcome, but still consider obstacles you might meet on the way. The students who applied this principle were more likely to achieve their set goals.[143]

STEP 1: Which achievements and characteristics are important to you and what future you would like to realize? First, distinguish between the three domains of personal, relational and professional and choose one to start with in this sit-up.

STEP 2: Write down the vision of the future you desire. Take your time, and remember, it's not going to be published, your grammar doesn't matter.

STEP 3: Visualize that future and then focus on potential positive feelings that arise. Experience them.

STEP 4: Imagine potential obstacles (too little time, an unwilling colleague, an unavailable product) and the way in which you can deal with these constructively. 'What makes you happiest?' is a question you may consider when dealing with these obstacles.

SIT-UP

This sit-up will strengthen your short-term optimism[144] (the experts are still investigating whether it also has a long-term effect). The exercise is most effective if you practise it several days in a row. Continue to describe different visions of the future (for different domains) to keep the impact fresh. If you want to continue using the same future scenario, then skip Step 2 (the writing down bit) after your first attempt.

✖ WATCH OUT!

One of the traps when trying to visualize a rosy future is that you feel a discrepancy between your current state and your future state. Consequently, your discontent increases. It's best to dream of your future from within an acceptance of the current situation – like a satisfied farmer who tills his or her land hoping for a good harvest.

OPTIMISM ABOUT YESTERDAY

Optimism about the future depends on your explanation of good and bad events in the past: do you see them as temporary or permanent,

global or specific, and do you explain them by internalizing or exter-
nalizing them?

Imagine you were leading a team building session and you accidentally overheard a conversation about you in the toilets. 'Wasn't
that boring! I wish I had recorded it – that voice works better than
sleeping tablets!' A person who is a pessimist at heart would respond
to this as a permanent state ('I never do things right; my presentations are hopeless'), globally ('I'm not particularly good at anything')
and internally ('They're right: I am boring'). An optimist's reasoning
is quite the opposite (temporary, specific and external): 'It was not
my best performance, but I know I can do it. Colleague X obviously
had a bad day, so I will take his opinion with a pinch of salt.' If it had
been a story full of praise, then the pessimist would have dismissed it as temporary, specific and external, while the optimist would
say: 'I do indeed deliver good presentations, and of course I'm very
capable. Thanks to my excellent preparations and talent for bringing
people together, I got this session sorted.'

In short, pessimists see themselves as the guilty person in negative
events,[145] and if the latter are positive, they say: 'It was sheer luck' (the
circumstances were responsible, not the pessimist). In addition, they
believe that negative consequences will always prevail and that the
problem is entrenched in their (unchangeable) personality. Optimists
attribute success to themselves and failure to others (or fate). They see
themselves as the trigger of good events, believing that their qualities
are permanent and stable, blaming bad events on circumstances or
something unexpected. You can train to be more optimistic.

SIT-UP

Write down a pleasant event that happened recently and practise
the optimistic perspective: permanent, global and internal. For
example: 'I received such a nice card. This is because I am nice
(internal), many people think so (global), I'm sure it will always
be that way (permanent).' Now try a negative event from an
external, specific and temporary perspective. Don't exaggerate:
try to connect with what you really believe.

The beauty of optimistic explanations is that you can step back from 'results achieved in the past'. Imagine you had an unpleasant, insecure childhood, then this kind of perception shows that you are no longer the little boy or girl from the past and that you can shed the adopted feelings of victimization.

✖ **WATCH OUT!**
The danger of this technique is that if you go too far, you will never take responsibility for your actions. You will always blame your failures on others or coincidences, and you pat yourself on the back after each success, even if it was your sibling/colleague/employee who deserves the praise. You need to find a balance between 'lying to yourself' and harsh reality: this is flexible optimism. Be realistic about risks and your own mistakes, while still believing that you can create a better world. For example, a flexible optimist paralysed in the legs after an accident, knowing that he or she will never walk again, sees new opportunities, and faces the future with confidence. Attention training clears the mind and helps you understand the appropriateness or inappropriateness of optimism.

SAVING AS

Often you exaggerate how happy you felt at special moments – you think back to your holiday in France and you conveniently forget the diarrhoea, the delay and argument on the Paris Boulevard Périphérique – and underestimate feelings of happiness on normal days such as last Tuesday morning in the office at the coffee machine. Another tendency of the brain is the so-called beginning–peak– end rule. The first dive in the pool on holiday, your goal during the otherwise boring football match and the last time you had sex with your ex: your brain hangs on to the beginning and even more strongly to the end and (emotional) peak moments of an event. This is how you cultivate distorted memories, and these may unconsciously cause wrong decisions in the future.

Your awareness of this and being more realistic about your experiences will help you create a better foundation for future decisions.

You could also benefit from this knowledge by cultivating additional positive memories.

Would you like to have good memories of your city trip to Berlin? Make sure that the trip doesn't become unadventurous and plan a 'peak' moment, such as a meal in a Michelin-starred restaurant or bungee jumping (or whatever suits). And save the best for last. Not only will you have a more positive memory of the trip, but you'll also be able to recall the positive feeling; your brain is like a woolly jumper permeated with positive memories.

SIT-UP

Give yourself one peak moment today and end the day on a happy note.

CONSOLIDATION

Your brain likes to wear a raincoat against positive emotions: joy or enthusiasm just roll off like raindrops; a good feeling is lost very quickly. Negative emotions are more like a woolly jumper: irritation, anger and sadness linger in the knit. Fortunately, your brain is flexible (see Introduction) and can be programmed. Emotions to which you pay attention will grow and strengthen.

Every day, happy moments (catching a train by the skin of your teeth, a card from a loved one, the sun popping through the clouds) are stored in the short-term memory. But if you don't pay any attention to the experience, it will be erased. You want to achieve a lasting change in your internal hard drive, so, if you spend enough time (at least eight seconds) focusing your attention on the good experience, the information will loaded onto your long-term memory and your brain is programmed positively.[146] The more often you do this, the easier it will be, and the more receptive your brain is to positivity. And the bonus is that the brain likes to wear the raincoat against negative emotions more often.

HEAL

The psychologist Rick Hanson has developed a technique that helps you recognize good experiences – even during the leftovers meal on a Monday evening – and to absorb them and store them by programming your brain differently.

His HEAL method consists of four steps:

HAVING A POSITIVE EXPERIENCE

You have a positive experience like a welcome guest. The experience arrives spontaneously (the sun on your skin or an unexpected conversation) or is evoked by your imagination or by a conscious action, for example by complimenting somebody or tidying up your house. Don't focus on the clean kitchen, but on the experience. How does it affect you, how (good) are you feeling now?

ENRICHING THE POSITIVE EXPERIENCE

Now enrich that positive experience – offer a chair to your welcome guest and something to eat. Be fully open to the positive feeling and consciously hold on to it for 10–15 seconds longer than 'usual'. Try to savour it. Focus on all your senses; it intensifies the experience.

Explore new insights during this step, especially those that make the experience personally relevant to you. It will make the experience last. For example, explore how reading a novel, watching a cycling race, or having a lively conversation with a refuse collector enriches your life and makes a difference. A different angle or the fresh perspective will only take root if you reflect on it in a relaxed way and enrich the experience.

ABSORBING THE POSITIVE EXPERIENCE

Now make a conscious decision to let the experience embed itself in your mind. The welcome guest can spend the night; you store the experience in your brain. Your imagination can help you now: try to imagine how the experience can enter your heart or be saved by pressing Ctrl-S. You may feel the positive experience flowing through your body or imagine your brain putting on its woolly sweater

THE 12 WEEK MIND WORKOUT

specially for the occasion. Think of an image that will help you, that works for you. The more strongly you can experience these emotions in your body, the more deeply they will be embedded in your brain. Hold on to this step for 15–20 seconds.

LINKING POSITIVE AND NEGATIVE EXPERIENCES
Sometimes negative experiences, ranging from a painful break up to a serious accident, pop up uninvited and without function. Letting go of them can be difficult. But did you know that you can override a negative memory with a (current or recent) positive experience? *Neurons that wire together, fire together.* You could even invite that unpleasant guest who put his feet on your table, because their behaviour will have less effect on you as the welcome guest is there, too.

This step (Step L) makes you link the positive experience to a negative experience from the past. This is how you recognize fear and helplessness, anger or sadness, but no longer allow yourself to be carried away by them. You offer the welcome guest a king-size bed and you offer a stretcher to the unpleasant guest. It might be wise to check (beforehand) in the core needs schedule, near the start of this chapter, which positive counterpart can modify your negative feelings. For example, you could link gratitude to disappointment, relaxation to insecurity and appreciation to jealousy.

Shine a light on the positive experience and leave any negative ones in shadow. Hold onto this step for at least 15 seconds and end with a full focus on the positive experience. If the negative experience re-emerges in the (near) future, you will find it easier to activate the positive experience sooner and more easily. It is like playing cheerful music to accompany a painful scene. You can make sure that the positive feeling is not overshadowed by the negative feeling by rethinking the positive – or at least neutral – experience repeatedly for another 15 seconds, within the first hour after Step L.

In this step, start with unpleasant experiences that are easy to deal with, such as a parking fine or a broken phone. If Step L is too difficult for you, don't worry; just leave it for now. HEA is quite an achievement; and is in itself healing. Don't introduce traumatic even-ts in Step L, as these would require professional coaching.

Try to receive the positive feelings in a relaxed and grateful mood, and notice, without judgement, when they fade away and the corners of your mouth drop again. This will lengthen and intensify your positive experience. Don't try to overanalyse things. If you spend more time thinking and less time on experiences in the HEAL phases, simply take note without judgement and refocus your attention on your body and the positive sensations.

When practising HEAL you may find that negative moods often arise (see Step L) – in other words the unpleasant, annoying guests. You may also find that you have difficulty allowing yourself to have positive emotions. Once again, pay compassionate attention to whatever is there, or let go of the difficult experience, allowing your attention to return to the pleasant experience.

Practising HEAL strengthens the attention muscle. If your monkey mind starts playing havoc with you again, you should patiently focus attention on your body or on the point of focus at that moment. The more often you practise HEAL, the more it will appeal to you and the easier it will be.

TRAINING

Whether you are in the gym, on a walk, in the kitchen, how much time do you spend exercising your body? Happiness requires just as much input. And it will really pay off. This week you will practise noticing and evoking more positive emotions. You will also learn how to stay connected longer.

Optimistic thinking and the value of gratitude are not new to you. Practising them, however, might be new. So, don't let doubt or scepticism prevent you from going through the open door.

▮▯▯ LIGHT

This week choose one of the following three exercises every day to prevent injury.

EXERCISE 1: REPEAT FINE MOMENTS

Choose a quiet moment, sit down and make yourself comfortable and spend a couple of minutes browsing the photo album in your mind. Relive happy moments in your life; use all your senses. Try not to analyse but focus on the experience and cherish emerging positive emotions.

EXERCISE 2: GRATITUDE TRAINING

Take one of the gratitude exercises in the sit-ups and practise it several times a day. You could try alternating different exercises to keep things fresh. This sit-up has to be fun.

▶ TRAINER'S TIP

Chocolate spread on your sandwiches every day would become rather boring. This also applies to gratitude (training): keep it fresh by alternating exercises and don't overdo it. A compliment or expressions of gratitude will lose their value if they are said too often, from the point of view of the recipient as well as the giver. So be alert: if gratitude (training) becomes a routine activity, you need to change its frequency or format. Replace the gratitude text sit-up with the silver lining sit-up, or – preferably – create your own gratitude exercise.

EXERCISE 3: OPTIMISM

Write down three positive events every day and analyse them from an optimist's point of view: internal, global and permanent. Also write down one negative event and review it externally, specifically and temporarily.

None of these exercises take much time, but all bring about substantial and lasting change. In short: little effort, great benefit.

ıl MEDIUM

EXTENSION TO LIGHT

Start a happiness album. Fill a booklet with precious photographs, mementos, poems, funny cards, pictures and love letters: all the things that made you feel good in the past. Leaf through the book several times in the coming week and relive those moments of happiness. If you get a bit blasé about it, you may be doing this too often. In that case, keep the album closed for a few days.

ıll INTENSE

EXTENSION TO LIGHT + MEDIUM

EXERCISE 1

Do you feel you need some intensive training this week? Then besides the daily light training, perform a silent gratitude meditation. Set a timer for ten to fifteen minutes and simply allow yourself to get in touch with the things you are grateful for.

EXERCISE 2: THANK YOU LETTER

Think of somebody you never thanked properly. Don't choose your loved one or somebody you have a crush on or whom you feel you still 'owe' a thank you, but someone for whom you feel sheer gratitude. Write them a thank you letter on a sheet of A4 (handwriting the letter will be more effective). Take your time to express clearly why you are so grateful, and what you appreciate about them. Write it over several days, as this will enrich the message. Then invite the other person to come round or drop by and read out the letter. Don't give the reason beforehand; just say you would like to meet up. Read your thank you letter slowly and with empathy, in a face-to-face situation. Give time and space for the message to land and wait for a response. Then hand over your letter, in a pretty envelope or maybe even framed – whatever suits you. This can one of the most intense examples of positive psychology in action, one in which you are open and vulnerable. But the positive impact makes it all worthwhile!

COOL DOWN

Some people have goose pimples when they watch a tennis rally, while others are indifferent, though they become quite emotional when listening to a piano recital. People differ in their responses to the exercises in happiness skills, and the intensity of the effects varies from person to person. Maybe not every happiness strategy suits you (now), or works for you, or meets your needs. It's good to check which exercise worked for you, which was most helpful or struck you as being the most powerful. Maybe you were not greatly affected during the entire week. In that case, it's particularly important that you read on to see whether any of the following weeks will suit you better.

Ask yourself if you have achieved any of the following in Week 9:

- ↔ Do you recognize positive emotions and can you evoke those you need?
- ↔ Have you managed to experience gratitude in everyday situations? And how about in difficult situations?
- ↔ Can you now absorb and retain the good and the positive for longer periods?
- ↔ Has it become easier to explain events from the past wearing your optimistic cap?
- ↔ Can you be (more) optimistic in the way you view the future?

IN CONCLUSION

This chapter shows that many of our positive emotions are derived from being satisfied with what we have, and that we are fortunate that we can experience what 'enough' is.

'The little things? The little moments? They aren't little.'

JON KABAT-ZINN

WEEK

10

BEING HAPPY WITH
OTHER PEOPLE

'Those who are not looking for happiness are
the most likely to find it, because those who are
searching forget that the surest way to be happy
is to seek happiness for others.'

MARTIN LUTHER KING

After initially exercising your own positive emotions, this week
you will focus on one of the main sources of happiness: relationships. Christopher Peterson, one of the founders of positive
psychology, summarized his theory of happiness in two words:
other people. To seven billion people you are the other person.
This week you will start working with the good-relationship recipe, in which trust, kindness and connective communication are
the core components.

WARM-UP

Aristotle said: 'No happiness without friendship.' This classic sta-
tement resonates with large amounts of research: having a strong,
well-functioning circle of friends and acquaintances is what makes
the difference between people who are averagely happy and the
happiest 10 per cent of people. If you feel connected to others, your
chances of feeling happy are four times greater.[147] The reverse is also
true: happy people have better relationships than their unhappy
counterparts.[148]

There are many kinds of relationship therapy to help you if there
are problems within your family or between you and your partner.
However, people do not often engage in relationship training to celebrate their relationship or to take it to an (even) higher level, whereas
you will only have a full sense of happiness when you enrich your
relationships – both in love and in friendship. Think back to the
positivity ratio in Week 9.

But how can you develop peaks in relationships that are trundling along OK? Attentiveness, genuine interest and investing in other people underpin any relationship. The motives of happy people go beyond this, transcending the ego. They give without expecting anything in return (the brain circuit of altruism). In the good-relationship recipe, happy people incorporate three (interrelated) main ingredients: trust, kindness and connective communication.[149]

How often do you use the words 'me', 'my' and 'I'? Overuse of these brings risks. A study at the University of California found that people who talk a lot about themselves are more at risk of fatal heart attacks.[150] Frequent use of the word 'I' appeared to be an even stronger predictor of heart failure than smoking or high blood pressure. The follow-up study showed that people who often speak in the first person are more likely to feel depressed than those who use 'us' and 'we'.[151]

EYE-OPENER

TRUST

Imagine you are a business manager and are interviewing an applicant. He passes you his CV: a blank sheet of A4. The man says he has just been released from prison, after serving 15 years for murder. He pulls up his T-shirt and shows his gang tattoos. At the end of the interview, you congratulate him on his new job. Can you imagine this happening? You don't have to: such managers really do exist. They work at Greyston Bakery, in Riverdale, New York. The business is known for its open contracting policy. It's not interested in an applicant's background, but trust in his or her abilities. Greyston Bakery has been running successfully for years – and their employees are unusually happy.

DISTRUST IS HUMAN

Trust keeps relationships together, but mistrust, its counterpart, is embedded in us. First, this is because it is how our brain is tuned: it's better to be safe than sorry. We have an elephant's memory when it comes to deceit and unpleasant surprises, but it's a sieve when it comes to times when trusting somebody was the right thing. Mistrust is drummed into us. As a child you were probably told a hundred times, 'Don't speak to strangers!' It's not a recipe for happiness, and often it's wrong-headed (at least for us as adults). Research shows that talking to strangers makes people happy.[152]

The positivity ratio of trust is big: you need five good experiences to forget one bad one. After that one bad experience when you bought a damaged drill on eBay, it will take a long time before you dare buy a second-hand lawnmower.[153]

Media coverage also fuels our mistrust: *if it bleeds, it leads*. We prefer to see blood to birds (unless they come with the bees) due to our omnipresent threat system. The media colours our perception and tunes our brain to danger, baddies and mistrust. In the USA, a 12-year-old will on average have already witnessed in one way or another 12,000 murders – in the newspapers, on TV but mainly on YouTube or online.[154] How many murders have you witnessed in real life? How many murder victims have you known personally?

And of course, there's the combination of self-fulfilling prophecy and contagiousness that plays a part in enhancing our distrust. The more suspicious you are of your environment, the harder it is not to be affected. And the more mistrust around you, the less safe your environment eventually becomes. In effect, our consideration should not in the first place be whether your neighbour is (un)trustworthy, but you should ask yourself: do you trust him or her or not?

The tendency to mistrust others is usually not consistent with reality. Research shows that people are much more reliable than we think.[155] Purity and goodness are underestimated; maliciousness and evil are overestimated. We tend to forget innumerable interactions when people help, comfort and support each other; we remember the time our phone was stolen or the customer who walked out without paying, whereas the number of altruistic acts is many times greater than selfish and/or wicked actions. If there had been more conflict than cooperation, humanity would have become extinct long ago. Instead, humans have been able to successfully take control of the animal kingdom and the world of technology because of our exceptional ability to cooperate. Have you ever seen a lizard (the greatest egoist in the animal kingdom) cruising along in an electric car?

> Is trust or mistrust stronger in your life? (You can break this up into the main areas of work, personal life and social life.) Do you recognize your reflex to mistrust or trust in your reactions to minor or unexpected events, such as a knock at the door (an election canvasser or a friend?) or your impulse whether or not to leave your belongings unattended in a café when going to the toilet?

SIT-UP

EFFECTIVE TRUST

How do you gain the trust of others and how do you ensure you won't get cheated? The answer is both simple and difficult: trust. It's like the smallholder who uses an honesty box to sell eggs: he or she trusts that we will leave enough money in the box. Various studies have shown that the smallholder is right: people who are trusted usually live up to that trust.[156] The smallholder's proactive trust creates a win-win situation. The smallholder is confident he or she can put all his eggs in one basket. And if the smallholder loses out to that one idiot who stole the eggs, he or she is more than compensated because he does not waste valuable time physically selling the produce – and of course by the customers in whom he trusts.

Karma Kitchen (which operates in various cities and under various guises around the world) is an example of a wonderful initiative that inspires trust. There are no prices on the menu. When they give you the bill, it always states £0.00 and it says: 'Your meal was a gift from somebody before you. To keep this chain of gifts going, we invite you to pay for the meal of the person that follows you.'

Although they are a significant minority, there will always be people who embrace you to steal your necklace. You want to arm yourself against those thieves, but at the same time you love receiving hugs. How do you ensure that you have lots of reliable relationships while minimizing the risk of being cheated? You must learn to trust effectively if you want to be like the smallholder. Try to strike a happy medium between trust and mistrust. Effective trust consists of five elements[157] that help you transform the tendency to mistrust into proactive trust, all while keeping an eye out for the odd bad apple.

1. AWARENESS

The first step to effective trust is knowing how you score on the trust scale (test yourself at <happysmarts.com/scale/trust-scale>). Are you often cheated because of your gullibility, or do you tend to mistrust others as a matter of course? In either case, you can move along the scale towards a more balanced position.

Most people overestimate the times they are cheated; so be fair and also consider the moments when trust was (or would have been) justified.

2. BE ALERT TO TRUST AND DISTRUST

Remind yourself explicitly that people can be trusted. The single rotten apple in the basket is the exception. Notice your suspicion with kindness without condemning yourself for having it. Avoid watching violent television programmes and – if you can – minimize fixating on the news and learn to take breaks from it. As a counterbalance, take note of your own capacity to trust and take a proactive approach to bestowing it on others. Give your trust to the honest person who found your phone and handed it back to you, and to your partner who kept their promise to massage your feet. Believe your daughter when she says she will tidy her room; trust the painter and decorator who's promised to meet the deadline.

3. FRAME YOUR MIND IN TRUST

Be inspired by objects, images and people that inspire your trust. From inspirational quotes, books and documentaries to the people in your community, soak up anything that has human goodness at the core. Repeatedly think of the benefits of trust. The great bonus of your proactive trust is that it will be easier for others to trust you, and therefore they are more trustworthy.

4. POSITIVE EMOTIONS

Notice and/or evoke positive emotions associated with reliable interactions. Use the HEAL method to reflect on and embed them (see Week 9). In this way, you can turn trust into a lasting trait rather than a fleeting emotion.

5. MINIMIZING PAIN

Don't let that one rotten apple spoil the entire fruit bowl. Your mistrust you felt when you fished a rotten apple out of the bowl should not be allowed to outweigh the feeling of happiness you gained through your heartfelt belief in the good. Just take the pain of that one rotten apple on board. Compassion training should have given you more resilience to deal with pain and potential self-condemnation. You are prepared to take more risks because you're not afraid of the inevitable 'blisters'. And if you do get cheated, don't condemn yourself for being gullible, but be proud that you were open to the good in others. Do call people to account for their behaviour and give them a second chance to prove their reliability.

If they don't respond (well), take a healthy distance. You don't need to forget their actions, but it's wise to forgive the people who have committed them (see Part 2 on compassion). Where bitterness leads to mistrust, forgiveness is the key to proactive trust.

KINDNESS

The plane shudders and shakes; the woman in 6C has been in her cramped seat for hours. She looks out of the plane window and her eyes show fear: the wings are bouncing up and down in the strong wind and heavy rain. A fellow passenger observes the restless woman. He gets up and moves to the empty seat next to her. The man points outside with confidence and reassures the woman: 'Don't worry. I'm a flight engineer and a shaking wing is quite normal on this type of aircraft.' The woman's shoulders drop, and a faint smile appears on her face. In reality, the man is a tax adviser without any practical skills; satisfied with a job well done he returns to his seat. His white lie has done the trick.[158]

Not only confidence, but kindness is indispensable for satisfactory social relationships. Your willingness to help someone – a stranger or a loved one – makes you happy. Kindness is close to compassion. The main difference is that, while compassion focuses on alleviating suffering, kindness also aims to increase happiness. Like compassion, you can train yourself to express sincere kindness – the idea 'that my niece, a little devil from birth, will never change' just isn't true.

Like compassion, the whole concept of kindness also faces scepticism. There are loads of nice people around, sure, but will they help you when your house is on fire? Maybe you (unconsciously) associate leadership with the raging Trumps in this world, rather than the empathic Obamas. However, the power paradox[159] shows that the most effective leaders are kind and concerned with serving others,[160] and that kindness is the decisive factor that distinguishes the best-performing managers from the worst-performing managers. Being loved and kind cannot be separated from performance and efficiency. Companies that are generous and caring towards their employees prove to be more successful.[161]

The Brazilian company Simco's participatory leadership is a prime example. Every employee, from manager to cleaner, decides on their own work hours and salary. You might be thinking that this is cloud cuckoo land – the company will go bankrupt in no time. On the contrary, the company has flourished for years. Simco's approach is a textbook example of participatory leadership and the power of kindness.

Even in highly competitive markets, it's not so much the law of the strongest as the law of the kindest. In other words, the kindest is the strongest. For example, research at the Kellogg School of Management shows that kind and cooperative negotiators conduct the best business deals.[162]

HELPFUL SELF-IMAGE

Self-compassion, we've seen, is the foundation of being kind to others. If you are at ease with yourself, you will also be able to care about and be kind to others. Part of this is your self-image, which should not hinder but help you. Of course, you have both a dark and an altruistic side, but a helpful self-image requires a focus on the latter. Acknowledge and cultivate your own goodness. It helps you like yourself more, and therefore be kinder to others.

THE SECRET OF KINDNESS

The motivation behind your kindness makes all the difference. Are you selfless when you give a helping hand or pat someone on the back? Or are you doing it for your own benefit, expect something in return? If you act kindly only to ease your own discomfort or because you would secretly like something in return, then you are highlighting your own self-interest at the expense of the other. If you pay a compliment to receive one in return, your 'kind' act will fall flat.

'You don't get anything for nothing' is a bartering principle used by the Ik-people of north-east Uganda. Imagine that a neighbour, acquaintance or relative comes to dig over the garden or build a wall without being asked, not out of kindness, but to make you indebted to them. It means that the 'giver' can then ask the debtor for redemption of time and effort when it suits the 'giver'. The 'kindness' is only shown in anticipation of a reward.

The key to kindness consists of doing something for someone without expecting anything in return. Regardless of your own expectations, kindness is apparently reduced if the other person offers *you* a reward. For example, the frequency of altruistic acts decreases if we are informed about the (material) rewards in advance.[163] In countries where blood donors receive a reward, the overall donation is less.[164] Heroes who rescue people from a burning building or a from a car sinking into a river rarely do so in anticipation of recognition and appreciation. The usual explanation is: 'I was just doing what I felt I had to do.' If it probably leaves them with a good feeling, that's a nice bonus. What I said about compassion in Part 2 also applies to kindness: it's infectious.

> *'It is one of the beautiful compensations of life that no man can sincerely try to help another without helping himself.'*

RALPH WALDO EMERSON

SIT-UP	Today, show some kindness to somebody without them noticing – preferably to an acquaintance or a stranger, rather than a friend or relative! Pick up a fallen bicycle, clear leaves in someone's garden, compliment your colleague anonymously on paper, put some money in the letterbox of your less well-off neighbours, or donate anonymously to a charity. Cherish the pleasant emotions that arise, though don't be concerned if no such feelings arise.

KINDNESS IN PRACTICE: GIVING

An interesting study shows how five volunteers with multiple sclerosis were selected to do voluntary work: to be buddies for other MS patients. Three years later, the volunteers were happier about their lives and had a greater sense of control than the other MS patients. Obviously, the patients benefited from the support, but the volunteers benefited seven times more from giving support than their patients did from receiving it.[165] Giving makes us happier than taking, from a material (clothes, toys and food) as well as an immaterial (love, time and interests) perspective.

This is mainly because you are not constantly worrying about yourself. It improves your self-image, reinforces optimism and makes others more generous to you (because of the infectious effect). It makes you thankful because you realize how much you have to give. Most importantly, each time you give something away, you let go of that little bit you frantically call 'mine'. You free yourself from the prison called greed.

GIVING CAN BE LEARNED

What happens to you when you consider giving something away? Think of something precious, such as your last piece of cake, your favourite sunglasses, or a half day off while you are extremely busy. The anxious greedy little grabber whispers in your ear:

'Don't give it away, because you won't have enough for yourself!'

Training in giving means using DANC(E) (see Week 3) to help you become familiar with your greed. You will notice a tendency to put yellow sticky notes everywhere with 'me' on them when your attention is open and non-judgemental. Rather than being taken hostage by that forceful greedy grabber, you use your magic quarter-second and you step out of the automatic 'must have', 'buy' and 'grab' pattern. You don't have to wait for the moment that you feel fine, happy or calm. It works the other way: giving, or the trigger to do so, will bring calmness and happiness.

> *'Happiness depends on what you can give,*
> *not on what we can get.'*

ARISTOTLE

Giving doesn't mean you shouldn't be greedy, but it's about embracing greed and kindly saying no instead of pushing it away. It's important that it doesn't come from a sense of duty or 'because it's the right thing to do', but because it's a desire deep inside you.

SIT-UP

Today, give something away, such as time, money or an object. It should be something you find difficult to part with. Even though the very thought of letting it go might make you feel anxious, focus on the part of you that really wants to give it away. Register those feelings beforehand as well as your thoughts of fear, greed and doubt, without judgement. Afterwards, note which thoughts and feelings arise after giving it away. Then cherish any emerging positive emotions.

�֎ **WATCH OUT!**

A man opens his newspaper and sees all the misery in the world – war, natural disasters, people dying of famine. He decides to give all his money away for those who need it. After his donation, he still thinks it's not enough. He donates all his belongings, including his house. Now he's homeless and lives on the streets. Then one day he sees a newspaper with the headline 'SHORTAGE OF DONORS'. He goes to the hospital and donates one of his kidneys. After the operation, the man still thinks his donation is inadequate and he asks the surgeon to take his other kidney, his liver, heart and lungs, in fact, all his organs. The surgeon refuses: 'I can't do that: it equates to murder.' When the man leaves the hospital, he gives the last thing he can give: his life. A completed donor declaration form is found beside him.[166]

Givers are more likely to experience happiness and success, but they are also more prone to failure and unhappiness. This seeming contradiction is because there are two kinds of givers: the reckless giver, who gives more than they can afford materially, mentally and physically, and the clever giver, who judges wisely when, how frequently, and to whom they can afford to give. Adam Grant, a professor of psychology, an expert on giving and author of the bestseller *Give and Take*, concludes that clever giving is not only healthier for us than reckless giving, but it is also more beneficial to others.

Clever givers are clued up about two aspects of giving:

They are efficiently effective. Clever givers don't serve 20 bowls each with a different kind of soup, but make one extra-large pan to serve everyone at once. They optimize their support to avoid being overworked or ending up with empathy fatigue.

They are emotionally balanced. Clever givers cherish arising positive emotions such as pride and gratitude (for example with HEAL). It gives them an energy boost and the motivation to continue giving. Clever givers will then proactively discern the outcome of their good deeds, such as the other person's smile, which will give them more positive emotions. Actively checking the outcome is quite different from giving for the sake of self-interest (selfish giving), which is counterproductive. If you have helped a good friend choose new clothes or decide on a house makeover, then you should visit them the following day – not because you are proud of your achievement, but because you're pleased for her. It's a bonus if you can be part of her happiness.[167]

CONNECTIVE COMMUNICATION

Celebrating a wedding anniversary is quite common, but how often have you and a friend raised a glass to your friendship, or given a party for many years of friendship? The five following techniques for connective communication do not only focus on connecting with a potential life partner, but also – and particularly – on connecting with friends and acquaintances.

1. LOOK AT EACH OTHER

We humans are good at discussing, arguing and generally talking bullshit, but how often do we just look at another person. Place your hand over your mouth or just shut it, and look around; look at others in silence. An older man did this, observing his wife in silence for five minutes. He was so moved that he said to her: 'When I look at you like this, I realize how much you mean to me.' It was the first time in 55 years of marriage that he had something like this out loud.[168]

Research shows that this man isn't exceptional. When a couple look at each other in silence for five minutes, there will be more mutual sympathy and a feeling of connection. This is 'brain Bluetooth': during eye contact the brains of both individuals synchronize; it stimulates the feeling of connection.[169] Incidentally, this also happens when two strangers do this (go on, I dare you!). In an experiment, the psychologist Arthur Aron asked two people to look at each other in silence for four minutes after they had asked each other 36 personal questions. The pair fell in love with each other. Many couples followed suit, after going through the same procedure, though not in the laboratory setting.[170]

> **SIT-UP**
>
> For this exercise, you need to ask your partner, friend or relative to work with you. Sit down facing each other. Set a timer for five minutes (and put your phone out of sight). What do you notice in the beginning? Is it embarrassment or do you immediately feel at ease? What does it feel like at the end? Do you feel more connected after those five minutes?

2. CAPITALIZATION

This may sound like a boring financial product, but it's much more exciting than that: capitalization means sharing the good things that have happened to you with others.[171] This could range from 'My partner and I are getting married' to 'My mother has completely recovered from her illness' to 'I was in Amsterdam for a city break last weekend and I fell in love with the place': share your joy, and you, the narrator, will find an increase in your positive emotions.

And, *more is more* (as long as you don't forget to listen to their stories as well!), because the more people you tell your story to, the more you will enjoy it. Your enthusiasm is infectious.

> Think of a positive event you experienced recently and share it with an acquaintance (especially with someone you wouldn't normally share experiences with). Make it lively and engaging.
>
> **SIT-UP**

3. APPROPRIATE RESPONSE

You rush home to tell your partner at the top of your voice: 'Today I won a toaster and an alarm clock at the bingo, and again with 14, my lucky number!' Instead of cheering along, your partner responds: 'Darling, please don't shout, I'm reading the newspaper.' It's a downer, isn't it? And if this kind of let-down keeps recurring, it won't be conducive to your relationship.

Shelly Gable, a US professor of positive psychology, came to the same conclusion. Her large-scale research – she questioned thousands of couples – showed that responses to good news have a significant impact on the length and quality of a relationship, and that they have a greater impact than responses to bad news.[172] These results also apply to friendships or relationships at work: if your boss never responds when you have attracted a new client or commission, or is unkind, or shows no interest in you or your work, you will soon find yourself scrolling down LinkedIn job vacancies. An enthusiastic response and show of interest (listening actively by asking many questions) will reinforce your relationship. And, of course, it will also make you feel better. You will increase the number of positive interactions, which then give you a feeling of happiness. In addition, it helps you share in the other person's good moments.

An active and constructive response is the best medicine for envy. I'm not suggesting you will no longer feel that emotion, but frequent active and constructive responses to others will strengthen your sincere joy and your jealousy will fade away. And if it doesn't, verbalize your feelings in your response in a respectful manner. For example, if someone has taken the job you wanted, or has a baby while you (and your partner) are still trying to conceive, you could say, 'I do envy you, but that's such cool news!' and then ask a follow-up question: 'When will you start the job?' or 'How do you feel about it?'

SIT-UP	Notice how you respond to your partner, to your colleague, to your friends or family. Your responses often depend on the speaker. Today, try to respond actively and constructively at least once, especially to people to whom you do not normally respond well.

4. FLOURISHING FEEDBACK

The Russian literary giant Leo Tolstoy compared flattery to the grease that makes a wheel turn smoothly. Paying attention to other people's strengths will give them more happiness and energy. But you will benefit, too: you practise your optimistic view, which makes you quicker to recognize your own strengths, and it will boost the relationship with the receiving party. How can you do this? Follow these three steps: recognition, identification and enhancement.[173]

1. *Recognize.* When you consciously pay attention to someone, you recognize their strengths. Only then do you notice: your mother's patience, your girlfriend's broad cultural interests, your father's caring nature, your boss's creativity.
2. *Express.* It's not always easy to pay a compliment. Sometimes you feel inhibited: you're afraid they'll think you're a creep, or the recipient will be indifferent, or that so much praise will make them lazy or arrogant. Note your threshold(s) in a kind

manner and then make a conscious decision to express the positive trait(s) to the other person.

3. *Enhance*. The third step is often forgotten, and yet it's so important. You want to see their pride made visible in their face; you want the other person to shine.

Unfortunately, the recipient may try to deflect the compliment with: 'Anybody could do this' or 'It was no trouble at all.' But even those who find it difficult to receive praise will often show their pride, joy or gratitude in micro-expressions.[174] Their look may last for only a fraction of a second, but, as ever, paying attention is key. If you notice any glimmer of joy, radiance or pride, encourage the other person to (re)connect with that expression. For example, by asking: 'I think I saw a sparkle in your eyes, am I right?' And maybe follow this up with: 'I see it again, right now. Did you notice, too?'

If you haven't been able to spot joy or pride, you could try to lead them towards it. 'I have a feeling that you find it difficult to accept/ believe this compliment. Do you recognize that?' Or you could make a suggestion: 'It looks as though what I said needs a little time to sink in. Am I right?' Another way to enhance the compliment is to draw attention to the impact of their response to it on yourself or others: 'It's fantastic to see how you opened up; everybody was so touched' or 'If anybody were to highlight such a quality in me, I would be absolutely delighted, too.'

Today, choose one person and tell them about their strengths. Have you managed to help the other absorb the feedback? And what kind of thoughts and feelings arise when you give flourishing feedback? Cherish potential positive emotions.

SIT-UP

5. HAVE A GAME WITH OTHER PEOPLE

When did you last play a game with somebody? Was it a long time ago when you played football with friends in the park or a board game? Ageing brings its own imperfections, and one of them is our to-do-list addiction. Our heads become full with small mundane tasks, for work and home and we end up thinking that washing the car is more important than having fun; having a good time is not given priority. It may seem paradoxical, but having fun is necessary, too: it brings happiness and health, wellbeing and fruitful relationships. So, take note: make time for each other and be serious about having fun together.

SIT-UP

Get on the phone now and arrange to meet up with someone to play that board game.

TRAINING

You may have felt that previous weeks have been like mental boot camps. In that case, be at ease: this week's training is like a play-ground. You will learn to connect at a high level, but light-heartedly and creatively.

▮▮▮ LIGHT

Make sure you do the exercises that suit you; don't force yourself to do all of them. It's better to do one exercise well than several half-heartedly.

EXERCISE 1: TRUST

Try to trust one person proactively every day and take account of the five elements of effective trust.

EXERCISE 2: KINDNESS

Every day choose and perform one of the kindness sit-ups:

- ↔ Secret kindness.
- ↔ Giving something away, in the face of your greed and doubt.
- ↔ Giving something away, and checking on the impact of your generosity.

EXERCISE 3: CONNECTING

- ↔ Share a positive event with someone else every day, something you have experienced and enjoyed. As you don't get promoted or win the lottery on a daily basis, it can be something quite small, such as receiving a compliment or a discount you were given in a shop.
- ↔ Respond actively and constructively to someone else's story. Take note of your reactions and consciously respond actively and constructively. Show your interest and ask lots of

questions. Practise this with people whom you find difficult to relate to.

↔ Every day point out a strength or strengths to someone you meet and compliment them. Vary the people you 'target': pay compliments to acquaintances, loved ones or people you meet for the first time. Use the three steps of recognize, express and enhance (see Week 10). Take note of any positive emotions you feel after paying compliments.

↔ Share fun with others. Even if it's only for a minute, laugh, play or have fun!

▮▮ MEDIUM

EXTENSION TO LIGHT This week, in addition to the light training, try to do something with somebody else which pleases both of you (you could even find a couple of occasions). It could be going ten-pin bowling, going to the pub or cinema, or going for a bike ride. And remember, it shouldn't be one of those mundane tasks on your to-do list!

▮▮ INTENSE

EXTENSION TO LIGHT + MEDIUM If you would like to do some intensive training this week, then do this additional exercise. It's based on the work of the psychotherapist Nathaniel Branden.[175] It will help you gain some new insights into your relationships with others – especially if you do this daily – because it throws a spotlight onto your unconscious at work.

Complete four sentences every day. Choose from the following sentences or go to

<www.nathanielbranden.com/sentence-completion-i>

↔ If I want to give my relationships a 5 per cent boost...
↔ 'Loving' means...
↔ If I increase my responsibility regarding my choice of friends by 5 per cent...

↔ If I pay more attention to how I interact with people today...
↔ If I want to be a better lover and partner...
↔ If I want to bring love into my life...
↔ If I want to add 5 per cent more happiness to my love relationship...
↔ If I want to add 5 per cent more happiness to my friendships...
↔ If I allow myself to fully experience love...

Choose sentences which are your best triggers.[176] Complete each sentence six to ten times. For example: 'Loving' means...

↔ being there for each other;
↔ giving each other a hug;
↔ making concessions;
↔ supporting her even when I do not agree.

Write down your completed sentences, record them or share them with another person. Say or write down what comes to mind. Don't think too much about them; send your inner critic on holiday. If the task has taken more than ten minutes, it means that he hasn't packed his bags yet. And you are probably overanalysing stuff. At the end of the week, review your new insights and write them down once more for your own benefit. In Week 12, you will learn how to use the tools to transform insights and intentions (e.g. giving more time to friends) into behaviour (making more phone calls, going to the pub for a weekly drink, etc.).

COOL DOWN

If you consider that you spend 70–80 per cent of your waking hours on interaction every day, you will certainly have enough practice material.[177] You may have noticed how pleasant and meaningful it is to consciously celebrate relationships, and not to take others for granted. Maybe you encountered restrictive patterns that upset the potential happiness in your relationships. Accept this as gain: you can now see what might otherwise have become a festering wound.

As Carl Jung said: 'What we do not make conscious emerges later as fate.' Now you can deal with these things constructively.

New insights often come with anger and sadness, for example because you have denied happiness to yourself (and others). Allowing that pain to enter can be restorative. You now have fresh eyes and will make space to strengthen and deepen your relationships.

Maybe you've asked yourself the following question: 'All this about stuff being kind to one other is great, but when am I going to focus on the sticking points in a relationship?' You must remember that celebrating relationships does not mean avoiding difficulties, but that you are trying to find a balance between celebrating and conflict management. Let your relationships flourish so you can develop greater resilience in climbing over the difficult hills in life, together.

Ask yourself whether you have achieved any of the following in Week 10:

↔ Have you learned to trust others (more) effectively?
↔ Have you learned to show more kindness, partly through clever giving?
↔ Can you now connect with others and spark positive emotions by sharing with them, responding constructively, bringing out the best in them and having fun together?

IN CONCLUSION

A young family was travelling through the American west. On Christmas Day their car broke down and, while they waited for a mechanic, they went for a meal in a virtually empty restaurant. There was one customer in the classic American diner. The old man had an ashen face, a long unkempt beard, and was mumbling something to his empty, cheap bottle of wine. Oh dear, a rough sleeper, the mother thought. The youngest child, four-year-old Eric, waved cheerfully to the man and shouted a friendly: 'Hi!' The man waved back, and Eric grinned. Eric's mother was not particularly happy. She tried to distract her little boy and ushered him away, but Eric wouldn't give up. He kept turning back to connect with this grubby-looking man. 'Do you like fries too?' he asked the little boy. Eric nodded enthusiastically. Partly embarrassed, partly annoyed by this contact, Eric's parents decided to leave and look for another restaurant. As they walked past the dishevelled man, Eric raised his arms to indicate he wanted a hug. The man's eyes begged the young woman to allow him to do so, but before she could decide the little boy threw himself into the arms of the rough sleeper. Tears ran down the man's cheeks when Eric rested his head on his shoulder. The man put down the boy and said to his mother: 'Take good care of this child. Thank you so much, from the bottom of my heart; this is the most beautiful Christmas gift I could wish for.' The mother was deeply touched and went outside with her family, mumbling, 'God, forgive me.'[178]

WEEK

11

THE SWEET SPOT
OF HAPPINESS

'We become what we think about. Energy flows
where attention goes.'

RHONDA BYRNE

Happiness is more than a party, a new car, or winning a game of
cards. Contributing to something that is bigger than your own
'self' is indispensable to a fulfilling life. Last week you were exercising your happiness skills in relationships; this week you will
look for your strengths, for meaning and a sense of purpose, and
you will discover what gives you joy. When pleasure, strengths
and meaning come together, when you are fully absorbed in what
you are doing, you experience a positive flow. And this gives you
lasting happiness.

WARM-UP

In the Belgian absurdist film *The Brand New Testament* (2015), directed by Jaco Van Dormael, God's computer is hacked. Everybody on
Earth receives a text message telling them how many years, months
or days they still have left to live. How does humankind respond:
there's panic and consternation, which soon turns into a 'Let's make
the most of it' free-for-all. Not many sit down to open Facebook.

DEATH AND A RICHER LIFE

Whoever faces up to their mortality wastes less time on trivial pur-
suits. It would be great if we could experience this without receiving
distressing news from a doctor or receiving a text message from
above. Although we know rationally that it is a shame to waste our
time, when it comes to an emotional level all of us probably bury our
heads in the sand. The following exercise encourages you to do the
opposite: instead of running away, you will face your death – and so
enrich your life.

WEEK 11: THE SWEET SPOT OF HAPPINESS

Sit or lie down comfortably. Reflect on the following questions, preferably with your eyes closed. Spend at least a minute on each question. See what surfaces, and remind yourself that there are no wrong answers.

- If you knew you would die within five years, what would you do, what would be most important to you?
- If you had one year to live, what would you do, what would be most important to you?
- And if you only had one month to live...?
- And if you only had one week to live...?
- And if you only had one day to live...?
- And if you only had one minute to live?
- And if you only had one breath left, how would you like to experience it?

SIT-UP

Maybe this exercise makes you feel emotional. Don't worry – this means you are involved. Notice your emotions with kind attention. What are you feeling, what is happening in your body? Think about it and focus on those sensations. When you are ready, write down your answers to the sit-up questions in a notebook (or on your computer). You don't have to take action immediately or do anything else. Put the list away then a few days later bring it out again and reread your answers. It will give you a real, urgent sense of what's important to you.

> *'Most importantly do not forget what
> is most important.'*
>
> ANONYMOUS

YOUR FINAL MONTH

At George Mason University, students were asked to imagine that they were running out of time. The students must ask themselves the same question every day: 'What if this were my final month?', and then once a week they should do something that was still on their bucket list (such as a mountain trek, bungee jumping, visiting a loved one across the world or just drinking a cup of coffee in the sun). This exercise significantly improved the students' happiness. They also blossomed in their daily activities.

> 'Remember that there are two kinds of lunatics:
> those who
> don't know that they must die, and those who have
> forgotten that they're alive.'
>
> PATRICK DECLERCK

Bronnie Ware, an end-of-life counsellor, made the following list in her book *The Top Five Regrets of the Dying*. These regrets were most expressed on people's deathbeds:

1. I wish I had had the courage to live a life in which I remained true to myself, instead of living up to other people's expectations.
2. I wish I had worked less hard.
3. I wish I had had the courage to express my feelings.
4. I wish I had kept in touch with friends.
5. I wish I had allowed myself more feelings of happiness.

SIT-UP

In which of these five regrets do you see yourself? Maybe there is a sixth regret that applies especially to you? What could you do right now to prevent potential feelings of regret? 'I wish I had a better relationship with my mother': ring her now. 'I wish I had had a healthier lifestyle': make an appointment with the dietician now. 'I wish I had read more': get a book. You need to act first to prevent regret.

MPS MODEL

It's an illusion to think that you and I will not have any regrets at all on our deathbeds. We are all pretty good at deceiving ourselves. It's how we avoid facing the important things in life. You avoid seeing your brother because he's such a pain. Or you procrastinate: 'I will resume my studies when the children are older.'

What you can do is reduce your feelings of regret, for example by addressing the imbalance between meaning (or a sense of purpose), pleasure (or enjoyment) and strengths.

The Harvard lecturer Tal Ben-Shahar describes three measurable components which you need to experience happiness. If we focus too much on one of them, and thus neglect the other two, it makes us feel unhappy. However, if you focus on activities in which these three converge, as in the MPS model,[179] it takes you to the flow spot. Before you learn how to enter a positive flow, we will highlight three concepts.

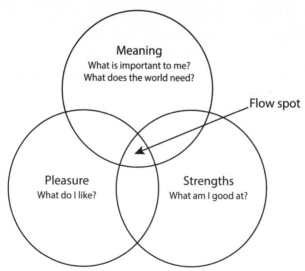

Figure 11.1
Source: Based on Tal Ben-Shahar, *Happier: Learn the Secrets to Daily Joy and Lasting Fulfillment* (McGraw-Hill Education, 2007)

MEANING

A significant part of our life is about having a sense of purpose or meaning: being intrinsically motivated helps you contribute to something greater than yourself. You do not need to be a monk, an imam or a doctor to know this. A person who becomes a doctor, just to have a high salary and an expensive home, may have less sense of purpose than a refuse collector who works to make our world a cleaner place.

Feelings of dissatisfaction, frustration and fear often arise from the realization that you are not living according to your values; that you are living a worthless life. Meaning and a sense of purpose give you something to hold on to as well as direction, especially in the midst of life's vicissitudes. You can discover your meaning by realizing what is important to you and by recognizing your values. The next step is to put them into practice, which is your contribution to helping the world become a better place.

You do not create these values; you discover them and expose them. Some call this a vocation, as if a higher power is calling them to fulfil their mission in this world.

Maybe the notions of a 'sense of purpose' or 'vocation' make you feel uncomfortable, because you associate them with climbing mountains barefoot or founding a rescue centre for destitute donkeys. You should remember, though, that an individual's sense of purpose varies from person to person. You, personally, may look for meaning in collecting vintage cars or pulling the perfect pint of draught beer. You should also note that a sense of purpose is a quest, not a destination. Ten years after that perfect pint of draft beer, your job as a dietician could make your life purposeful, because you help others to live healthy lives. In short, the questions 'What are my values?' and 'What is meaningful to me?' are more important than any standard answers, and they are as fluid as beer. Try to live with the inconvenience of uncertainty and welcome it as a crucial part of your quest. If you manage to do this, it will be easier for you to find your meaning and values.

Would you like to try to work out what your values are? If you do, you need to be inquisitive and proactive – being horizontal in front of the TV, scoffing pizza won't help. You can apply what you learned in Week 10: Connecting with others. Talking to a friend, a life coach, a second cousin and even a casual acquaintance can give you an idea of your values, provided you are prepared to listen and see. Another way to discover your values – just as powerful – is to reflect on your life and to imagine your own death. Why? As I wrote before, a deeply felt realization of your own mortality will give you a better idea of what matters in your life.

Write your own funeral speech. You could write it from your perspective, or a loved one's. How would you like to be remembered? What would you like people to say about you? What are the hidden values?

SIT-UP

So long as you're not a classic car fanatic, you probably won't want to be remembered for the leather upholstery in your vintage Porsche. You'd prefer to be remembered as a good father, a thoughtful son, a visionary, a great colleague, a good storyteller, a loyal and entertaining friend, or a loving partner.

Whatever people say, it always boils down to you having made a (positive) difference to the lives of others.

PLEASURE

The second component of the MPS-model is enjoyment. What gives you real enjoyment? Your brain will have a ready and 'perfect' answer to this kind of question. It will be something you are used to saying, what you expect yourself to say, or what you think others will expect you to say. But your subconscious has deeper desires which you can explore and discover. Once you know them, you can act accordingly.

'Must' is the greatest enemy of pleasure. While the amateur actor loves going on stage, many professional actors have to drag themselves to the theatre night after night. Parties, trips to theme parks or romantic dinners can also feel like obligations. You are expected to have fun, and that expectation itself sometimes deprives you of any pleasure you might have had. Being unconstrained is a prerequisite for real enjoyment. So get rid of that addiction to always being useful and effective that we came across in Week 10!

You need to multiply the number of times you do something just for the fun of it. But how do you find what that something is for *you*?

Have a look at Figure 11.2: the idea is that you will want to reach the smallest of those circles. The next two sit-ups are an initial step to getting closer to that innermost circle.

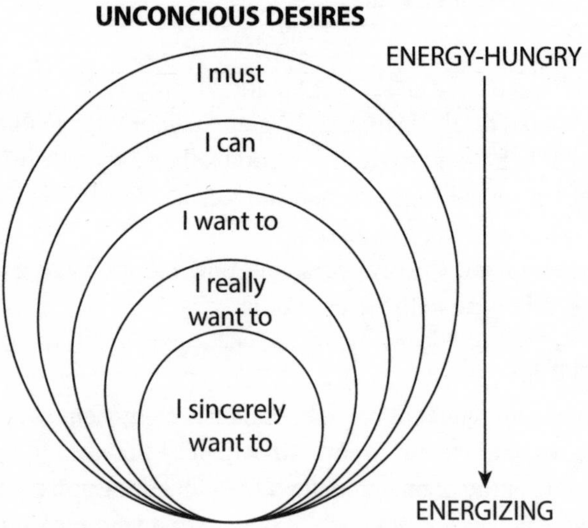

Figure 11.2
Source: Based on Tal Ben-Shahar, *Happier: Learn the Secrets to Daily Joy and Lasting Fulfillment* (McGraw-Hill Education, 2007)

Set a timer for 5–10 minutes. Sit down, relax, close your eyes and focus on your breathing. After a couple of inhalations and exhalations repeat the following question internally on each inhalation: 'What do I long for?' Don't try too hard, but wait for answers to emerge during the exhalations.

You could also do this exercise without focusing on breathing. Repeat the question several times at a pace that suits you: 'What do I long for?' and wait for answers to come. If you prefer to write then take a pen and paper to answer this question. Just keep writing, particularly if your thoughts stop coming (and record that on paper, too). Either way, continue for 5–10 minutes. Take note of any distractions, kindly and without judgement, and return to the exercise.

SIT-UP

You could also find out together with someone else what really gives you pleasure. Ask the other person to continue repeating the following sentence: 'Tell me what you long for', and you answer the question. Some playing rules apply:

↔ The person asking the question mustn't interrupt; they should just listen silently.
↔ When the questioner feels that your answer is complete, they say: 'Thank you.'
↔ They will then repeat the sentence, without changing the stress pattern.
↔ Don't have any expectations, but let the answers just pop into your head and out of your mouth. Don't worry, either, if nothing pops up; that's its own answer, too.

SIT-UP

The strength of both sit-ups here lies in the repetition of the question. Just as you think nothing is surfacing, and the question is starting to annoy you, your deeper desires emerge. If the sit-ups don't work today, try again tomorrow. And the day after tomorrow. And the day after. And the day after that. Once again, the strength lies in the repetition.

STRENGTHS

For years we have thought that we could develop by strengthening our weaknesses. It appears from research that this takes an enormous amount of energy and that usually you don't manage to convert your weaknesses into strengths.[180] Two years of ballet is unlikely to turn you into a ballerina if you are heavy-footed. And if you're tone deaf, years of practice will not help you hit the right notes – though you might just manage 'Baa, Baa, Black Sheep'. Instead, it's best to focus on your strengths and you will create a win-win situation: your performances will be of a high standard and those around you will benefit. Moreover, in contrast to weaknesses, strengths do increase exponentially.

> *'A person can perform only from strength. One cannot build performance on weakness, let alone on something one cannot do at all.'*
>
> PETER DRUCKER

Positive emotions from within your strengths are the third factor in the MPS-model. They provide long-lasting pleasure and give you energy. Of course, this doesn't mean that you should run away from your weaknesses; on the contrary you should accept and manage them – with compassion! In Part 2 you learned how to be at peace with yourself, inclusive of your weaknesses, mediocrities and strengths. Self-acceptance should not prevent you from paying focused attention to your strengths. As the

Austrian-born American professor of management Peter Drucker rightly said: 'Manage your weaknesses, focus on your strengths.'

FLOURISHING FEEDBACK ON YOUR OWN CHARACTER STRENGTHS

What are your character strengths? The steps in Week 10 used to feed back on the power of your character strengths will help you find out. You must first recognize your strengths, then (dare to) name them and, finally, deepen them. The fourth and main step of the process is the practical implementation.

1. RECOGNITION

Often some of your strong qualities get snowed under or forgotten. The next sit-up allows you to go back to and explore your core: who you are, what gives you pleasure, and what you can do.

> Browse your childhood photo album. What can you see? What are you doing? What good qualities would you attribute to that little girl or boy?
>
> **SIT-UP**

We will now look at the *values in action* (VIA) model developed by Christopher Peterson and Martin Seligman to help you identify your strengths. They describe strengths as 'a way of thinking, feeling, and acting that leads to excellence and optimized functioning'. The VIA model subdivides strengths into six virtues. Each virtue includes several core qualities, also known as key competencies.

Table 11.1   Character strengths

Virtues	Core qualities
Wisdom	Creativity, inquisitiveness, judgement, natural curiosity, bilateral thinking
Courage	Courage, persistence, sincerity, diligence
Solidarity	Love, kindness, social intelligence
Moderation	Forgiveness, modesty, thoughtfulness, self-regulation
Righteousness	Cooperation, honesty, leadership
Spirituality	Appreciation of beauty and excellence, gratitude, hope, humour

Source: Christopher Peterson and Martin Seligman, viacharacter.org/www/Character-Strengths[181]

SIT-UP

Have a look at the 24 competencies listed in Table 11.1. Find your most typical competency or competencies by asking yourself the following questions:

↔ Does this competency give me energy and inspiration when I use it?

↔ Do I experience this competence as an essential part of who I am – do I feel incomplete without it?

↔ Do I want to apply this competency to as many areas as possible?

↔ If I use this competency, will it feel like personal growth?

↔ What are my top five most typical character strengths?

You can take the strengths test at <www.viacharacter.org>. Fifteen minutes of your time will give you a lot of self-insight that will be helpful for the rest of your life.

2. EXPRESS

Modest people tend to downplay their strengths. 'I persevere, but sometimes I find it hard to stop.' It is safe to put yourself down. But only when you recognize and fully embrace your strengths by naming them will you benefit most.

> Name your top five typical competencies aloud to yourself. For example: 'I am brave. I have a sense of humour. I am creative. I have leadership qualities. I have a natural curiosity.' Without judgement, take note of any tendency to use lots of 'buts' or mention associated pitfalls. Maybe you find it easier to name a situation? Instead of saying 'I am creative', you could say, 'People often ask me to think along with them' or 'I often have different ideas.' Don't say, 'I have a sense of humour' but 'I often make people laugh at lunchtimes.' If you find it easy/easier to name your strengths aloud, it will also be easy/easier to tell others about them, without immediately playing them down.

SIT-UP

3. ENHANCE: GOING DEEPER

Many training courses and coaching programmes forget the following step: going deeper. Sometimes we go on and on and on discussing our strengths, but we do not properly feel them. Pointless waffle won't inspire you. The following sit-up will take you a step in the right direction.

> Sit down, relax and focus on your breathing. After several inhalations and exhalations recall a moment when you were brimming with enthusiasm or were completely absorbed in what you were doing. Picture the moment as vividly as possible. Which of your top five core qualities do you recognize? Feel how this affects you.
>
> Without judgement, note the thoughts and feelings that sometimes block the core quality: self-criticism, unwillingness to take centre stage, being matter of fact, or worried about what others might think. Recognize and acknowledge these are unjustified obstructions and try to let the core quality enter. Create as much space as possible to experience the core quality, both in mind and in body. Maybe you feel yourself sitting up straight, adopting a more open posture, possibly with a smile on your face? Identify the effect of your core quality on yourself as well as your environment.

SIT-UP

TRAINER'S TIP

Do you find it difficult to accept somebody complimenting you about your qualities? Then imagine inhaling the compliment. Try it out and see what happens!

4. IMPLEMENTATION

Research shows that the positive impact of identifying strengths soon disappears. It is not until you implement them that you find you are still benefiting from the process more than six months later.[182] You need to expand the implementation to optimize your gain. If you have leadership qualities, don't use them just at that conference you led but also as the captain of your local football team (and delegate washing-up duties to someone else at home).

> **SIT-UP**
>
> Think back to your top five core qualities again. Which ones would you like to use more often? Select one or two and add them to your repertoire today/this week. Also think of new situations and new contexts (work, love, friends, strangers, parenting) where you would use your core quality/qualities. What is the effect? And who benefits?

FLOW

Your flow spot is where meaning, pleasure and strengths meet.

The first person to research flow was the Hungarian/American psychologist Mihaly Csikszentmihalyi (don't ask me how to pronounce it). It surprised him how artists could forget time: they could paint for hours at a stretch without feeling hungry or thirsty or being distracted, as if they were carried away on a powerful current (flow). After questioning tens of thousands of people, he came up with six characteristics of flow. If you are in the flow, the following happens:

1. Time seems to pass both quickly and slowly. A two-hour tennis match seems to last ten minutes. But when the ball is returned after a hard serve, it is as if the time is delayed, as though the ball is coming at you in slow motion.

2. You forget yourself. There is no observer of the experience. You are not bothered by a distracting monkey mind.

3. You find yourself completely in the moment. Your attention is not focused on an end goal, but you are absorbed in the activity of the moment. You are not trying to win the tennis match; your sole focus is on hitting that ball.

4. You have a clear goal. Although you are not consciously trying to achieve an end goal, you do have a concrete goal in mind which is the final result of the activity: the final game, a beautiful painting, reaching the summit, appreciation...

5. You are intrinsically motivated. You enjoy doing the actual activity; it's not only about potential results.

6. Your strengths and the activity are balanced. If a task is too difficult and not in line with your skills, it frustrates you. If it is too easy, you are bored. Halfway between these – where there's enough challenge, but not too much – you experience flow.

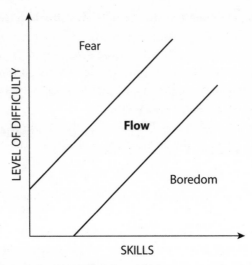

Figure 11.3 Mihaly Csikszentmihalyi's flow model
Source: Mihaly Csikszentmihalyi

HEALTHY AND UNHEALTHY FLOW

When do you experience flow? Maybe when you are cooking, are on Facebook, playing a ukulele, kissing, coding, watching a TV serial, drawing, playing volleyball, doing a wood carving, or gaming? This list of activities shows that flow might not be effective per se, make you healthy or happy. Flow can take over to such an extent that you neglect other 'duties' such as sleeping, healthy eating or loving others (think of gaming addicts or workaholics). In addition, the activity that gives you a sense of flow might not even be useful; it can even turn out to be destructive. For example, a gambler at the roulette table can experience the same sense of flow as a doctor performing a lifesaving operation. A whole day of binge-watching Netflix series might give a freelancer a sense of flow, but it will not yield much cash flow.

A healthy flow is found where meaning, pleasure and strengths overlap: this is the flow spot. Imagine you do something you like, something you can do well, the task is challenging but not too difficult, and you find it meaningful. In this situation, you not only feel your activity as pleasant at the time, but you also create long-term benefits. And a healthy flow makes you happy: it is pleasant, partly because it may even silence your chattering brain. Another advantage is that your performance is optimized when you are in a healthy flow. You learn and grow.

It can be frustrating and demotivating playing chess against a chess grandmaster, while having a game of chess with your eight-year-old nephew can be rather boring. Nonetheless, you do learn from playing when your opponent is just that little bit better than you. And once you have raised your game to their level, you will try to go one notch higher.

You will always need a greater challenge to reach the desired flow. Result: you grow.

HOW DO YOU PRACTISE A HEALTHY FLOW?

You can't force a healthy flow; it emerges. But you can create the conditions to be in that flow. A strong attention muscle underpins a healthy flow because it helps you fully concentrate on the task where meaning, strength and enjoyment meet.

If your mental bandwidth is preoccupied with future carrots and sticks – a.k.a. reward or punishment – instead of focusing on the task of the moment, your experience of flow is still far away. You undertake the task from within your drive or threat system, and thus block the flow. We have already come across this in Part 2 – self-criticism is not motivational and your performance deteriorates.

What is motivational? Self-correction from within kindness. A playful attitude, from within the soothing system is what you need to be in the flow. A final product (a perfect piece of music) isn't your goal; instead, you concentrate fully on the task in front of you (fiddling, strumming – in short, practising). Flow helps you live in the now instead of being dissatisfied because you're too busy looking through binoculars at future goals, not yet achieved.

If you stop to think about all the routine tasks that make up your life, it can seem quite depressing. Your alarm goes off, you have a shower, you travel to work, you ring your mother/grandmother/best friend, you have a cup of that awful vending machine coffee, you go for a walk at lunchtime, and so forth and so on. But this shouldn't make you depressed. You can take advantage of your humdrum routine and give it a happy ending.

FLOW IN ROUTINE

One way to have more flow in your life is to convert those routine tasks into moments of flow. How? First, focus on that routine. Stop multitasking and keep distractions at bay. Then consider how you could deploy your strengths in a typical routine job and give it meaning. Even ironing can become an occasion for flow if you are able to deploy one of your strengths (e.g. orderliness) and imbue it with meaning (a more aesthetical world). Any activity could be viewed from this perspective: driving, taking children to football, cooking dinner, greeting a passer-by, a meeting. You increase your chances of experiencing flow.

And even if you don't achieve it, it makes the activity more agreeable and your performance more efficient.

> **SIT-UP**
>
> Choose a routine task today and carry it out with full attention, while consciously applying your strengths and meaning and adding pleasure. Here is an example: John is washing up and paying attention, and in so doing he deploys his strength (orderliness) and listens to some good music.

WORKFLOW

At an early age, children learn to distinguish between work and play, which continues all the way to retirement (or until the day they die).[183] This observation led to the following experiment undertaken by Donald Hebb. Six hundred students aged between six and fifteen were given an engaging task: if they were disobedient or misbehaved, their 'punishment' was being sent to play outside. If they followed the rules, their reward was that they could do more work. It appeared that most of the children preferred to work than to play outside.

Actually *wanting* to work is a position you'd like to be in as an adult, isn't it? Worldwide there appear to be twice as many dissatisfied as satisfied employees.[184] That's a great pity if you consider that a healthy UK employee works an average of 84,171 hours in their career.[185] Are you also part of this largely dissatisfied cohort? Maybe you think that happiness at work can never be your lot? Well, hey presto – you proved yourself right. As soon as you think something will be a certain way, your thoughts conspire to make it true, as a self-fulfilling prophecy. The good news is that, if you let go of those thoughts, it's quite possible to find flow at work (although maybe not in your current job).

HOW DO WE SEE OUR WORK?

> If money (and status) didn't matter, how would you fill your days? Answer honestly – nobody's judging you. In what respect does it differ from your current situation?
>
> **SIT-UP**

You can look at your work from three different perspectives, in three different ways.[186] The first is that you work only to receive a payslip, to fund that new motorbike or your weekend bowling nights. Your work is just a means to an end. At best, you are indifferent to your duties, and at worst you hate them.

They don't give you any pleasure, you don't have the opportunity to deploy your strengths and they don't give you any sense of purpose.

The second perspective is that you are committed to your career and consciously deploy your strengths. Your monthly payslip is important to you, but so too is promotion. Future rewards – status, more money and power – drive you. Success, rather than the journey, gives you pleasure, but your work is essentially meaningless for you. Once you've reached your ceiling and find yourself sitting in the oversized desk chair as a CEO, boredom and dissatisfaction set in.

The third and most desirable possibility is that work is your vocation. You do your work with dedication and pleasure; the goal is higher than yourself. Your work is challenging, it gives you much energy, and, regardless of salary or promotions, it is more than satisfying.

SIT-UP

What does work mean to you? Is it a job, a career or a vocation? Which concrete steps could help you experience your work as a vocation?

If your answer is 'job' or 'career', try to imagine yourself with (more) wrinkles and grey hair and with a regret nagging away at you from the back of your mind: 'If only I had had a job that gave me satisfaction.' Does that mean you should change course completely, or could you find flow in the work you're doing now? Together, we will check out both options.

JOB RENOVATION

A change of employer, retraining or going back to uni, a complete change of profession – in the quest for job happiness and satisfaction, the first thought often is to completely change course. But sometimes it's only the sails that need repositioning to cruise the course of satisfaction and flow.

Anna was a student who had a temp job in a service station. She was mainly doing this for money and benefits; she hated the work, especially the 'upselling' ('Our special offer today is coffee and cake for only £3'). During a training session I asked her to recall a moment when she was in the flow, deploying her strengths. She immediately mentioned organizing a surprise party for her sister. While talking about it, her eyes lit up.

We both discovered that she had deployed two of her core qualities: creativity and social intelligence. The 'homework' I gave Anna was to use those qualities in her job, too, so that she could replace the challenge of garnering extra profit with that of making customers smile. A week later, she was pleasantly surprised at the result. It had become a kind of game to cheer her customers up. Of course, this didn't work with every customer, but most responded well (and she also sold more snacks than ever). The job isn't exactly Anna's dream career, but now that she's using her strengths, it gives her more pleasure and a sense of purpose.

Let's be honest, some jobs are more suited to having a sense of purpose than others. An official working in a stuffy booth on a toll bridge will find it harder to see meaning in their work than a doctor or a sports instructor. However, you can have an influence over your sense of happiness in any kind of job.

Martin Seligman, for example, tells us about John, a committed hospital cleaner. The wife of a coma patient noticed him repeatedly scrutinizing the rather dismal black-and-white photographs on one of the ward's wall. Then, soon after, she spotted him again, this time with two paintings under his arm: one of a meadow with a rising sun, another with the picture of a dancing couple. He removed the black-and-white photos on the wall and prepared to hang the paintings.

'What are you doing?' the patient's wife asked.

'Although I'm only the cleaner on this ward, I also feel responsible for patients. Your husband has been in a deep sleep for weeks. When he wakes up, I want to be sure that the first thing he sees is something beautiful.'

The trick is to be creative, like this cleaner: how do you apply your strengths? If you like writing, try to become responsible for the company newsletter. If you love organizing, and your current job does not offer any scope for this, why not suggest you organize team days out or teambuilding sessions. And keep reminding yourself every day, just like Anna and John, what makes your work important. It is how you transform a dull job or routine work into something that gives you satisfaction.

CHANGING JOBS

But maybe you've tried every to get satisfaction from your job, and still you have to drag yourself to work every morning? Then it's time to take more steps. 'But if I gave up my job now...' I hear you thinking.

After all, you've still got rent or mortgage to pay, your own mouth and maybe several others to feed. In her book *Working Identity*, Herminia Ibarra recommends us to 'Take small steps'. If the job that doesn't satisfy you isn't damaging your mental health, then keep it and decide to do new things several hours a week. Do activities that are fun, meet people that inspire you, whose work or actions you find meaningful.

This strategy prevents you from falling into the black hole of unemployment and poverty – which would certainly not motivate you to realize your dreams of having a wonderful job – but also helps you replenish the energy you expend on your current job. It's the first cautious step to another job.[187]

LIVING SIMPLY

Perhaps you don't like taking small steps? Do you want to swap your parking attendant's uniform for that of an airline pilot (or vice versa)? In other words, do you want to make a complete switch? You need to realize that, if you do switch careers, it will require making some compromises. Because, regardless of the potential opportunities in your new career, you will be inexperienced immediately after the switch. It will show in your status and responsibilities – and potentially on your payslip, too.

Think first how much you will need to make ends meet. And does your 'need' have a sneaky tendency to acquire noughts at the end? How essential are the latest iPhone, groceries from a more exclusive supermarket, and the umpteenth pair of trainers and fourth holiday this year?

You need far less than you think and – as you read in Part 2 – excess doesn't make you happy; it can be a source of gloom and depression. If you simplify your life and consider what you really need, it creates the space for you to align your work with your flow spot. You will then no longer experience your work as a duty, but as a privilege because you can contribute to a larger whole.

TRAINING

Even if you know what gives you pleasure, what you are good at and what gives you a sense of purpose, it might still be difficult to find the healthy flow spot. The training session this week will help you do just that.

ıll LIGHT

This week, the emphasis is on changes you can immediately implement in your daily activities. They will help you bring more meaning, pleasure and strengths to your tasks – and all with more consciousness.

EXERCISE 1: IN YOUR DIARY

This week you should add more meaning and pleasure, and strengths to:

↔ one routine task (cooking, flossing, bathing your children);
↔ one (challenging) activity at work;
↔ one moment during a social get-together with friends, your housemate, partner or relatives.

Schedule this exercise in your diary. For example: on Tuesday you focus on flossing, on Wednesday on that boring weekly work meeting, and on Friday on your after-work drinks.

EXERCISE 2: ON PAPER

Draw three overlapping large circles on a piece of paper (this is the MPS model we looked at earlier). In each circle write down your strengths, what gives you enjoyment (your pleasures), and what creates meaning for you. Use this week's sit-ups to discover them. Put the diagram on your noticeboard at home and complete the diagram as the week goes by.

Figure 11.4 shows the MPS model drawn up by Christian, a father, sports lover and banker.

Christian takes pleasure in coaching people, finds an outlet for his social intelligence and sense of humour, and it connects with education, which gives him a sense of purpose. So teaching and supervising touch his flow spot. Maybe he could adapt his current role (as a manager) or would he want to change job. Thanks to this model he has more clarity for taking action.

Christian's MPS model

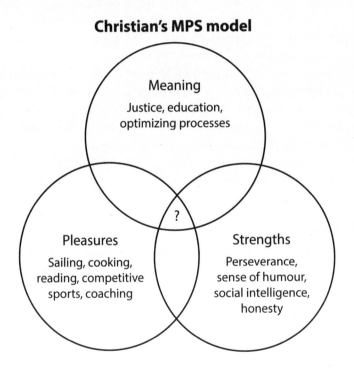

Figure 11.4

ıl| MEDIUM

EXTENSION TO LIGHT

On the left side of a sheet of paper, write a list of up to 30 activities
you perform on an average (working) day – for example getting up,
having a shower, having breakfast, getting dressed, cycling to work,
making a phone call, meeting a customer, doing an employee appraisal, having a violin lesson, and picking up the children from a
swimming lesson. Consider the following in each case: Does it give
you a sense of meaning? Can you engage your character strength(s)?
Does it give you pleasure (enjoyment)? According to your answers,
write an M, E and/or S after the activity.

Next, create a concrete action plan in which on every working day
you add meaning, pleasure or strengths (and preferably all three) to
one of your existing activities. Don't do this only for routine tasks,
but also for activities that are challenging or energy-consuming, or
which you find difficult. For example, if you don't like conducting
appraisal interviews, try to put more strengths, meaning and/or
pleasure into that activity.

ıl| INTENSE

EXTENSION TO LIGHT + MEDIUM   In the intensive training
version you go for the bigger picture. It gives you a helicopter view of
your life where you consider big decisions about work, your studies
and love.

EXERCISE 1: COMPLETE THE SENTENCES (PURPOSEFULLY)

Complete four sentences every day. Example sentences might include:

↔ To me a purposeful life means...

↔ If I accepted 5 per cent more responsibility for my deepest desires, I would...

↔ If I added 5 per cent more meaning to my work (or relationships, marriage, parenting), I would...

↔ If I wanted more core qualities in my life, I could...

There are more examples of sentences in Week 10. Choose the sentences that suit you right now, those you would like to have answers for. Set ten minutes on a timer. Take the first sentence, write down six to ten answers, and then move on to the next. Write down what comes to mind. Practise at set times, for example before you go to work. Read your answers at the end of the week. Allow yourself (at least) half an hour to reflect in silence; on a sofa, at the kitchen table or, preferably, while out on a walk. An alternative option would be for you to discuss your answers with a loved one, acquaintance or colleague. Then create an action plan for the next two weeks and set out small steps that will bring you closer to your goal.

EXERCISE 2: ADVICE FROM YOUR OLDER SELF

Give yourself at least 15 minutes to complete this visualization exercise.

The tragedy of life is that it's only with hindsight that you realize how you should have dealt with a situation or behaved. Imagine you are 80-plus and give your younger self advice. Write this down, or imagine it without writing it down – whatever works for you.

If you tend to think more in images than in words, that's fine: try giving your younger self a symbolic gift, or accompany yourself to a place that is particularly meaningful to you.

Try to turn the wisdom you gain from this exercise into something concrete, something you can change right now. For instance, daring to be yourself; giving yourself more time; spending more time with a loved one; making up with an old friend; doing voluntary work; taking a first step to making your work more satisfying...

COOL DOWN

This week was all about self-reflection: what do you do well, what gives you pleasure, what do you find important? Was discovering all this a good experience? Or did you find it frustrating, because you don't know how to fill that flow spot?

Remember that a single week is too short a time to discover your vocation. So be proud that you have taken the first step. And realize that asking yourself the right questions is more important than finding the answers. In your quest, try to use your strengths and derive meaning and pleasure from them, such as pride (because you show courage, because you are active) and fun (laugh at your 'wrong' choices, enjoy meeting new people). Remember that all anybody is really doing is muddling through and messing around. The trick is to derive enough pleasure, meaning and happiness from this 'muddling through' and 'messing around'.

Ask yourself whether you have achieved any of the following in Week 11:

↔ Are you looking for more fun by doing the things you really want to do?
↔ Do you have a better idea of your core qualities and do you put them into practice in different contexts?

↔ Do you have a better idea of your values, what a sense of purpose means to you and whether you are acting accordingly?

↔ Have you also managed to find fun and meaning, and to use your strengths in ordinary, everyday or boring tasks?

12

Over the past 11 weeks, you have been exercising your mental fitness so as to make your life more pleasurable and purposeful, on your way to a sustainable mindset of happiness. But you need to keep up this workout, just like you have to keep going to the gym. So, this week you are going to strengthen your willpower. More willpower doesn't only make you happier, but using it efficiently also allows you to integrate mind workout exercises into your daily life. You will become your own personal trainer as you create a meaningful and happy life.

WARM-UP

The champagne is flowing, you hear the crackle of fireworks, and your New Year's resolutions are resounding through your brain: 'Less Facebook / a healthier diet / not overworking myself / going to bed earlier...' Although some are sceptical about these kinds of resolutions, apparently people who set themselves goals like this are ten times more likely to change their behaviour than those who don't. Indeed, the majority of people who make New Year's resolutions keep them up for months. Problems arise after six months when approximately 60 per cent call it a day. And by 31 December only 8 per cent can raise a glass to having made a successful behavioural change, such as healthier eating.[188] The 92 per cent who were unsuccessful reward themselves with a bout of bitter self-reproach. And herein lies the vicious circle of unhappiness. How can you manage to maintain your behavioural change for months, years, for ever? By not perceiving persistence as persistence.

THE WILLPOWER MUSCLE

Roy Baumeister, a scientist and willpower expert, claims that you should see willpower as a muscle.[189] Here's an example that illustrates this concept.

> Researchers at the University of Copenhagen followed 60 men 'with spare tyres' who were trying to lose weight in 13 weeks by exercising every day. After all those weeks the scales showed an average weight loss of 3.6 kg among those who really had exerted themselves for half an hour each day. However, the men who had been exercising every day for a full hour (with a similar level of exertion) did not lose more weight, but less: on average they lost 'only' 2.7 kg. This surprising difference was due to overload – not of their abdominal or calf muscles, but the willpower muscle. Those who exercised for half an hour retained more motivation to develop a healthy lifestyle in addition to their exercise routine. They often cut out desserts and would travel by bike instead of by car. The willpower muscle of those men who exercised for an hour every day was overloaded. They had less motivation to live more healthily.[190]

EYE-OPENER

Willpower is used for various tasks and can easily get used up. If you get up early in the morning to go to the gym, to tidy up the house, and have one of those long phone calls to Aunty Moaning Myrtle, you may end up consuming a full bottle of wine in the evening. The good news is that, just like your actual muscles, willpower can be trained. The trick is to strengthen your willpower muscle without overloading it – and this starts with you setting appropriate goals for yourself.

ELIXIRS FOR WILLPOWER

Culturally, we are programmed to think in terms of having 'goals'. What would you like to be when you grow up? Where would you like to be in five years' time? What is your target time in the marathon?

How many children would you like to have? What is your target turnover for the next year? How many kilograms do you want to lose? (All this probably sounds horribly, wearingly, familiar.) The problem is that, once you have set your goals, you punish yourself if you don't manage to achieve them within a certain timeframe and you praise others when they do. Programmes such as *The Voice*, books such as *The Secret* and numerous financially unfeasible start-ups (the word start-down is more befitting of the truth) all suffer from the deadly 'if only you put your mind to it' virus. It's a dangerous virus because a) it's easy to stuff your life full of unrealistic goals, and b) you'll inevitably kick yourself when you don't achieve them.

Of course, what I'm not saying here is that you should forget about your dreams and eliminate your goals. It's good to dream and set goals, but *what* you dream and aspire to is more important.

Many people aim for wealth, status and power (a.k.a. success), hoping it will make them happy. These are not helpful goals, because – as we saw in Week 11 – they are counterproductive: success does not make you happy; it's happiness that brings success. The best thing would be for everything you do to be in alignment with your ultimate goal: a happy and meaningful life. Your willpower muscle will grow and develop accordingly.

Just think of the stamina of passionate people, whether they are teachers, chefs, lawyers, parents, doctors or artists. They are driven by their ultimate goal, and this shapes their lives. Along the way, they set concrete goals, ranging from gaining Michelin stars to winning lawsuits. We all need those milestones, but they shouldn't be our focus and they shouldn't get in the way of our *ultimate* goal – for example, the healthy bank account that obscures the wish for complete freedom. Take small steps and don't lose sight of your ultimate goal; this is the elixir of willpower.

RESERVING WILLPOWER

Everyone knows that a muscle can be overworked, so you should consciously determine how you use it. Reserve your willpower for activities that contribute to a happy life. The following five tips will help you.

1. LIMIT YOUR GOALS

Setting feasible goals is important, but regular adjustment or even letting go of goals is just as important. Time is the most precious gift you can give yourself. It gives you mental energy and therefore insight and willpower to make the choices that really matter. And if suddenly, out of the blue, you begin exercising your attention, working more efficiently, going to bed earlier and cutting out sugar... chances are that on day two you'll find yourself sending texts at 1am, watching Netflix, using Facebook and eating syrup waffles.

> Think back to the past month (or look back at your diary) and see which (recurring) goals you can specify. Which ones could you give up? Maybe you are exercising too much, attending too many meetings, or arranging to see more people than you really want to. What have you said 'yes' to when 'no' would be desirable? This coming week, resolve to let go of at least one goal.
>
> **SIT-UP**

2. TAKE SMALL STEPS

We have discussed this before: small changes require less willpower and consequently have a greater chance of success. Goals are most effective and powerful if they are well phrased and quantifiable, achievable, but also time restricted.

3. EMBRACE ROUTINE, MINIMIZE CHOICE

Left or right? Pasta or rice? Who shall I ring first, A or B? You make many choices in a day, and this has a disastrous effect on your willpower, says Barry Schwartz[191] in his book *The Paradox of Choices*. Routine and regularity, on the other hand, help maintain your willpower. For example, flexible fitness memberships sound a sensible idea, but in fact they undermine your available willpower: you may spend all your time deciding exactly when and whether you will exercise. If you know that you are going to go boxing on Tuesday nights and running on Thursday mornings, there are fewer uncertainties; you are more at ease and retain your willpower.

I am sure you have caught on that automatic behaviours are not always desirable; rituals, however, are an exception. Tony Schwartz and Jim Loehr explain in *The Power of Full Engagement: Managing Energy, Not Time* how rituals can bring about sustainable change. According to them, the ritual has three characteristics: the action is described accurately; its timing is specific; and its performance is underpinned by deep personal values. The exercise in Part 2 in which you were asked to write down every day five things for which you are grateful is an example of such a ritual. Always do this exercise just before bedtime, at the kitchen table, listening to the same background music, in the same book, and based on your value(s), not because you 'have to'. If you use the power of automatic behaviours and routines, you circumvent your willpower, which you can then save for the moments and activities that are most important to you.

4. MAKE USE OF THE POWER OF LANGUAGE: I WANT TO, I CAN, I AM GOING TO (AND IF YOU DON'T: NO PROBLEM)
The way you speak to yourself makes a difference, even when it comes to your willpower. In a case study, 80 per cent of the subjects who motivated themselves by saying, 'I am not going to... [eat sweets, drink alcohol, etc.]', managed to maintain their intentions compared to only 10 per cent of the subjects who repeated the mantra 'I must not...' to themselves. Clearly, finger-wagging did not work as well as the neutral sentence. It shows that language that arises from within the drive and threat systems provides only short-term motivation, whereas language from within the soothing system is motivational and lasts longer.

Refer to Week 6 for an overview of the words and phrases used in the three emotion regulation systems.

The positive approach has a similar impact: that is, if you use 'I would like to' instead of 'I don't want to'. It's better to tell yourself 'I want to live more attentively' instead of 'I do not want to do any more multitasking'. Why? The brain finds it difficult to process negative words such as 'not' because it requires mental energy to think of what you should be doing instead. In relation to this you should pursue your goals from within self-acceptance and self-correction (motivated from within the soothing systems) and not from within self-criticism (drive and threat systems). Self-criticism undermines your mental energy and absorbs your willpower in no time. A feeling of guilt increases your chances of making the same mistakes.[192]

> Reflect for ten minutes on what (or which behaviour) you would like to change. Think of three things. And then investigate if you are convinced that you won't be satisfied with yourself until they have changed. Can you set your goal from within the acceptance of your current situation?
>
> **SIT-UP**

5. ACTIONS SPEAK LOUDER THAN WORDS (AND THOUGHTS)

If you have been thinking of doing something for days (e.g. 'I must update my website, arrange the holidays, etc.') without doing anything, it eats into your willpower. When you think of it, your brain concludes that you have already started working on it. Therefore, you can be 'working on it' for hours, days, weeks, years without producing anything. Attention (training) makes you aware of this behavioural pattern. You then have three options: acting, cancelling, or reassuring your brain that you will not forget to put it on your to-do list. It helps you put willpower and energy aside for other decisions.

STRENGTHENING YOUR WILLPOWER

Having consciously chosen the target for which you need your will-power, you can also strengthen your willpower muscle. Once again, there are five tips.

1. SHARE YOUR TARGET AND YOUR SUCCESSES

Do you want to stop smoking? Share your intention with friends and/or post your intention on Facebook. Does that sound scary? Yes, maybe, but it's also an extra motivating factor. As well as setting your intention, you've organized a support team. Your friends may send you messages such as 'You can do it!' and 'Wow, fantastic!' And if you've not smoked for six months? Then share this success with others. Research confirms the positive impact of external support and encouragement.[193]

2. DON'T FORGET THAT YOU ARE IN CONTROL

The feeling that you are in control will increase your willpower. Even the illusion of being in control boosts your willpower – fewer people feel afraid of driving a car than being in a plane. You lose willpower when you don't have a sense of autonomy; you become anxious or quit. In particular, an awareness of inner control boosts your willpower; in other words, the realization that you can deter-mine your own responses and behaviour. The realization that you can control your disappointment (see Part 2 about compassion) after an unsuccessful application will motivate you to try again in the job market. The (often unrealistic) concept of external control (thinking that you can make the HR manager do what you want them to do) tends to have a demotivating effect and reduces willpower.

3. CHANGE YOUR AUTOMATIC BEHAVIOURS

Embrace your automatic behaviours, not only to avoid wasting willpower, but also to exercise it. Start exercising easy habits. Do you always brush your teeth with your right hand? Now try your left hand. Practise standing on both feet instead of putting all your weight on one foot, try sitting straight at your desk, waiting at least a minute before you eat something tasty, parking your car in the same space (or a different space) every day. This is a playful way to practise your willpower on small tasks. If it starts to irritate you or bore you, take a break or choose an alternative. Choose activities that are not too demanding, but require some effort (and which you do not necessarily have to 'change', such as brushing your teeth with the other hand).

4. PUT YOUR LAZY SELF TO THE TASK

Does it disappoint you when, at the end of your working day, you review your achievements? Surely, you think, I could have done all that in less than two hours if I hadn't been checking my mailbox or phone. If this is a common occurrence, the 20 seconds rule[194] may help you. You use ingrained human laziness to get rid of bad habits by creating obstacles before you can carry them out. For example, log out of your email account and create an almost-impossible password – such as 'IcanonlyCheckmyemailsonceEvery3hoUrs!' – which will take up more time each time you want to check your inbox. It sounds clumsy and time-consuming, but in the end you will not log in as frequently because it requires 'so much' effort. It will soon put an end to your tendency to check emails. The 20 seconds rule can be applied to all kinds of bad habits. For example, put your phone with all its distracting apps in a drawer in a cupboard in your bedroom. Or do you want to eat less bread? Put it in the freezer, which means it first needs defrosting and then toasting: 'Too much trouble, forget it!' Putting your lazy self 'into action' increases your awareness of occasions when you are not doing well.

We all know that checking your smartphone before you go to bed will affect your sleep. And that it's not a good idea to start the day checking the news and sending messages, either. So, ban your phone from the bedroom – and, if necessary, buy an old-fashioned alarm clock.

SIT-UP

The 20 seconds rule can also be used in reverse to learn good habits. So you want to do more sports? Get your sportswear ready in the evening. You'd like to meditate regularly? Create a comfortable little area in your home with all you need already in place. You only need to stop and sit down.

5. VISUALIZE DANGER

In a moment of calm you may think 'I'll never again open a bottle of wine on a weekday', and you are full of good intentions. But come Tuesday evening, and you're exhausted, stressed and emotional after a horrible day at work, those intentions quickly drop away. Science calls this the 'hot–cold empathy gap', which is your inability, even when you are at your most rational and calm, to estimate your reduced level of self-control at difficult moments.

That gap will always be there, but you can try to visualize danger in advance. Imagine being offered delectable snacks at a drinks party and still saying firmly, 'No, thank you'. By visualizing the situation and your powerful response you are more likely to respond like this in real life.

GIVING YOUR WILLPOWER RECOVERY TIME

'Stress is not the greatest enemy of great achievements, it's the absence of recovery,' says the performance psychologist Jim Loehr. Treat willpower as if it were an achievement: recovery is crucial to build your willpower. Here are five tips to help you.

1. EAT HEALTHILY

Willpower needs glucose (energy) just like your muscles. Getting up early, rejecting a piece of cake, walking instead of taking a bus – when you apply your willpower, you use glucose. Your body wants to replenish it as quickly as possible. Sugar, sweets and other fast-absorbed carbohydrates are the quickest way. After this kind of energy boost, your glucose level drops even faster. You know the feeling: you end up tired and exhausted. At such moments, your willpower is at its weakest: you do not have the energy to drive yourself. You often find your 'solution' in quick-sugar foods: a bag of jelly babies or a cornet of chips... The vicious circle begins. Sugars are absorbed more slowly in foods with slow-absorbing carbohydrates. Your glucose level remains constant over a longer period, and your energy levels are balanced, which is a good, reliable source of willpower.

2. GET ENOUGH SLEEP

Yawn, surely we're not going to get that old lecture on sleep again, are we? Well, yes, you are, because, although much has been written about it, we continue to underestimate the need for a good night's sleep. In the old days, only parents with young children would have been caught nodding off at work, but now it's pretty much everyone. And the guilty party – the blue light from our laptops and smartphones, of course. But did you know that even making a phone call, watching television, or simply reading a magazine or a book slows down the production of melatonin (the hormone that makes you sleepy)? Your sleep deprivation makes you want quick-sugar foods the next day, because you need a quick boost of energy and because a lack of sleep obstructs the storage of glucose.

3. TAKE A BREAK

'I'm so busy!' In Western societies, this is now a common reply to the question: 'How are you?' And it's pretty much accurate of the state of affairs. The problem is running from one appointment to the next doesn't give your willpower a chance to recover. Try to embrace a more laid-back ethos by taking breaks. If you find that difficult, then go back to Part 1 about attention, where you will find plenty of techniques to help you.

4. USE LITTLE TRICKS AND TOOLS

Apply the 'Don't waste your money' motivation. We are all programmed to avoid loss. You're not exempt. Our suffering when we lose a thousand pounds is greater than our happiness if we win the same amount. Imagine you want to read three books this month. Place a substantial sum of money (e.g. £50) in an envelope, give it to a friend and agree that, if you are unsuccessful, your friend will give the money to a charity or cause you do not support. For example, if you normally vote Conservative, then give it to the Greens, or vice versa. Then discuss with a friend or your loved one what you will do with the money if you do read those three books: you could give them a present or take them out. This is a double gamble: you feel uncomfortable at the thought of giving a donation to your least favourite political party and you do not want to disappoint your friend.

EYE-OPENER

The SnūzNLūz alarm clock works on the same principle. The clock punishes you for (the unhealthy habit of) snoozing. The alarm clock is linked to your bank account via WIFI. Each time you hit the snooze button, a fixed amount gets deposited into the account of a designated charity you certainly wouldn't wish to support – the committed carnivore donates to the Vegan Society, the ardent atheist gives to the Church.

5. REWARD YOURSELF

The essential fuel for willpower is a reward to yourself. Did you clean the windows, and would you like to clean them frequently? Give yourself a little reward: a magazine, half an hour's downtime, or – OK, go on – a bar of chocolate. Next time it will take you less time to find the squeegee. Give yourself plenty of time for the reward, even if you think you do not have any. You will notice that it pays off at the end of the day; you will have more energy and willpower to go for that early-evening run.

SIT-UP

Make a little list of (healthy) rewards. Pin it on your noticeboard at home. If you think of other things over the coming days, add them to the list.

TRAINING

The integration of techniques that promote attention, compassion and happiness in your life depends entirely on willpower, which in turn relies on routine. This week you will use routine to exercise your willpower.

ıٍ LIGHT
EXERCISE 1: ROUTINE 1
Choose a daily routine which you are going to change. When you are used to the new routine, choose another routine and change that one...

EXERCISE 2: ROUTINE 2
Choose an activity which you often put off (e.g. a trip to the swimming pool, an attention exercise, cleaning, maintaining your website, ringing your grandmother) and choose a set day and time (or set days and times). Write down this activity in your diary. The more routine the activity becomes, the easier it will be for you to fulfil it.

EXERCISE 3: VISUALIZE DANGER
Take five minutes a day to visualize an obstructive pattern you want to break (e.g. checking your phone, unhealthy eating).

Imagine your constructive behaviour, vividly and concretely. If possible, stay with one pattern for several days.

EXERCISE 4: TWENTY SECONDS
Choose one habit you want to stop and apply the 20 seconds rule (detailed earlier in this chapter).

ıٍ MEDIUM

EXTENSION TO LIGHT Write a letter to yourself. Be encouraging, don't wag your finger, and record what you hope to take from these past 12 weeks and use over the rest of your life. Don't browse back through the book, but try to recall ideas and activities from memory. What comes to mind will be what you value most. What would you like to remember and what would you like to blend into your everyday life? Share some of your new insights.

Put the letter in an envelope, address it to yourself and attach a stamp. Then give it to a friend, a loved one or a relative, and tell them to post the letter whenever it suits them – at the latest after two months.

When you unexpectedly receive this letter from yourself, give yourself enough time to read it through carefully. It should act as a refresher and a boost. You could respond by writing a new letter to yourself – and so on.

ıll INTENSE

EXTENSION TO LIGHT + MEDIUM Leaf through the whole book again. Take your time. Underline, highlight, read actively. You may get something new out of passages you skipped over before, or find examples that give you fresh inspiration or insights. Write down which exercises you found most helpful. Which exercises would you like to continue using or do more often? Make it concrete using tips from this final chapter. Always keep that first tip, 'Limit your goals' in mind.

COOL DOWN

Sustainable change is made by making small changes to consciously chosen everyday routines; it doesn't occur in an epiphany when everything suddenly seems to fall into place. If you're waiting for a big moment of revelation, forget it – better still, throw it in the bin. Don't give up, but embrace any difficulties and inconveniences that arise when exercising your willpower and consolidating good, healthy habits. But stay alert: too much inconvenience can injure your willpower muscle.

Ask yourself if you have achieved any of the following in Week 12:

↔ Can you bring your self-imposed goals into alignment with your ultimate goal, a meaningful and happy life?
↔ Can you set goals from within self-correction instead of from within self-criticism?
↔ Do you know how to apply your routines to boost your willpower?
↔ Can you now see clearly how you can retain your willpower?
↔ Have you learned more tricks and exercises to strengthen your willpower?
↔ Do you realize the importance of giving your willpower recovery time?

IN CONCLUSION

In a hundred years' time we will probably look back on this time with amazement, just as we now look back at the witch hunts of the 15th–17th centuries with disbelief. We will wonder why on earth our culture, educational systems, organizations and governments were so fixated on material prosperity and economic growth. Why did our institutions unnecessarily fuel our evolutionary propensity for greed and selfishness? Why on earth was profit given more importance than life?

The Scientific Revolution has given us so much. With those little devices in our pockets we can reach anybody in the world; we fly in huge metal machines; we produce clever medicines; we live and work in buildings where you can literally touch the clouds and soon, perhaps, a holiday trip to the moon will be just like going to the Costa del Sol. In the West at least, we have experienced an unprecedented time of peace, and the average person enjoys a higher quality of life than the nobility or even the kings and queens of the past. Sonja Lyubomirsky puts it like this in *The How of Happiness*: 'We can produce convincing arguments that the degree of material comfort we currently enjoy is equal to that of the top 5 per cent who lived only half a century ago.'

That's great, but we need to move on from this: we are in the middle of the next step of our development from material to spiritual prosperity. We need to build a new society in which material wealth supports meaningful happiness, and not the other way around. A society in which we are not merely obsessed by short-term goals, but the ultimate goal, which is happiness itself, and the joy of our journey towards that goal. A society/world in which support and care for each other are the norm, and in where the term 'voluntary work' no longer exists, because it has become superfluous. A society, in short, built on a healthy, well-exercised mind.

It's an illusion to think that it will be an easy, quick and smooth process. In Arnold Bennett's words 'Any change, even a change for the better, is always accompanied by discomforts.' We need to abandon old systems and thought patterns to create a society based on greater happiness and meaning. It will be accompanied by a lot of discomfort. The witch-hunt phenomenon did not disappear overnight. But our history proves that it's possible and reasonable to hope. The number of violent crimes and wars has fallen dramatically over the past thousand years, and the freedom, health and life expectancy of many people have increased. If we continue to pursue this trend, our institutions, educational establishments and governments will eventually understand that material prosperity supports spiritual prosperity, the highest achievable goal. Sustainability, climate conservation and long-term perspectives will be the rule rather than the exception.

Perhaps this sounds like a pipedream, but remember, just thinking that thought is undermining. We are quick to blame the inadequacy of our system, as if we were its victims. In fact, we ourselves are the system, our minds are the source of the system; in other words, how we view the world makes that world. It may sound like a paradox, but the more we are concerned about our inner world, the more we care about the world around us. If we change our view of the world, then the world will change.

It is this relationship between mind and reality that explains why the happiness revolution can have a major impact on our world. Change is not imposed on us from the outside by interfering governments, dictators, rebel groups or terrorist organizations. It is a revolution from within. It is matter of a voluntary, personal and individual choice. If it were not, we would immediately undermine the happy society. Many revolutions are repulsive, but this revolution will have a magnetic effect, because our deepest core longs for happiness. Of course, talking about it (or reading a book about it) isn't enough; it requires action. And therein lies the challenge. In theory, many agree that a meaningful, happy society is the ideal, but not many are prepared to work towards it. The only way this revolution can gain momentum is if we begin it within our minds.

We are entirely responsible for our own minds, and our mind is something we can influence better than anything else. A healthy, happy mind does not happen to you; you train and shape it. And remember: if you don't exercise, it's not your breath but your head that will smell! You will be improving not only your own life but also the world around you. If you don't want to do it for your own benefit, do it for your family, your children, your friends.

Mind training requires discipline, resilience and courage, if you're not to give up on the bumpy road. You have to look inside yourself and let go of your old ideas. Choose courage over convenience. And if you ever wonder when's a good time to start, remind yourself that there's only one moment, the only moment that matters, the only moment you will ever have: NOW.

'Life is like a camera. Focus on what's important. Capture the good times. And if things don't work out, just take another shot.'

ZIAD K. ABDELNOUR

REFERENCES

1. mhfaengland.org/mhfa-centre/research-and-evaluation/mental-health-statistics/
2. www.centreformentalhealth.org.uk/publications/mental-health-work-business-costs-ten-years
3. Lyubomirsky, Sonja, Laura King and Ed Diener. 'The benefits of frequent positive affect: Does happiness lead to success?' *Psychological Bulletin* 131.6 (2005): 803–55. De Neve, Jan-Emmanuel, et al. 'The objective benefits of subjective well-being.' In Helliwell, John, Richard Layard and Jeffrey Sachs (ed.). *World Happiness Report* 2013. New York: Sustainable Development Solutions Network, 2013: 54–79.
4. www.adformatie.nl/nieuws/we-zien-377-reclames-dag (6 July 2017). www.quest.nl/artikel/hoeveel-reclame-zien-we-in-ons-leven (6 July 2017).
5. 'The brain is remarkable when it comes to collecting information and processing it. The more you feed it, the hungrier it gets. Technology is now feeding it an ever-expanding diet.' Bruce Morton, researcher at the University of Western Ontario's Brain & Mind Institute. See nationalpost.com/news/canada/canadians-now-have-shorter-attention-span-than-goldfish-thanks-to-portable-devices-microsoft-study (13 March 2016).

6. Davidson, Richard J., et al. 'Alterations in brain and immune function produced by mindfulness meditation.' *Psychosomatic Medicine* 65.4 (2003): 564–70.

7. Goyal, Madhav, et al. 'Meditation programs for psychological stress and well-being: A systematic review and meta-analysis.' JAMA, *The Journal of the American Medical Association* 174.3 (2014): 357–68.

8. www.pnas.org/content/102/51/18626. (7 October 2016).

9. Loukopoulos, Loukia D., Key Dismukes and Immanuel Barshi. *The Multitasking Myth: Handling Complexity in Real-World Operations.* Farnham: Ashgate Publishing, 2009.

10. Wegner, Daniel M., Alexis Broome and Stephen J. Blumberg. 'Ironic effects of trying to relax under stress.' *Behaviour Research and Therapy* 35.1 (1997): 11–21.

11. www.fsw.leidenuniv.nl/nieuws-2011/lorenza-colzato-en-peter-buwalda-in-pavlov-over-creativiteit-en-mediteren.html (7 February 2017).

12. Smallwood, Jonathan, Daniel J. Fishman and Jonathan W. Schooler. 'Counting the cost of an absent mind: Mind wandering as an underrecognized influence on educational performance.' *Psychonomic Bulletin & Review* 14.2 (2007): 230–6.

13. 'Watch the 'Door' Study by Daniel Simons and Daniel Levin at www.youtube.com/watch?v=FWSxSQsspiQ (15 June 2017).

14. Bradt, Steve. 'Wandering mind not a happy mind.' *Harvard Gazette* 11 (2010).

15. Wansink, Brian and Jeffery Sobal, 'Mindless eating: The 200 daily food decisions we overlook.' *Environment and Behavior* 39.1 (2007): 106–23.

16. Del Percio, Claudio, et al. 'Neural efficiency of athletes brain for upright standing: A high-resolution EEG study.' *Psychological Bulletin* 79.3 (2009): 193–200.

17. Jamieson, Jeremy P., Matthew K. Nock and Wendy Berry Mendes. 'Mind over matter: Reappraising arousal improves cardiovascular and cognitive responses to stress.' *Journal of Experimental Psychology: General* 141.3 (2012): 417–22.

18. Bechara, Antoine, et al. 'Deciding advantageously before knowing the advantageous strategy.' *Science* 275.5304 (1997): 1293–5.

19. Kraft, Tara L. and Sarah D. Pressman. 'Grin and bear it: The influence of manipulated facial expression on the stress response.' *Psychological Science* 23.11 (2012): 1372–8.

20. These estimates are still controversial, but the consensus is that it runs into tens of thousands of thoughts a day. Estimate based on the National Science Foundation. See https://www.huffpost.com/entry/healthy-relationships_b_3307916 (8 November 2017). Research at Loni Laboratory of Neuroimaging even estimates 70,000 thoughts per day.

21. Mehl, Matthias R., et al. 'Are women really more talkative than men?' *Science* 317.5834 (2007): 82.

22. Wilson, Timothy D., et al. 'Just think: The challenges of the disengaged mind.' *Science* 345.6192 (2014): 75–7.

23. Bushman, Brad J. 'Does venting anger feed or extinguish the flame? Catharsis, rumination, distraction, anger, and aggressive responding.' *Personality and Social Psychology Bulletin* 28.6 (2002): 724–31.

24. Creswell, J. David, et al. 'Neural correlates of dispositional mindfulness during affect labeling.' *Psychosomatic Medicine* 69.6 (2007): 560–5.

25. Vago, David R. en Silbersweig A. David. 'Self-awareness, self-regulation, and self-transcendence (S-ART): A framework for understanding the neurobiological mechanisms of mindfulness.' *Frontiers in Human Neuroscience* 6 (2012): 296.

26. Tashani, O. A., D. Burnett, and G. Phillips. 'The effect of brief mindfulness meditation on cold-pressor induced pain responses in healthy adults.' *Pain Studies and Treatment* 5 (2017): 11–19.

27. Greenberg, Jonathan, Keren Reiner and Nachshon Meiran. '"Mind the Trap": Mindfulness practice reduces cognitive rigidity.' *PloS ONE* 7.5 (2012): e36206.

28. Taken from John Keats. See Keats, John. 'Selections from Keats's Letters (1817).' *Poetry Foundation* (2009).

29. Frankl, Viktor. *Man's Search for Meaning.* London: Rider, 2004.
30. Chiesa, Alberto and Alessandro Serretti. 'Mindfulness-based stress reduction for stress management in healthy people: A review and meta-analysis.' *The Journal of Alternative and Complementary Medicine* 15.5 (2009): 593–600.
31. Carver, Ronald, Raymond Johnson and Herbert Friedman. 'Factor analysis of the ability to comprehend time-compressed speech.' *Journal of Literacy Research* 4.1 (1971): 40–9.
32. Duhachek, Adam, Shuoyang Zhang and Shanker Krishnan. 'Anticipated group interaction: Coping with valence asymmetries in attitude shift.' *Journal of Consumer Research* 34.3 (2007): 395–405.
33. Wacker, Katherine and Katherine Hawkins. 'Curricula comparison for classes in listening.' *International Journal of Listening* 9.1 (1995): 14–28.
34. Stauffer, John, Richard Frost and William Rybolt. 'The attention factor in recalling network television news.' *International Journal of Listening* 33.1 (1983): 29–37.
35. Janusik, Laura and Andrew Wolvin. 'Listening treatment in the basic communication course text.' *Basic Communication Course Annual* 14 (2002): 164–210.
36. Carver, Ronald, Raymond Johnson and Herbert Friedman. 'Factor analysis of the ability to comprehend time-compressed speech.' *Journal of Literacy Research* 4.1 (1971): 40–9.
37. Scharmer, Otto. *Theorie U.* Zeist: Uitgeverij Christofoor, 2010, 157–261.
38. Huber, Cheri. *The Key: And the Name of the Key is Willingness.* Keep It Simple Books, 1998.
39. Study by Stanford psychologist Brian Knutson in 2008, repeated later using brain scans. The results will be made public.
40. According to Kristin Neff's model.
41. Buss, David. 'Sex differences in human mate preferences: Evolutionary hypotheses tested in 37 cultures.' *Behavioral and Brain Sciences* 12.1 (1989): 1–14.
42. For interesting compassion research, see http://ccare.stanford.edu/research/peer-reviewed-ccare-articles.

43. Lutz, Antoine, et al. 'Long-term meditators self-induce high-amplitude gamma synchrony during mental practice.' *Proceedings of the National Academy of Sciences of the United States of America* 101.46 (2004): 16369–73.

44. Taylor, Shelley. 'Tend and befriend: Bio-behavioral bases or affiliation under stress.' *Current Directions in Psychological Science* 15.6 (2006): 273–7.

45. McGonigal, Kelly. 'How to make stress your friend.' TEDGlobal, Edinburgh, 2013.

46. Kohn, Alfie. *The Brighter Side of Human Nature: Altruism and Empathy in Everyday Life*. New York: Basic Books, 2008.

47. Neff, Kristin and Christopher Germer. 'A pilot study and randomized controlled trial of the mindful self-compassion program.' *Journal of Clinical Psychology* 69.1 (2013): 28–44.

48. Baumeister, Roy, et al. 'Does high self-esteem cause better performance, interpersonal success, happiness, or healthier lifestyles?' *Psychological Science in the Public Interest* 4.1 (2003): 1–44.

49. Ratner, Kyle and David Amodio. 'N170 responses to faces predict implicit ingroup favoritism: Evidence from a minimal group study.' *Social & Affective Neuroscience Society Meeting* 10 (2009), www.wjh.harvard.edu/~scanlab/SANS/docs/SANS_program_2099.pdf.

50. Frank, Robert H. *The Economic Naturalist: In Search of Solutions to Everyday Enigmas*. New York: Basic Books, 2007.

51. Leary, Mark, et al. 'Self-compassion and reactions to unpleasant self-relevant events: The implications of treating oneself kindly.' *Personality and Social Psychology Bulletin* 92.5 (2007): 887–904.

52. Neff, Kristin, Kristin Kirkpatrick and Stephanie Rude. 'Self-compassion and adaptive psychological functioning.' *Journal of Research in Personality* 41.1 (2007): 139–54. Neff, Kristin and Roos Vonk. 'Self-compassion versus global self-esteem: Two different ways of relating to oneself.' *Journal of Research in Personality* 77.1 (2009): 23–50.

53. Mischel, Walter and Ozlem Ayduk. 'Willpower in a cognitive-affective processing system: The dynamics of delay of gratification.' In Baumeister, Roy and Kathleen Vohs (ed.). *Handbook of Self-Regulation: Research, Theory, and Applications*. New York: Guilford, 2004: 99–129.

54. Nørgaard, Marianne, Preben Pedersen and Merete Bjerrum. 'Visualisation during ablation of atrial fibrillation – stimulating the patient's own resources: Patients' experiences in relation to pain and anxiety during an intervention of visualisation.' *European Journal of Cardiovascular Nursing* 14.6 (2015): 552–9.

55. Ibid.

56. Mondaini, Nicola, et al. 'Finasteride 5 mg and sexual side effects: How many of these are related to a nocebo phenomenon?' *The Journal of Sexual Medicine* 4.6 (2007): 1708–12.

57. Dijksterhuis, Ap and Ad van Knippenberg. 'The relationship between perception and behavior, or how to win a game of trivial pursuit.' *Personality and Social Psychology Bulletin* 74.4 (1998): 865–77.

58. Tifanny Field, Touch in Early Development. Hove: Psychology Press, 2014.

59. Spitz, Rene A. 'Hospitalism: An inquiry into the genesis of psychiatric conditions in early childhood.' *The Psychoanalytic Study of the Child* 1 (1945): 53–74.

60. Kraus, Michael, Cassey Huang and Dacher Keltner. 'Tactile communication, cooperation, and performance: An ethological study of the NBA.' *Science* 10.5 (2010): 745–9. 0345 300 8844

61. Linden, David. *Touch: The Science of Hand, Heart, and Mind*. London: Penguin Books, 2016.

62. Guerrero, Laura and Peter Andersen. 'The waxing and waning of relational intimacy: Touch as a function of relational stage, gender and touch avoidance.' *Journal of Social and Personal Relationships* 8.2 (1991): 147–65.

63. Ibid.

64. Neff, Kristin and Christopher Germer. 'A pilot study and rando-mized controlled trial of the mindful self-compassion program.' *Journal of Clinical Psychology* 69.1 (2013): 28–44.

65. Swann, W. B., Jr. 'To be adored or to be known? The interplay of self-enhancement and self-verification.' In E. T. Higgins and R.M. Sorrentino (eds). *Handbook of Motivation and Cognition: Founda-tions of Social Behavior*, Part 2. New York: Guilford Press, 1990: 408–48. Joiner Jr, Thomas, Mark Alfano and Gerald Metalsky. 'Caught in the crossfire: Depression, self-consistency, self-enhancement, and the response of others.' *Journal of Clinical Psychology* 12.2 (1993): 113–34.

66. Swann, W. B., Jr. 'The trouble with change: Self-verification and allegiance to the self.' *Psychological Science* 8.3 (1997): 177–80.

67. Pink, Daniel. *Drive: The Surprising Truth about what Motivates Us*. London: Penguin Books, 2011.

68. Neff, Kristin, Ya-Ping Hsieh and Kullaya Dejitterat. 'Self-compassion, achievement goals, and coping with academic failure.' *Self and Identity* 4 (2005): 263–87.

69. Bandura, Albert. *Self-Efficacy: The Exercise of Control*. Belper: Worth Publishers, 1997.

70. Neff, Kristin, Ya-Ping Hsieh and Kullaya Dejitterat. 'Self-compassion, achievement goals, and coping with academic failure.' *Self and Identity* 4 (2005): 263–87.

71. Cacioppo, John and William Patrick. *Loneliness: Human Nature and the Need for Social Connection*. New York: W. W. Norton & Company, 2008.

72. Neff, Kristin, Ya-Ping Hsieh and Kullaya Dejitterat. 'Self-compassion, achievement goals, and coping with academic failure.' *Self and Identity* 4 (2005): 263–87.

73. This exercise is based on Paul Gilbert's work.

74. Werner, Oswald. 'Sapir-Whorf Hypothesis.' In Lamarque, Peter (ed.). *Concise Encyclopedia of Philosophy of Language*. Oxford: New York: Elsevier Science Ltd., 1997: 76–83.

75. Winawer, Jonathan, et al. 'Russian blues reveal effects of language on color discrimination.' *Proceedings of the National Academy of Sciences of the United States of America* 104.19 (2007): 7780–5.

76. Wood, Joanne V., W. Q. Elaine Perunovic and John W. Lee. 'Positive Self-Statements Power for Some, Peril for Others.' *Psychological Science* 20.7 (2009): 860–6.

77. Carson, James, et al. 'Loving-kindness meditation for chronic low back pain: Results from a pilot trial.' *Journal of Holistic Nursing* 23.3 (2005): 287–304.

78. Burton, Chad and Laura King. 'The health benefits of writing about positive experiences: The role of broadened cognition.' *Psychology & Health* 24.8 (2009): 867–79.

79. Burton, Chad and Laura King. 'Effects of (very) brief writing on health: The two-minute miracle.' *British Journal of Health Psychology* 13.1 (2008): 9–14.

80. www.cbs.nl/nl-nl/nieuws/2015/39/een-half-miljoen-mensen-voelt-zich-eenzaam (6 September 2017).

81. Cacioppo, John, et al. 'Loneliness as a specific risk factor for depressive symptoms: Cross-sectional and longitudinal analyses.' *Psychology and Aging* 21.1 (2006): 140. Luo, Ye, et al. 'Loneliness, health, and mortality in old age: A national longitudinal study.' *Social Science & Medicine* 74.6 (2012): 907–14.

82. www.youtube.com/watch?v=jD8tjhVO1Tc (4 February 2017).

83. Valdesolo, Piercarlo and David DeSteno. 'Synchrony and the social tuning of compassion.' *Emotion* 11.2 (2011): 262.

84. Klimecki, Olga M., Susanne Leiberg, Ricard Matthieu and Tania Singer. 'Differential pattern of functional brain plasticity after compassion and empathy training.' *Social Cognitive and Affective Neuroscience* 9.6 (2013): 873–9.

85. Lamm, Claus, Jean Decety and Tania Singer. 'Meta-analytic evidence for common and distinct neural networks associated with directly experienced pain and empathy for pain.' *Neuroimage* 54.3 (2011): 2492–502.

86. Klimecki, Olga and Tania Singer. 'Empathic distress fatigue rather than compassion fatigue? Integrating findings from empathy

research in psychology and social neuroscience.' In Oakley, Barbara, et al. (ed.). *Pathological Altruism*. Oxford: Oxford University Press, 2011: 363–7.

87. www.youtube.com/watch?v=apzXGEbZhto (18 August 2017).

88. Noë, Alva. *Out of Our Heads: Why You Are Not Your Brain, and Other Lessons from the Biology of Consciousness*. New York: Macmillan, 2009: 30–1.

89. Sroufe, L. Alan, et al. *The Development of the Person: The Minnesota Study of Risk and Adaptation from Birth to Adulthood*. New York: Guilford Press, 2005: 268.

90. Mikulincer, Mario and Phillip Shaver. 'Attachment security, compassion, and altruism.' *Current Directions in Psychological Science* 14.1 (2005): 34–8.

91. Stefanie Tignor and C. Randall Colvin. 'The interpersonal adaptiveness of dispositional guilt and shame: A meta-analytic investigation.' *Journal of Personality* 85.3 (2017): 341–63.

92. Davidson, Karina and Elizabeth Mostofsky. 'Anger expression and risk of coronary heart disease: Evidence from the Nova Scotia Health Survey.' *American Heart Journal* 159.2 (2010): 199–206.

93. Chodron, Pema. *The Places That Scare You: A Guide to Fearlessness in Difficult Times*. Boulder: Shambhala Publications, 2007.

94. McCullough, Michael and Charlotte Vanoyen Witvliet. 'The psychology of forgiveness.' In Lopez, Shane J. and C.R. Snyder (ed.). *Handbook of Positive Psychology*. Oxford: Oxford University Press, 2002: 446–55.

95. Worthington, Everett, Steven Sandage and Jack Berry. 'Group interventions to promote forgiveness.' In McCullough, Michael E., Kenneth I. Pargament and Carl E. Thoresen (eds). *Forgiveness: Theory, Research, and Practice*. New York: Guilford Press, 2001: 228–53. Harris, Alex and Carl Thoresen. 'Extending the influence of positive psychology interventions into health care settings: Lessons from self-efficacy and forgiveness.' *The Journal of Positive Psychology* 1.1 (2006): 27–36.

96. DePaulo, Bella et al. 'Lying in everyday life.' *Journal of Personality and Social Psychology* 70.5 (1996): 979–95.

97. Niedenthal, Paula. 'Embodying emotion.' *Science* 316.5827 (2007): 1002–5.
98. Watch the online documentary Story of stuff or visit www. storyofstuff.org.
99. www.oxfam.org/en/research/economy-1 (19 July 2017).
100. The World Bank. *Poverty Data: A Supplement to World Development Indicators 2008*. Washington, DC: The World Bank, 2008.
101. UNICEF. *Progress for Children: A Report Card on Nutrition*. New York: UNICEF, 2006.
102. Díaz, Sandra, et al. 'Biodiversity loss threatens human wellbeing.' *PLoS Biology* 4.8 (2006): e277.
103. Ellis, Erle, et al. 'Anthropogenic transformation of the biomes, 1700 to 2000.' *Global Ecology and Biogeography* 19.5 (2010): 589–606.
104. Norberg, Johan. *Vooruitgang*. Amsterdam: Nieuw Amsterdam, 2016.
105. www.independent.co.uk/voices/five-things-would-happen-if-everyonestopped-eating-meat-a6844811.html (21 March 2017).
106. www.youtube.com/watch?v=fyZQfop73QM (8 May 2017).
107. Gazzaniga, Michael. *Human: The Science behind What Makes Us Unique*. New York: HarperCollins, 2008.
108. Oveis, Christopher, Elizabeth J. Horberg and Dacher Keltner. 'Compassion, pride, and social intuitions of self-other similarity.' *Journal of Personality and Social Psychology* 98.4 (2010): 618–30. Sprecher, Susan and Beverley Fehr. 'Compassionate love for close others and humanity.' Journal of Social and Personal Relationships 22.5 (2005): 629–51. Weng, Helen Y., et al. 'Compassion training alters altruism and neural responses to suffering.' *Psychological Science* 24.7 (2013): 1171–80.
109. This is an idea by Christopher Germer.

110. Kashdan, Todd and Robert Biswas-Diener. *The Upside of Your Dark Side: Why Being Your Whole Self – Not Just Your 'Good' Self – Drives Success and Fulfillment.* London: Penguin, 2014.

111. A remark by Tal Ben-Shahar.

112. Lyubomirsky, Sonja, Laura King and Ed Diener. 'The benefits of frequent positive affect: Does happiness lead to success?' *Psychological Bulletin* 131.6 (2005): 803–55.

113. Ibid. Ferguson, Yuna and Kennon Sheldon. 'Trying to be happier really can work: Two experimental studies.' *The Journal of Positive Psychology* 8.1 (2013): 23–33.

114. Danner, Deborah, David Snowdon and Wallace Friesen. 'Positive emotions in early life and longevity: Findings from the Nun Study.' *Journal of Personality and Social Psychology* 80.5 (2001): 804–13.

115. Quote by Agnes Replier.

116. Boorstein, Sylvia. *Happiness Is an Inside Job*, audiobook. Ashland Blackstone Audiobooks, 2008.

117. Milton, John. 'Paradise Lost'. Samuel Simmons, 1667.

118. Goldsmith, Kelly, et al. 'Happiness in the workplace: Employees who focus on maximizing happiness become happier.' Working paper, Northwestern University, 2013. Available from SSRN: dx.doi.org/10.2139/ssrn.1979829.

119. Mauss, Iris B., et al. 'Can seeking happiness make people unhappy? Paradoxical effects of valuing happiness.' *Emotion* 11.4 (2011): 807. Schooler, Jonathan W., Dan Ariely and George Loewenstein. 'The pursuit and assessment of happiness can be self-defeating.' In Brocs, Isabelle and Juan D. Carillo (eds). *The Psychology of Economic Decisions*, part 1. Oxford: Oxford University Press, 2003: 41–70.

120. Mischel, Walter, et al. '"Willpower" over the life span: Decomposing self-regulation.' *Social Cognitive and Affective Neuroscience* 6.2 (2011): 252–6.

121. Lyubomirsky, Sonja, Laura King and Ed Diener. 'The benefits of frequent positive affect: Does happiness lead to success?'

Psychological Bulletin 131.6 (2005): 803–55. De Neve, Jan-Emmanuel, et al. 'The objective benefits of subjective well-being.' In Helliwell, John, Richard Layard and Jeffrey Sachs (eds). *World Happiness Report 2013*. New York: Sustainable Development Solutions Network, 2013: 54–79.

122. Harker, LeeAnne and Dacher Keltner. 'Expressions of positive emotion in women's college yearbook pictures and their relationship to personality and life outcomes across adulthood.' *Journal of Personality and Social Psychology* 80.1 (2001): 112.

123. Frijda, Nico H. *The Emotions: Studies in Emotion and Social Interaction*. Paris: Maison de sciences de l'homme, 1986. Lazarus, Richard S. 'Cognition and motivation in emotion.' *American Psychologist* 46.4 (1991): 352

124. Fredrickson, Barbara and Christine Branigan. 'Positive emotions broach the scope of attention and thought-action repertoires.' *Cognition & Emotion* 19.3 (2005): 313–32.

125. Crowley, Chris and Henry S. Lodge. *Younger Next Year: A Guide to Living like 50 until You're 80 and Beyond*. New York: Workman Publishing Company, 2004. Davidson, Richard J., Daren C. Jackson and Ned H. Kalin. 'Emotion, plasticity, context, and regulation: Perspectives from affective neuroscience.' *Psychological Bulletin* 126.6 (2000): 890.

126. Metaphor by Barbara Fredrickson.

127. Fredrickson, Barbara and Robert Levenson. 'Positive emotions speed recovery from the cardiovascular sequelae of negative emotions.' *Cognition & Emotion* 12.2 (1998): 191–220.

128. Dickerhoof, Rene Melissa. *Expressing Optimism and Gratitude: A Longitudinal Investigation of Cognitive Strategies to Increase Well-Being*. Riverside: University of California, Riverside, 2007. Fredrickson, Barbara, et al. 'The undoing effect of positive emotions.' *Motivation and Emotion* 24.4 (2000): 237–58.

129. Fredrickson, Barbara and Marcial Losada. 'Positive affect and the complex dynamics of human flourishing.' *American Psychologist* 60.7 (2005): 678–86.

130. Ibid.
131. Losada, Marcial and Emily Heaphy. 'The role of positivity and connectivity in the performance of business teams a nonlinear dynamics model.' *American Behavioral Scientist* 47.6 (2004): 740–65.
132. Although the mathematical model underpinning the 3:1 ratio has been questioned, the hypothesis that people with a high positivity ratio will flourish more remains valid. Also see Brown, Nicholas, Alan Sokal and Harris Friedman. 'The complex dynamics of wishful thinking: The critical positivity ratio.' *American Psychologist* 68.9 (2013): 801–13. Fredrickson, Barbara. 'Updated thinking on positivity ratios.' *American Psychologist* 68.9 (2013): 814–22.
133. Emmons, R. A. and C. S. Shelton. 'Gratitude and the science of positive psychology.' In Lopez, Shane J. and C.R. Snyder (eds). *Handbook of positive psychology.* Oxford: Oxford University Press, 2002: 459–71.
134. Sheldon, Kennon and Sonja Lyubomirsky. 'How to increase and sustain positive emotion: The effects of expressing gratitude and visualizing best possible selves.' *The Journal of Positive Psychology* 1.2 (2006): 73–82.
135. McCullough, Michael, Robert Emmons and Jo-Ann Tsang. 'The grateful disposition: A conceptual and empirical topography.' *Journal of Personality and Social Psychology* 82.1 (2002): 112–27. McCullough, Michael, Jo-Ann Tsang and Robert Emmons. 'Gratitude in intermediate affective terrain: Links of grateful moods to individual differences and daily emotional experience.' *Journal of Personality and Social Psychology* 86.2 (2004): 295–309. Algoe, Sara and Jonathan Haidt. 'Witnessing excellence in action: The "other-praising" emotions of elevation, gratitude, and admiration.' *The Journal of Positive Psychology* 4.2 (2009): 105–27. Bartlett, Monica and David DeSteno. 'Gratitude and prosocial behavior helping when it costs you.' *Psychological Science* 17.4 (2006): 319–25.

136. Ryan, Mary Jane. *Attitudes of Gratitude: How to Give and Receive Joy Every Day of Your Life.* San Francisco: Conari Press, 2009.

137. Gable, Shelly, et al. 'What do you do when things go right? The intrapersonal and interpersonal benefits of sharing positive events.' *Journal of Personality and Social Psychology* 87.2 (2004): 228–45.

138. Croft, Alyssa, Elizabeth Dunn and Jordi Quoidbach. 'From tribulations to appreciation experiencing adversity in the past predicts greater savoring in the present.' *Social Psychological and Personality Science* 5.5 (2014): 511–16.

139. Lyubomirsky, Sonja, et al. 'Becoming happier takes both a will and a proper way: an experimental longitudinal intervention to boost well-being.' *Emotion* 11.2 (2011): 391.

140. Giltay, Erik, et al. 'Dispositional optimism and all-cause and cardiovascular mortality in a prospective cohort of elderly Dutch men and women.' *Archives of General Psychiatry* 61.11 (2004): 1126–35.

141. Mount, Joan. 'Depression among lawyers.' *The Colorado Lawyer* 33 (2004): 35–7.

142. Piper, Alan T. '*Zukunftsangst*! Fear of (and hope for) the future and its impact on life satisfaction.' SOEPpaper No. 706, November 2014. Available from SSRN: ssrn.com/abstract=2533882 or http://dx.doi.org/10.2139/ssrn.2533882.

143. Oettingen, Gabriele, Hyeon-ju Pak and Karoline Schnetter. 'Self-regulation of goal-setting: Turning free fantasies about the future into binding goals.' *Journal of Personality and Social Psychology* 80.5 (2001): 736.

144. Meevissen, Yvo, Madelon Peters and Hugo Alberts. 'Become more optimistic by imagining a best possible self: Effects of a two week intervention.' *Journal of Behavior Therapy and Experimental Psychiatry* 42.3 (2011): 371–8.

145. Abramson, Lyn, Martin Seligman and John Teasdale. 'Learned helplessness in humans: Critique and reformulation.' *Journal of Clinical Psychology* 87.1 (1978): 49–4.

146. Hanson, Rick. *Geheugen voor geluk. Neem het goede in je op voor een beter leven.* Utrecht: Publisher Ten Have, 2014.
147. Diener, Ed and Martin Seligman. 'Very happy people.' *Psychological Science* 13.1 (2002): 81–4.
148. Lyubomirsky, Sonja, Laura King and Ed Diener. 'The benefits of frequent positive affect: Does happiness lead to success?' *Psychological Bulletin* 131.6 (2005): 803–55.
149. Inspired by Dutton, Jane and Emily Heaphy. 'The power of high-quality connections.' In Cameron, Kim S., Jane E. Dutton and Robert E. Quinn. *Positive organizational scholarship: Foundations of a New Discipline.* San Francisco: Berrett-Koehler, 2003: 263–78.
150. Scherwitz, L. and J. C. Canick. 'Self-reference and coronary heart disease.' In Houston, B.K. and J.C. Canick (eds). *Type A Behavior Pattern: Research, Theory, and Intervention.* Oxford: Oxford University Press, 1998: 146–67.
151. Zimmermann, Johannes, et al. 'The way we refer to ourselves reflects how we relate to others: Associations between first-person pronoun use and interpersonal problems.' *Journal of Research in Personality* 47.3 (2013): 218–25.
152. Stark, Kio. *Hoe praten met vreemden je leven kan veranderen.* Amsterdam: Amsterdam University Press, 2016.
153. Gottman, John and Nan Silver. Th*e Seven Principles for Making Marriage Work: A Practical Guide from the Country's Foremost Relationship Expert.* New York: Harmony, 2015.
154. Centerwall, Brandon S. 'Television and violence: The scale of the problem and where to go from here.' *JAMA* 267.22 (1992): 3059–63.
155. Bohnet, Iris and Richard Zeckhauser. 'Trust, risk and betrayal.' *Journal of Economic Behavior & Organization* 55.4 (2004): 467484.
156. Zak, Paul. *The Moral Molecule: The New Science of What Makes Us Good or Evil.* London: Random House, 2013. Berg, Joyce, John Dickhaut and Kevin McCabe. 'Trust, reciprocity,

and social history.' *Environment and Behavior* 10.1 (1995): 122–42.

157. Covey, Stephen. *Smart Trust: Creating Prosperity, Energy, and Joy in a Low-trust World*. New York: Simon and Schuster, 2012. Raj Raghunatha. Als je zo slim bent waarom ben je dan niet gelukkig. Amsterdam: Business Contact, 2015: 218–23.

158. Story from the documentary *(Dis)honesty: The Truth about Lies*. Salty Features, 2015.

159. Term by Dacher Keltner.

160. For a good overview, read Collins, James Charles. *Good to Great: Why Some Companies Make the Leap ... and Others Don't*. London: Random House, 2001. Keltner, Dacher. *The Power Paradox: How We Gain and Lose Influence*. New York: Penguin, 2000.

161. Numerous studies are cited to confirm this in Noelle Nelson, *Make More Money by Making Your Employees Happy* (Malibu: MindLabPublishing, 2012).

162. Kopelman, Shirli, Ashleigh Shelby Rosette and Leigh Thompson. 'The three faces of Eve: Strategic displays of positive, negative, and neutral emotions in negotiations.' *Organizational Behavior and Human Decision Processes* 99.1 (2006): 81–101.

163. Kohn, Alfie. *No Contest. The Case against Competition*. Boston, MA: Houghton Mifflin Harcourt, 1992.

164. Titmuss, Richard. *The Gift Relationship: From Human Blood to Social Policy*. New York: Guilford Press, 1997: 339. The experiment was reconfirmed in 2008 in Mellström, Carl and Magnus Johannesson. 'Crowding out in blood donation: Was Titmuss right?' *Journal of the European Economic Association* 6.4 (2008): 845–63.

165. Schwartz, Carolyn and Rabbi Meir Sendor. 'Helping others helps oneself: Response shift effects in peer support.' *Social Science & Medicine* 48.11 (1999): 1563–75.

166. Based on the story in the Fargo series.

167. Dunn, Elizabeth and Michael Norton. *Happy Money: The Science of Happier Spending*. New York: Simon and Schuster, 2014.

168. www.youtube.com/watch?v=Xm-T3HCa618 (8 April 2017).

169. Koike, Takahiko, et al. 'Neural substrates of shared attention as social memory: A hyperscanning functional magnetic resonance imaging study.' *NeuroImage* 125 (2016): 401–12.

170. www.nytimes.com/2015/01/11/fashion/modern-love-to-fall-in-love-with-anyone-do-this.html?_r=2 (16 August 2017).

171. Gable, Shelly, et al. 'What do you do when things go right? The intrapersonal and interpersonal benefits of sharing positive events.' *Journal of Personality and Social Psychology* 87.2 (2004): 228–45.

172. Ibid.

173. Korthagen, Fred and Ellen Nuijten. *Krachtgericht coachen*. Amsterdam: Boom Uitgevers, 2015.

174. en.wikipedia.org/wiki/Microexpression (9 May 2017).

175. For a more in-depth technique, read Branden, Nathaniel. *The Six Pillars of Self-Esteem*. New York: Bantam Dell Publishing Group, 1995.

176. Taken from Ben-Shahar, Tal. *Gelukkiger*. Amsterdam: Archipel, 2008.

177. Carver, Ronald, Raymond Johnson and Herbert Friedman. 'Factor analysis of the ability to comprehend time-compressed speech.' *Journal of Literacy Research* 4.1 (1971): 40-9.

178. Story inspired by the story read by Jack Kornfield on his summer retreats.

179. Inspired by Ben-Shahar, Tal. *Gelukkiger*. Amsterdam: Archipel, 2008.

180. Luthans, Fred. 'Positive organizational behavior: Developing and managing psychological strengths.' *The Academy of Management Executive* 16.1 (2002): 57–72. Also see Clifton, Donald and James Harter. 'Investing in strengths.' In Cameron, Kim S., Jane E. Dutton and Robert E. Quinn. *Positive Organizational Scholarship:*

Foundations of a New Discipline. San Francisco: Berrett-Koehler, 2003: 111–21.

181. Peterson, Christopher and Martin Seligman. *Character Strengths and Virtues: A Handbook and Classification*, part 1. Oxford: Oxford University Press, 2004.

182. Seligman, Martin, et al. 'Positive psychology progress: Empirical validation of interventions.' *American Psychologist* 60.5 (2005): 410–21.

183. Csikszentmihalyi, Mihaly. *De weg naar flow*. Amsterdam: Boom Koninklijke Uitgevers.

184. Adams, Susan. 'Unhappy employees outnumber the happy by two to one.' *Forbes* 10 (9 May 2017), www.forbes.com/sites/susanadams/2013/10/10/unhappy-employees-outnumber-happy-ones-by-two-to-one-worldwide/#1ca4f519362a.

185. www.independent.co.uk/life-style/british-people-work-days-lifetime-overtime-quit-job-survey-study-a8556146.html.

186. Wrzesniewski, Amy, et al. 'Jobs, careers, and callings: People's relations to their work.' *Journal of Research in Personality* 31.1 (1997): 21–33.

187. Ibarra, Herminia. *Working Identity: Unconventional Strategies for Reinventing Your Career*. Brighton, MA: Harvard Business Press, 2013.

188. Norcross, John, Marci Mrykalo and Matthew Blagys. 'Auld lang Syne: Success predictors, change processes, and self-reported outcomes of New Year's resolvers and nonresolvers.' *Journal of Clinical Psychology* 58.4 (2002): 397–405.

189. Baumeister, Roy and John Tierney. *Willpower: Rediscovering the Greatest Human Strength*. New York: Penguin, 2011.

190. Ibid.

191. Schwartz, Barry. *The Paradox of Choice: Why More Is Less*. New York: Ecco, 2004.

192. http://blog.ted.com/the-science-of-willpower-kelly-mcgonigal-on-why-its-so-dang-hard-to-stick-to-a-resolution (9 July 2017).

193. www.ideafit.com/fitness-library/science-willpower-0. (1 August 2017).
194. Inspired by Achor, Shawn. *The Happiness Advantage: The Seven Principles of Positive Psychology That Fuel Success and Performance at Work.* New York: Random House, 2011.

ACKNOWLEDGEMENTS

Wouter de Jong

Maud Beucker Andreae, I thank you from the bottom of my heart for your enormous commitment, talent, insight and friendship. Without you, this would have a book whose long-windedness would have given my readers a headache rather than spiritual enlighten- ment. Many thanks to the best publishing company I could have wished for – to Emma, Juliët, Lydia, Mariska, Sander, Dorien, Gabina and Evelien. Committed, alert, creative, you are a bunch of smart, cool guys. Thank you, Marja Duin, you have more than lived up to the title 'the Rambo among editors'. Judith Schoffelen, thank you for the enormous choice of book covers you provided me with. My friends Lubert, Died, Swank, Maarten, Jurrian, Peter, Eran, Lykele, Wouter (Ritmeester) and Marije (my big sister), thank you for listening to my waffle, giving feedback and even, in one case, ma- king a cover design. Thanks to all the great minds and thinkers who provided the foundations for this book. And to Frits Koster and Erik van den Brink – you have taught me that compassion is not for wimps but for heroes. I appreciate your generosity in allowing me to use some of the texts in your compassion exercises for the audio tracks. Thank you, Nico Tydeman: you have taught me to view all our messing about on planet Earth with wonder. My parents, Rob and Françoise, thank you for tying the knot on 3 May 1980, and for bring me up in such a loving environment. Dear Elise, my civil partner until death do us part, many thanks for your patience, trust and the most precious thing ever given to me, our daughter, Ava. She is my motivation for writing this book: a healthy mind for a better world for future generations.

Maud Beucker Andreae

Dear Maarten Beucker Andreae, Mick Peet and Pien Kooy: thank you so much!

Your support during the writing process of this book was indispensable. I am also extremely grateful to Anita de Vries because she realized that I wanted to write this before I did. Wouter, Juliët, Lydia, Emma and Sander, many thanks for your trust and our harmonious collaboration.